Learning to Ch

EUROPEAN STUDIES IN LIFELONG LEARNING AND ADULT LEARNING RESEARCH

Edited by Barry J. Hake, Henning Salling Olesen
and Rudolf Tippelt

Volume 5

PETER LANG

Frankfurt am Main · Berlin · Bern · Bruxelles · New York · Oxford · Wien

Barbara Merrill (ed.)

Learning to Change?

The Role of Identity and Learning Careers in Adult Education

PETER LANG
Internationaler Verlag der Wissenschaften

Bibliographic Information published by the Deutsche Nationalbibliothek
The Deutsche Nationalbibliothek lists this publication in the Deutsche Nationalbibliografie; detailed bibliographic data is available in the internet at http://dnb.d-nb.de.

ISSN 1860-787X
ISBN 978-3-631-58279-4

© Peter Lang GmbH
Internationaler Verlag der Wissenschaften
Frankfurt am Main 2009
All rights reserved.

www.peterlang.de

Contents

Acknowledgements

I would like to thank Brenda Wilson in the Centre for Lifelong learning, University of Warwick for patiently undertaking the hard work of preparing the book for Camera Ready Copy. Carolyn Garwes did the indexing and I would like to thank her for this. I would also like to thank Ute Winkelkötter and Michael Ruecker at Peter Lang for their help and support. Lastly I would like to thank the members of ESREA Steering Committee for supporting this endeavour and the members of the ESREA Access, Learning Careers and Identities Network for making this book a possibility.

Barbara Merrill
July 2009

1 Introduction: Moving Beyond Access to Learning Careers and Identity

Barbara Merrill

In recent years the nature of European adult education research has changed. There is now an increased interest in looking at the processes and experiences of adult learning in terms of a learning career across the lifecourse and its subsequent impact upon identities in a range of educational contexts rather than simply access issues. This reflects the growing concern about and focus upon identity within the social sciences generally as the uncertainty, risk and individualisation of life in late modernity makes the maintenance of identity problematic (Giddens, 1991, Castells, 1997, Beck, 1992). Individuals, groups and society are experiencing social, economic, political and technological changes which are making life unpredictable and unstable as the traditional linear lifecourse patterns of the past, such as a job for life, disappear (Bauman, 2005). Biographies of adult learners reveal this uncertainty and complexity of modern life as they juggle multiple identities and sometimes fragmented lives resulting in learning careers which may not always be linear. Research indicates, as evidenced by the chapters in this book, that engagement in learning and the development of a learning career has an impact upon the identity of the self and sometimes others (family and friends) in both individual and collective ways. Whatever context adults are learning in most leave a programme a changed person, some in more pronounced ways than others (West, 1996, Merrill, 1999). Some adults become 'hooked' on learning and progress through different levels from returning to learn to higher education study although not necessarily in a continuous fashion.

This book looks at the issues of access, learning careers and identities in a diverse range of settings with diverse groups of adult students across Europe largely through the voices of adult students themselves. Life history approaches or biographical approaches are now a favoured method of researching the access and experiences of adult students in contrast to the earlier quantitative studies using questionnaires such as Bourner et al (1991) and Woodley et al (1987). Most of the chapters in this book reflect this trend. Some of the chapters explore the learning experiences of adult educators and educators more generally and what this means for their identities as they find themselves in a changing adult education environment. A few chapters focus on institutional perspectives and how institutions and their cultures impact upon learning careers and identities.

A changing adult education

Adult education and learning now takes place in a diverse range of sites and contexts, both formally and informally such as in the family, community, civic society and the workplace. Sometimes there is a blurring of boundaries. In the UK, for example, many higher education programmes for adults are now taught in further education colleges (post compulsory institutions) and these institutions are now being referred to as the lifelong learning sector. Adult education is also no longer confined to educational institutions as other sectors and professions are showing an interest such as health services. What adult education is can no longer clearly be defined as it has become, as described by Edwards (1997), a 'moorland'.

At the same time there has been a policy push by national governments and the European Commission (EC) to open up opportunities for adults to learn through lifelong learning strategies. Some European countries have developed further along this road than others, particularly in relation to the higher education sector. While, for example, higher education institutions are relatively open in countries like Sweden and the UK they remain mostly closed in Spain and Portugal. Accessing formal adult education, therefore, is not always easy and varies by institution and countries. Despite the continuing policy push for lifelong learning the rhetoric continues to be stronger than the practice. What is happening is that adult education is being channelled into a particular and narrow direction, gradually changing the nature of adult education. The 'push' by governments, the European Commission (EC) and policy makers, though, is largely an economic one driven by technological changes and globalisation and the need to compete in the world market. (see John Field's chapter). As Edwards et al argue:

> Despite many controversies, however, the idea that the present is a period of intense structural and destabilizing change has become inherent in establishing policy contexts, to which there needs to be a response. Change and adaptation to change have become watchwords of policy, including educational policy (2002: p.526).

Liberal adult education and 'learning for learning's sake' is increasingly under attack in many European countries as marketisation and the stress on vocational learning, skills and competencies becomes more dominant. However, there are still spaces where learning is not vocationally focused as some of the chapters in this book illustrate. Importantly participating as an adult student in education can offer a space for individuals to work out different, changing or new identities in order to adapt to the transformations of life in late modernity.

There are wider benefits, therefore, to participating in education (Schuller et al, 2004) for both the self and society, including the possibility for self development, transformation and changing identity. For some this process will be more transforming than for others. The learning career and journey of an adult learner may not always be straightforward, and for some, keeping on going on may be difficult because of personal, institutional and structural pressures. In developing a learner identity (or not) the stories that adult students tell reveal the interaction of structure and agency in a person's life. Some of the chapters illustrate how individuals use their agency to both get into formal education and also to manage/cope within the educational institution against a background of structural factors such as class, gender, poverty, etc. Adult learners are not homogeneous and as a result learning careers and identities are shaped by issues of class, gender, ethnicity, disability and age. At the same time adult educators also face challenges in terms of their learning and identity as educators in a changing adult education world. This book aims to explore the learning journey and changing identities of adult learners and adult educators in a range of educational settings such as further and higher education, adult and community education, the workplace as well as informal spaces such as the family or civic society.

The story of this book

The European Society for Research on the Education of Adults (ESREA) provides opportunities for adult educators from across Europe to meet, discuss and exchange research ideas. ESREA has several research networks covering a range of adult education topics. This book has developed from the work of the ESREA Access, Learning Careers and Identities Network and the meeting of researchers from across Europe to discuss their research at Louvain-la- Neuve in 2006. The life history of this network reflects the changing nature of research in this field. This network started its life in 1996 as the Access Research Network and held its first network conference in Leeds, UK. The convenors were Chris Duke, Etienne Bourgeois and myself. As the publication -*Access, Equity, Participation and Organisational Change*- (Hill & Merrill, 1997) from the conference illustrates the theme of the network was a narrow one focusing only on higher education, access and participation. This focus dominated the themes of the next two network conferences in Barcelona and Edinburgh. Ten years later the network was re-launched under its new title of Access, Learning Careers and Identities to reflect the new and wider concerns in adult education research around the concepts of identity and learning experiences and processes. The emphasis was no longer on getting in and accessing an institution.

Moving to the chapters

As stated above the chapters in this book embrace a wide range of adult education contexts looking at the concepts of access, learning careers and identities. Although different European countries are represented in this book each with different histories the discussions reveal many commonalities as well as some differences in relation to adult education and student experiences. Some of the authors have worked together on several European, EC funded research projects (a TSER project on adult access to universities and LIHE and PRILHE both of which focus on the learning process and experiences). These are referred to in the chapters by Rennie Johnston and Barbara Merrill, Peter Alheit, Ewa Kurantowicz and Adrianna Nizinski and Ana Maria Ramalho Correia et al.

In chapter two John Field argues that many social theorists assert that late modernity is characterised by increasing change across all areas of adult life, leading to a continuing experience of transition in the adult life course. Education and training is one area which can provide a stimulus to further change in work or everyday life. The chapter explores the role of social networks in adults' strategies for coping with learning transitions. It draws on recent research into social capital and adult learning, which has pointed to a largely beneficial relationship between participation in learning and engagement in social and civic activity. It also addresses more intimate forms of social capital such as family life. Drawing on life history data from a large national UK study (*'Learning Lives: Learning, Identity and Agency'*) funded by the Economic and Social Research Council) on agency, identity and learning among British adults, a series of broad strategic categories are identified. These are explored through illustrative case studies of the life stories of three individuals. Field suggests that some combinations of social support seem better suited to promote successful transitions than others.

Chapter three, written by Michael Tedder and Gert Biesta, also focuses on research from the *'Learning Lives: Learning, Identity and Agency'* project. Using a biographical approach they explore how participation in learning enables people to learn from their lives. What is the meaning of these learning processes and how does such type of learning help individuals deal with processes of change and transition? In doing so Tedder and Biesta examine the concept of biographical learning by drawing on the work of Peter Alheit and Bettina Dausien. They illustrate their ideas through the case study and biography of one male adult learner. Using the transcripts of seven interviews they examine his learning career, identity and the transitions he experienced. His story illustrates how education enables people to find the space to acquire tools and reflect upon their life experiences through the process of biographical learning.

Simon Warren and Sue Webb also centre their chapter (chapter four) on biographical research and the narrative of a female adult student (Jenny) in a further education college in the UK. They look at how her life trajectory is shaped and given meaning through key events in her life. In Jenny's case her narrative is constructed around a key event of the death of her aunt. Warren and Webb illustrate the consequences of this event: Jenny's decision to enter social care work and then later to participate on a part-time Health and Social Care course at a further education college. They argue that her narrative highlights the causal relationship between these events. In theorising their work they examine how stories are 'socially organised' and 'saturated by social structure'. For them Bourdieu's concepts of habitus and field or structure and agency provide a means to develop a 'recursive methodology' which enables them to illustrate the particularities and richness of an individual life while also taking into account the role of social structure.

In chapter five Paula Guimarães and Amélia Vitória Sancho shift the focus of learning from adult students to adult educators. Through participation on a training programme they explore the meanings of learning experiences which adult educators have while working as practitioners in Portugal. Guimarães and Sancho focus on informal learning in the workplace. Informal learning is seen as an open, indeterminate, flexible and a not necessarily organised process. They argue that informal learning is not a linear process but rather one that is frequently interrupted, resumed, and discontinued which occurs in response to constraints, requirements or arbitrary or contingent possibilities. Informal learning in the workplace enables adult educators to change attitudes and behaviour. The narratives of adult educators are used to explore the practitioners' own 'ways of knowing' about the effects of workplace practices on learning. The narratives are drawn from an EC funded project involving eight European countries entitled '*A Good Adult Educator in Europe' project*' (AGADE).

Chapter six by Rob Evans also focuses on professionals and learning but from the perspective of looking at organisational discourse(s) of learning through the narratives and talk of employees working in international corporations in Germany. Evans argues that professional knowledge management and organisational/ intercultural learning processes takes place within the framework of globalising contexts. He also examines how the learning experiences of employees are enacted out between demands for tacit/informal and /or explicit /formal knowledge, whereby the former is mainly experiential and subjective while the latter is market-oriented and codified and dependent on specific (and changing) work-place profiles (Evans, 2001). Evans uses biographical narrative unstructured interviews as a means of critique to identify current deficits in organisational communication and intercultural learning.

Life history methodology is also the approach used in chapter seven by Patricia Gouthro. This chapter, however, takes us to Canada and to a study funded by the Canadian Social Sciences and Humanities Council which examines the learning trajectories of women learners. This involved forty female participants from across Canada. The women were asked to trace their lifelong learning trajectories and highlight any concerns they faced in continuing their formal education. For Gouthro, a key objective is to assess, using critical feminist analysis, existing educational policies and practices in adult and higher education in Canada. She argues that gendered differences are not addressed in adult and higher education policies and practices. Instead such institutions serve to reinforce structural barriers and hence perpetuate women's inequality in the learning society. Critical feminist perspectives also reveal that differences in lifelong learning trajectories are due to both individual and social contexts.

In chapter eight Tamsin Hinton-Smith continues with Gouthro's theme of looking at the experiences of non-traditional adult learners in higher education. In this chapter the focus is on lone parents studying a range of courses in further and higher education institutions in the UK for a longitudinal project funded by the Economic and Social Research Council (ESRC). Biographical approaches are used to illustrate the uncertainties and complexities of modern life which impact upon everyday life and learning careers of lone parents studying in higher education. Juggling and balancing roles and tasks characterise their lives as they take on multiple identities and struggle with the uncertainty and risk that studying as a lone parent brings. The chapter is set within a policy background of a declining welfare state and an increasing emphasis on individual economic self-sufficiency against a background of a national policy push towards widening participation.

Chapter nine again continues the theme of non-traditional adult learners in higher education. Rennie Johnston and Barbara Merrill explore, through two life histories (female and male), the learning experiences and learner identities of working class adult students. The stories are taken from an EU project entitled *Learning in Higher Education*. The chapter highlights the complexity of a learning identity in relation to working class adult students. Johnston and Merrill argue for the centrality of social class in UK society despite its recent downturn in popularity in UK sociology. They draw on the work of Bourdieu and in particular his concepts of habitus and capital in order to examine how learning identities are constructed. The role of agency and structure is also explored through two life stories to identify how a learner identity is shaped and transformed while at the same time maintaining working class roots.

Chapter ten centres on a different aspect and arena of adult education and on an under-researched area. Nalita James and Bethia McNeil discuss their research study on young adults (male offenders) involvement and engagement in a drama programme in prison. Funded by the Arts Council England and the Department for Education and Skills (DfES) the project explored the use of drama and theatre as a site for learning. In particular James and McNeil are interested in how participation in drama and the process of drama as tools may encourage the personal and social development of the offenders. They look at how the programme enabled the young men to act as agents in their own learning and development and offers the time and space to explore images and projections of the self and identity.

The institutional habitus and the symbolic power of German universities is the concern of Peter Alheit in chapter eleven. Specifically the chapter focuses on the role of gatekeeping in relation to non-traditional adult students but looked at through the stories of four academics in a range of hard and soft disciplines. In drawing on the work of Becher (1987) he examines the impact that particular soft and hard disciplines may have in shaping disciplinary cultures and the habitus of academics. Using Bourdieu's concepts of habitus and capital he identifies four different types of habitus enacted by the four academics interviewed. The 'exclusive habitus' of the pure and hard scientist, the 'ambivalent habitus' of the soft and pure sociologist, the 'pragmatic habitus' of the hard and applied of the mechanical engineer and lastly the 'inclusive habitus' of the soft and applied social scientist.

The theme of universities and non-traditional adult students is continued by Ewa Kurantowicz and Adrianna Nizinski in chapter twelve. This chapter takes us geographically further east in Europe to Poland. Like Peter Alheit they draw on research undertaken in the PRILHE project on the critical, autonomous and reflective learning of non-traditional adult students in higher education. The focus here is on Polish adult students. In order to understand the present they examine the history of Polish universities and the impact of the events between 1980 and 1989 in Polish society. Although universities are the fastest growing and changing institutions in Poland they explore why there is little debate on the learning process. Using life history stories and students' diaries collected through the PRILHE project they discuss the impact of higher education institutions in enabling (or not) non-traditional adult students to become reflective, critical and autonomous learners.

In chapter thirteen Ana Maria Ramalho Correia, Duce Magalhães, Ana Vristina Costa and Anabela Sarmento look at knowledge sharing and learning processes in a comparative study of technological schools and higher education institutions in Portugal in relation to adult students. The data for this study again draws on the European PRILHE research project. In Portugal there has been an increasing interest in adult learners over the last few years. They assert that while learners' biographies reveal uncertainty and sometimes a lack of confidence concerning their learning potential some do develop approaches to deal with these difficulties and become autonomous and independent learners. They argue that this may be related to pathways chosen during the course of their life. They examine whether or not the choice to study at either a technological school or a university is dependent on their biography and how the learning context may also affect their ability to become autonomous and independent learners.

In the final chapter – chapter fourteen – Jan Frederiksen takes us to northern Europe in a study of social educator students in Denmark. The chapter discusses how social educators who have extensive professional practice in the field become adult students and the opportunities that the professional training offers them. He applies theories of control to the grading of students and the role of grading as a social practice and explores what impact this has on the learning identities of the students. He draws on Bernstein's concept of pedagogical devices and Foucault's concept of governmentality to look at how a lenient and considerate grading system helps to develop the students' understanding of their professional and educational field. And also how students learn how to govern themselves without losing control in the classroom and lastly how self-governance provides a matrix for the subjective experience of becoming and being a social educator student.

References

Bauman, Z. (2005). *Liquid Life.* Polity: Cambridge

Becher, T. (1987). Disciplinary Discourse In: *Studies in Higher Education*, Vol. 12, pp. 261-274

Beck, U. (1992). *Risk Society: Towards a new modernity.* Sage: London

Bourner, T. Reynolds, A. Hamed, M & Barnett, R. (1991). *Part-time Students and their Experience of Higher Education.* Buckingham: SRHE/Open University Press

Castells, M. (1997). *The Power of Identity, The Information Age: Economy, Society and Culture.* Vol II, Oxford: Blackwell

Edwards, R. (1997) *Changing Places? Flexibility, lifelong learning and a learning society,* London: Routledge

Edwards, R. Ranson, S. and Strain, M. (2002). Reflexivity: towards a theory of lifelong learning. In *International Journal of Lifelong Learning,* Vol. 21, No. 6, pp525 – 536

Evans, K. (2001). Tacit Skills and Work Inequalities. A UK Perspective on Tacit Forms of Key Competences, and Issues for Future Research. In *ECER:* Lille

Giddens, A. (1991). *Modernity and Self Identity: Self and Society in the Late Modern Age.* Cambridge: Polity Press

Hill, S. and Merrill, B. (1997). *Access, Equity, Participation and Organisational Change.* University of Warwick, Université Catholique de Louvain and ESREA

Merrill, B. (1999). *Gender, Change and Identity: Mature Women Students in Universities.* Aldershot: Ashgate

Schuller, T. Preston, J. Hammond, C. Brassnett-Grundy, A. and Bryner, J. (2004). *The Benefits of Learning.* London: Routledge-Falmer

West, L. (1996). *Beyond Fragments: adults, motivation and higher education.* London: Taylor and Francis

Woodley, A. Wagner, L. Slowey, M. Fulton, O. and Bowner, T. (1987). *Choosing to Learn.* Buckingham: SRHE/Open University Press

2 Learning Transitions in the Adult Life Course: Agency, Identity and Social Capital

John Field

Introduction

Many recent social theorists stress the fluidity of everyday life in contemporary Western societies. As a result of rapid technological, economic, cultural and social change, they suggest that individuals are constantly faced with transitions in their personal circumstances. In turn, governments exhort their citizens to prepare for a life of permanent adaptation and flexibility. Education in adult life becomes both a resource for individuals seeking to promote their employability and mobility, and at the same time a cause of further uncertainty and risk.

This paper explores the relationship between adult learning and social networks in adults' lives. Recent studies of social capital and adult learning have examined the ways in which different kinds of community engagement influence people's attitudes towards, and participation and achievement in education and training, as well as the ways in which participation in learning appears to produce gains in the likelihood of civic participation (Field, 2005; Tett and Maclachlan, 2007; Schuller et al 2004). A number of other studies have shown that social connections and civic engagement appear to exert a positive influence on participation in education and training through adult life (Benn 2000; Strawn, 2003). This paper looks instead at the ways in which people seek to manage their social capital in the light of their learning experiences and aspirations. It draws on qualitative life history data collected in the course of a longitudinal study of identity, agency and learning in the adult life course, as part of the Learning Lives research project[1].

---

1 Further details of the Learning Lives project, including discussion of methodology and data analysis, can be found on its website, www.learninglives.org. The study is funded by the Economic and Social Research Council as part of its Teaching and Learning Research Programme, and involves repeated life history interviews with some 120 individuals as well as a detailed quantitative analysis of the British Household Panel Survey. The project is a partnership, based at the Universities of Stirling (Gert Biesta, John Field, Heather Lynch and Irene Malcolm), Leeds (Phil Hodkinson, Heather Hodkinson, Geoff Ford and Ruth Hawthorne), Exeter (Flora McLeod, Paul Lambe and Michael Tedder) and Brighton (Ivor Goodson and Norma Adair) I owe particular thanks to Heather Lynch and Irene Malcolm, who conducted the interviews on which this paper is based. Previous versions of the paper were presented at seminars at the Universities of Exeter, Kingston, Louvain-la-Neuve and Tübingen, and I am grateful to those who attended for their thoughtful comments.

Some influential social theorists suggest that people increasingly appear to treat their social networks as a resource which can be manipulated in the light of changing needs, and the paper presents evidence that this is indeed the case for some people. Equally, some people consciously decide not to pursue learning opportunities in case it might jeopardize their social ties. These findings suggest a degree of agency and reflexivity that have been largely neglected in much research into adult learning. Yet structural constraints also feature in the life histories, suggesting that the deployment of social capital is only part of the story, and that institutional and other structures – including those of class and gender – continue to exercise a significant influence on adults' life chances.

Social connections in late modernity

Adult education researchers have frequently drawn attention to the ubiquitous enthusiasm of western governments for policies designed to promote lifelong learning (Field, 2006; Green, 2003; Knoll, 1998; Schemmann, 2007; Schuetze, and Casey, 2006). Policy makers primarily base these policies on economic grounds, presenting them as a virtually obvious response to the twin challenges of globalization and technological change (eg Commission of the European Communities, 1994). However, these policies also seem to reflect other factors, including a shift away from provision-led models of welfare towards more active policies of 'insertion' (Rosanvallon, 1995), as well as wider social and cultural tendencies that are characterised by the steady – and even sometimes rapid – erosion of existing social relations and cultural patterns. Fundamentally, though, there is broad agreement that the probability of undergoing significant transitions in adult life has increased and continues to increase; that the nature of these transitions has become ever more complicated; and that an active approach towards learning across the lifespan constitutes a desirable strategy for coping with recurrent and complex transitions.

This perspective marks a decisive change from earlier perspectives on adult learning. Influenced by developmental psychology, as well as theories of andragogy as an intellectual underpinning of adult teaching, many adult education scholars took a view of the adult life cycle as a largely predictable series of passages, each of which produced its own learning tasks, thereby creating 'teachable moments' (Merriam, 1994, p. 79). One highly influential American scholar divided adult transitions into 'normative' events, which were more or less expected at particular times in the life span, and 'non-normative' events such as bankruptcy or the death of one's child; she also distinguished life events that were 'on-time' in terms of when they occurred in the life cycle from 'off-time' events such as a late pregnancy (Merriam, 1994, p.76-77). By contrast, social theorists such as Bauman, Beck and Giddens emphasise the extreme varieties of timing in adult life events, drawing attention to knowledge-driven possibilities like post-menopause pregnancy, as well as the increasing impact of unpredictable economic changes on the financial stability of individuals and organisations. We might add to these the prospects for 'off-time' education, whether in the form of organized pre-schooling or periodic returns to learning in adult life, as well as 'non-normative' adult learning in such cases as initial vocational training for redundant workers or parenting classes for people who are already parents.

A number of researchers have turned to theories of late and post modernity to account for these trends (Edwards 1997; Schemmann, 2002; Bauman, 2005; Field, 2006). Both theoretical frameworks emphasise the fluidity and pluralism of economic, social and political beliefs and institutions, and draw attention to the influence of globalization, new technologies, migration and rapid organisational and policy change on attitudes and behaviour. In particular a number of researchers have explored the implications of what has loosely been called 'reflexive modernisation' theorists, above all Ulrich Beck and Anthony Giddens (Schemmann, 2002). There are, of course, important differences between these two thinkers, but both emphasise the distinctive role of knowledge and information in driving change in contemporary societies. As Giddens puts it, the reflexivity of modernity consists in "the susceptibility of most aspects of social activity, and material relations with nature, to chronic revision in the light of new information or knowledge", in a way that is not just incidental to modern institutions "but constitutive of them" (Giddens, 1991, p.20). In contradiction to the expectations of Enlightenment thought, modernity's reflexivity creates uncertainty and doubt, and even manufactured risks, rather than security, in ways that are "*existentially troubling* for ordinary individuals" (Giddens, 1991, p.21, emphasis in original).

One reason that modernity is so troubling is that institutionalised reflexivity, according to Giddens and Beck, exposes all social practices and arrangements to doubt and revision. And this applies in the private and intimate sphere as much as in the open and public sphere, to family life and love as much as to work and politics. Change is so pervasive that the self becomes what Giddens calls 'a reflexive project', which must be constantly explored and (re)constructed (Giddens, 1991, p.32-4). In circumstances where the "proportion of life opportunities which are fundamentally close to decision-making is decreasing and the proportion of the biography which is open and must be constructed personally is increasing", individuals must continually produce and re-produce their own biographies (Beck, 1992, p.135).

In turn, reflexive modernisation theorists suggest the individuals must also continually (re)produce their social connections. Networks of associates, friends, relatives and loved ones are similarly increasingly based on elective decisions, and less and less on habit and routine. Even within families, according to Beck, individual members are likely to choose their own separate relationships and live in networks of their own, rather than simply accepting the body of ascribed relationships that 'come with' family membership. He goes on to connect this with his hypothesis of increasing individualisation:

> The newly formed social relationships and social networks now have to be individually chosen; social ties, too, are becoming *reflexive*, so that they have to be established, maintained and constantly renewed by individuals (Beck, 1992, p.97).

And again:

> In the individualised society the individual must therefore learn, on pain of permanent disadvantage, to conceive of himself or herself as the centre of action, as the planning office with respect to his/her own biography, abilities, orientations, relationships and so on. Under those conditions of a reflexive biography, 'society' *must* be individually manipulated as a 'variable' (Beck, 1992, p.135; emphasis in original).

This paper is concerned precisely with the 'manipulation of society', and the reforming of social relations, in the light of learning transitions in adult life.

Adult learning and social connections

There has been considerable interest in recent years in the relationship between social connections and adult learning. Some of this literature has explicitly conceptualised social connections as a form of social capital (Field 2005; Tett and Maclachlan, 2007; Schuller, et al 2004; Strawn, 2003), seeing social networks as a valuable asset. People's networks are not solely of immediate advantage, moreover, but can provide a basis for social cohesion because they enable people to co-operate with one another – and not just with people they know directly – for mutual advantage (Putnam 2000). A series of studies confirms that social connections facilitate reciprocity in respect of knowledge sharing and information exchange, as well as in the transmission of skills and know-how; and that they function in this way both during childhood (Ball, 2003; Coleman, 1998-99; Dika and Singh, 2002) and in adult life (Field, 2005; Kim and Nelson, 2000; Maskell, 2000). This influence of social capital on learning can be double-edged, in that some types of connection – frequently close personal bonding ties – tend to favour informal pooling of knowledge and know-how, while more heterogeneous connections tend to foster positive engagement with the education and training system (Field, 2005). Conversely, it has also been shown that participation in learning tends to enhance social capital, by helping develop social competences, extending social networks, and promoting shared norms and tolerance of others (Schuller, et al 2004; Tett and Maclachlan, 2007).

Previous research has largely focused on social capital in relation either with participation in learning or with its outcomes. Studies of social connections and learning transitions have so far largely concentrated on transitions in young adult life. One study of contemporary youth transitions in Germany, for example, considered the role of informal networks in relation to 'destandardized' youth transitions (Walther, Stauber and Pohl, 2005). This study concentrated on two groups of young adults: those with 'risk biographies', who had disengaged to a greater or lesser extent from the formal support system, and people with 'choice biographies' who had combined informal and formal mechanisms to go beyond conventional transition expectations. This study noted that most young people's transitions were rather more messy and complex than easily fitted a neat typology, and it also found that both of these groups were characterised by a broadly critical view of the education and training system. it found that 'choice biographies', while including access to intimate ties who offered high trust and respect for autonomy, were generally characterised by access to broad and heterogeneous networks (Walther, Stauber and Pohl, 2005, p.225-7). Young men and women with 'risk' biographies, meanwhile, tended to reject the formal support system and rely on informal contacts to find work, but could only draw on a relatively narrow and homogeneous set of ties, which led them into precarious forms of employment (Walther, Stauber and Pohl 2005, 330, p.31; see also Emler and McNamara 1996).

Higher education transitions also affect social capital and are affected by it. Mary Stuart has recently examined young university students' networks, noting that some individuals are only able to achieve academic success if they abandon some existing contacts and build a new peer group (Stuart 2006). There are also references to social capital resources as success factors in Merrill and Alheit's study of participation and persistence among mature students (Merrill and Alheit, 2004).

These studies confirm the importance of social capital during transitions. From them, it seems that elective transitions (choice biographies, in the words of the authors) are supported by a combination of strong ties and heterogeneous connections. Together, these appear to provide access to and understanding of diverse information, a sense of belonging, security and trust, and command of important interpersonal skills (Walther, Stauber and Pohl 2005, p.223). Yet although these findings may be relevant to adults' transitions more generally, we should be cautious in generalising from studies of early adult life. Despite increasing tendencies towards destandardisation, most youth transitions are generally unilinear, characterized by precise age-stage expectations, and occur within the context of a broadly based and well defined structure of public support. Transitions in adult life, by contrast, are frequently multiple and multilinear; the adult life course is ever less defined by precise age-related stages; and support mechanisms are fragmented, and spread between the public and – increasingly so – the private sector. Further, according to Bauman, in late modernity

> Conditions of action and strategies designed to respond to them age quickly and become obsolete before the actors have a chance to learn them properly (Bauman, 2005, p.1).

Of course, like Beck, Bauman is making an assertion rather than summarizing from evidence. The question of whether adults consciously manipulate their own social relations in order to cope with learning transitions therefore remains an open one.

Social networks in adults' learning lives

Social capital, for the purposes of this analysis, can be defined as:

> the sum of resources, actual or virtual, that accrue to an individual or a group by virtue of possessing a durable network of more or less institutionalized relationships of mutual acquaintance and recognition (Bourdieu and Wacquant, 1992, p.119).

In itself, this definition differs little from those proposed by Coleman (1998-89) or Putnam (2000). Rather, it is Bourdieu and Wacquant's wider analytical framework that is distinctive in the social capital literature, emphasising as they do the role of social networks in underpinning inequalities and sustaining privilege, as well as enabling co-operation for the wider benefit.

As noted above, researchers have already shown that social capital has some influence on participation and achievement in adult learning, and that participation in learning in turn leads to new and wider social networks. For this paper, the focus is on the ways in which people build and their social networks in order to cope with learning transitions. By learning transitions, I mean both people's transitions between types, forms or levels of learning, and also the transitions that occur in other life spheres as a consequence of their learning. In both cases, I am interested in agency and identity – that is, the extent to which people are and feel able to control their social networks – and in the structural background that shape capacities for action.

In summary, we can hypothetically distinguish between four broad ideal types of individual strategies. These are:

- Maintain old networks, no new network
- Maintain old networks, build new networks
- Abandon old networks, no new network
- Abandon old networks, build new networks

Further, we may distinguish between different types of ties. Social capital theory has become increasingly sensitive to the need for a differentiated analysis, distinguishing particularly between what one prominent scholar (Woolcock, 1998) defines as bonding ties (horizontal and homogeneous), bridging ties (horizontal and heterogeneous) and linking ties (vertical and heterogeneous).

- Maintain family ties and wider networks
- Adapt family ties, maintain wider networks
- Adapt wider networks, maintain family ties
- Adapt family ties and wider networks

The first case is Fraser Smith[2], who has radically changed his family ties and built a new set of social networks. Fraser, in his mid-30s at time of interview, works with young homeless people in a highly urbanized community in the West of Scotland. He had a broken educational trajectory, which he resumed with success in adult life. He took a milk round while in secondary education, spending money on alcohol and developing a network of friends who were older than he was; his mother was a single parent, his father having disappeared from his life. He achieved little in school, and was arrested for violent behaviour before being expelled and placed under supervision. Following this he was incarcerated for assaulting a police officer. On release, he joined a martial arts centre and found work, initially as a trainee painter and decorator and then as a production worker in a factor. He also married, and in his twenties has a young family. Aware of the risks of redundancy, Fraser enrolled on an evening course in computing that his trade union had set up; he also worked voluntarily with young people, particularly by running martial arts courses, and become interested in homelessness. Following redundancy, he took a Higher National Certificate course in social care at a local further education college, and moved into full time social work, supplementing his HNC with an in-service national vocational qualification and a counselling course.

Fraser's story, told in summary form, might sound deceptively smooth. Yet it is full of 'non-normative' transitions (incarceration, significant change of

---

2 Interviewees' names have been altered to protect their anonymity. Where participants spoke routinely in Scottish, the interview transcripts reflect this. Quotes are therefore not translated into standard English.

occupation) and 'off-time' transitions (particularly initial vocational training as an adult, as well as a move in adulthood from unskilled manual work to semi-professional status). In negotiating these transitions, Fraser drew on a number of resources, including social support networks. His interest in martial arts he owed to a developing friendship with a cousin, as well as to encouragement from staff in the secure unit who urged him to take up sports. At the same time, he cut ties with his old friendship network, developing new ties through martial arts and his work. These new ties also helped him find new jobs, first in the factory and then in youth work.

As well as building new friendship networks and extending his bridging ties, Fraser also transformed his family life. Having acquired a new girlfriend after his release, he cut his ties with his mother, and moved in with his girlfriend's family. This girl became his wife, and her mother became effectively a second, replacement mother for Fraser; he also described himself as close to his father in law, but did not seek advice from him on education and jobs. On a number of occasions, he refers to the support and encouragement of his wife and her mother for his learning; he describes both women's views as crucial in reaching the decision to pursue youth work as a career, rather than finding another factory job. Equally, it was the thought of his wife's disappointment that kept him attending the evening class in computing, helping him to overcome what he describes as a very considerable fear of this unknown and challenging experience. By contrast, he saw "it as a good thing being away and no having any contact with my mother, she was, she used to always bring negatives, my mum would try to bring you down and stuff" (Fraser Smith, Interview 3, 4/12/2006).

So far, then, Fraser's story is one of social capital abandoned and renewed. Old, limiting ties were dropped; new ties were created, constituting a mixture of more heterogeneous and loose ties through work and sport, and closer intimate and homogeneous ties through his new family. In their turn, these new ties were now holding Fraser back from further educational progression. Aware of the need for a degree if he was to move up the career ladder, yet having lost his own father at an early age, Fraser decided that he would stay with his current employer, and look for opportunities to learn by expanding his role. Formal adult education, he said, had "no been a big headache or anything, my lecturer at the college said that as well, 'You would nae have a problem I think in doing it', but I wouldnae take away that time fae my kids" (Fraser Smith, Interview 3, 4/12/2006). So for the time being at least, Fraser had called a halt to formal participation in learning. Nevertheless he had a strong sense of achievement and a clear direction, and was deeply satisfied with his working life, family life and sporting activities.

Kathleen Donnelly, the second case, also became a youth worker in urban West Scotland. Like Fraser, she had a broken educational trajectory, and had resumed learning in adult life with partial success. After enjoying primary school, high school came as a shock and from the third year on, "I would dae anything, I'd sit doon the railway line, anything rather than go intae that school". At fifteen and a half Kathleen entered a youth training programme in the post office, a job that she hated but tolerated for the income, and stayed there for the next twelve years. In her free time, she engaged in what she called a "magazine lifestyle" of frantic clubbing and partying coupled with "quite a few boyfriends" and frequent use of recreational drugs (Kathleen Donnelly, Interview 2). Eventually she started dating a boy regularly, then moved in with him and became pregnant. As she tells it, "the first year wis great, brilliant, and then we decided tae get married and I got married on the Friday and by the Sunday I wis abused, he wis intae physical violence in a big, big way" (Interview 1, 16/1/2006). A regular coke user, her husband also stole and ran up debts. After ten weeks the marriage was over, but – against the strong advice of her mother - Kathleen decided to have the baby. After calculating that she would be better off financially on income support than trying to balance work and child care, she left her job.

After more than two years of full time child care, she decided to go to college. She had already enrolled in an office administration course but found it boring, and after a break she started a Higher National Diploma in social science, a subject that she pursued with increasing enthusiasm. Kathleen's interest in social science was in part because it helped her explain and describe her own life: "all of a sudden like ye get these theories and ye thought, I used to be astounded, 'God, that's me, is that maybe the reason why I didnae do well at school'". As examples, she described the effects of her teachers' attitudes in terms of labelling theory, and attributed her shock at her husband's violence to the expectations laid down by her own father ("Nae matter whit, I think ye dae relate tae yer relationships tae how yer dad treated ye"). College, she said, "wis so brilliant for me and when I came oot I'm like that, 'I'm telling everybody'. I telt my mum, 'Get to college, get a wee volunteer placement, it'll change yer world'".

At the time of our interview, Kathleen's mother was indeed at college, taking an HNC in counselling, and was phoning her daughter with questions about Freud; her father, by contrast, was "quite feart ae her learning" (Kathleen Donnelly, Interview 1, 16/1/2006). Kathleen had also put her new skills to good use, investigating housing legislation and lobbying successfully to be moved out of her tower block flat into a new home. She then registered for the final year of a degree course, but dropped out shortly before the examinations; although she talked about switching to the Open University, she had not done so. She was studying for a national vocational qualification at time of first interview, but struggled with the placements, which required her to engage with young people who were hostile to her, and by time of second interview she had withdrawn.

She was seeking permanent employment, after a number of short term posts - leaving one because she found the manager "derogatory" – but what she really wanted, she said, was to work for Women's Aid.

Again, social connections form an important part of the story. In part, Kathleen's decision to return to education was simply a response to loneliness. She had "lost aw my pals" through her marriage, and "all of a sudden yer in the hoose wi' a small baby and naebody to talk tae in the tower, and my maw's no just like roon the corner and everything wis an effort tae even go and meet somebody" (Interview 1, 16/1/2006). College itself widened her social connections, and also allowed her to create a new friendship network, but it was a small Thursday evening study group, meeting at Kathleen's home, "just me and three other lassies", who included single parents like herself (Interview 1, 16/1/2006). Her social science training also gave her new ways of understanding and describing her social relationships. She remained close to her mother, and indeed shared her educational interests with her, and took a close interest in her sister's daughter. But Kathleen still looked back to her old friendships and "magazine lifestyle" with nostalgia. She had broken her old connections through a failed marriage and single parenthood, rather than as a result of her own choice, and while loving her daughter, she had strong regrets.

So Kathleen had continued in an interrupted trajectory. Although she had a clear aspiration – working in Women's Aid – she had not worked out a strategy to achieve this goal, and was unable to settle to any of the placements that she was undertaking as part of her latest course. Despite having completed her HND, she had dropped out of her degree, while the new friends she had made in the study group were away at university. Although she was now happy in a new relationship, she continued to suffer from anxiety and depression, and after spending much of her adult life away from the town of her birth, was now back there again. Kathleen had retained her core intimate relations, and, unwillingly losing her existing friendship network, had replaced it with a smaller group of fellow students who had then moved away to pursue their studies. Unable to settle in a new job, she had no wider network which might have provided the emotional and informational resources that could help her find work that she enjoyed. So her trajectory remains a broken one, and she is experiencing only partial success in her learning transitions.

The third and final case is Willie Cotter, a Glaswegian in his fifties who trained as a chef but is currently unemployed. He lives still in Glasgow, in a large council housing scheme, where he has become involved as a volunteer in the local community centre. Willie has taken a number of courses, mainly lower level skills and general studies, but including some short higher education courses. He had a troubled childhood, suffering extreme poverty, undergoing violent abuse and experiencing a range of family difficulties. He has a background of addictive behaviour, and at each interview reported faithfully on his struggle to give up alcohol. He is married with two daughters; his son had been killed some time before we met; his wife works shifts at a local hospital, and Willie continues to do most of the cooking.

All of Willie's adult education and training has been undertaken in local settings. Some of the courses were run by his local community centre, while others were offered in local facilities by a further education college. A large number of these courses were either skills programmes designed to prepare people for re-entry to the labour market, or self-development courses aimed at improving their 'soft skills', but he had also taken more general subjects like creative writing. At the time of the sixth interview, for example, he had been attending a stress management course, but had stopped and switched to a two-day motivation course called Goals. As ever, he had enjoyed the course:

> *It wis quite good, it wis quite educational, anything that's gaun tae be educational tae me I'll take it, as they say, knowledge is power* (Interview 6, 20/9/2006).

But although he fully grasped the message of the course, could describe its content in detail, and would "like tae dae a full week on something like that, ye know, tae pick up a lot mair", he saw little immediate relevance to himself:

> *I didnae need anything, just tae educate myself, I've nae goals, my goals is a Wednesday and a Saturday, know, the fitba' or the lottery, cause that wid change it, that wid gie ye goals aw right* (Interview 6, 20/6/2006).

As well as community based courses he also belongs to a local alcohol support group, through which he has learned about a range of topics from addictive behaviour to the history of alcoholic drinks.

Willie finds his immediate family relations a source of anxiety. He is desperate to please his wife, and stays reasonably close to his daughters. He mourns his lost son. He yearns for grandchildren, but fears that neither daughter – one a 'workaholic', the other a drug addict – is likely to have a child. At the time of the sixth interview his friend's grandson had given him a nine-week old puppy. Willie had considered getting a dog for some time beforehand:

> *Just tae get oot and aboot, walks, just go walks ye know, plus the satisfaction ae the dug an aw, pet, ye know whit I mean, but after a certain time it's no a pet, it's part ae the family ye know* (Willie Cotter, Interview 6, 20/9/2006).

Family is paramount for Willie, but it is problematic. It offers some emotional support, but in troubled ways.

He does of course have friendship networks, but these too are tricky. One part of his wider friendship network is bound up with drinking, and his contacts with this group depend on whether or not he is trying to stay dry. His involvement in the community centre also varied according to his drinking, as his role was in the local branch of an alcohol programme. He was briefly chairman of the local group, but resigned after a fortnight when he went back on the drink. Nevertheless, he maintained his connection with the group, and is clearly proud of what it is trying to do:

> *I wouldnae bring any shame tae the project or anybody that works, anybody that belongs tae it, ye know, but I still go doon and keep contact wi' them, ye know, cause I've made a lot ae good friends doon there, ye know* (Interview 6, 20/9/2006).

However, what this means is that "quite a lot" of Willie's friends are also alcoholics.

More generally, Willie's wider social networks are fragile and often fleetingly temporary. Unemployment has, as is often the case, been an isolating experience. Willie watches a lot of television and DVDs, particularly westerns and football. He does meet others through education, but they are from similar backgrounds to himself, and are familiar to him. Indeed, the experience of local community provision often confirms his hostile views of certain of the neighbours. For example, four of the men taking the motivation course had particularly upset him by making constant sexual references on the first day; on the second day, "they didnae come back, thank fuck, ye know whit I mean, idiots". Once they had gone, though the participants – who included women as well as two younger men whom Willie suspected of being sent by the courts - related well to one another: "it wis a good group, and we were aw hitting aff one another, ye know" (Interview 6, 20/9/2006). But it is hard to see how these wider connections can bring any new emotional or informational resources.

So Willie is a multiple participant in formal learning, but with little or no sense of direction. His trajectory is broken and flat, and his education appears to be compartmentalised from the rest of his life. It forms a kind of entertainment, providing knowledge which he values but seems not to use. It does extend his social networks, but mainly among people who are in the same situation as himself. He clearly learns a great deal, and can expound at length on the content of the courses, while drawing no immediate impetus for other areas of his life. In many ways, this can be seen as a realistic adjustment to structural constraints: age, geography, and skillset mean that almost any job he finds will leave him no better off financially than he is at present. In these circumstances, the local and known nature of community based provision creates a comfort zone in which Willie acquires new skills and knowledge, but will not be required to use them. The transitions are merely educational, and lack any direction other than keeping things as they are until and unless he wins the lottery.

Networks and success strategies

It has been argued in the context of youth transitions that, given the weakening influence of public institutions and parents in late modernity, access to informal networks is increasingly decisive in determining outcomes (Stauber, Pohl and Walther, 2007, 9-11). This paper has explored evidence which suggests that adults similarly make use of social networks to support transitions. However, it indicates that success strategies may require a multiple combination of family bonds, selective continuation of old looser ties, and the creation of new networks of more heterogeneous loose ties. This combination appears to provide access to a number of resources, including emotional support and confidence, as well as informational and knowledge assets, and more practical everyday support. Yet even the closest example here to a pure success strategy – Fraser Smith – was willing to prune his networks so far and no further; he was certainly not keen to pursue higher education if it were to put his family relationships at risk, despite the encouragement of his wife (and his mother-in-law).

This study also suggests that certain combinations of social capital are unlikely to promote transitions, but are more liable to put people into a holding pattern. Willie Cotter remained within an educational comfort zone of short courses, covering a wide variety of skills and knowledge, offered within local community settings, and attracting familiar faces from the local community. While he remained close to his immediate family, he was anxious about his marriage and feared for his daughters' future. His friendship networks were limited, and consisted of people in a very similar situation, whose access to wider information and knowledge assets was restricted to the immediate locality (as well as constrained by their alcohol dependence). This is not to criticise Willie's values or behaviour, or even his networks; from his perspective, remaining as he was can be seen as entirely rational, given the alternatives, and given the context – which he can hardly challenge – of a highly unequal society. However, Willie's learning life should challenge easy assumptions about the nature and meaning of educational participation. Willie's enjoyment of courses simply in themselves is a kind of 'flow', but a narrow and limited one when viewed against the backdrop of transition and transformation in late modernity.

This is of course a limited study, based on primarily qualitative evidence. Further, three case studies – however valuable for illustrative purposes – can prove very little in themselves. This paper may therefore be best seen as providing a basis for more systematic analysis in the future. Nevertheless, the analysis outlined here does indicate that some people may indeed 'manipulate society' in the way that Beck suggests, provided that we understand 'society' as referring to their own immediate relationships. Of course, taken together, the larger effects of countless individuals rearranging their social networks to support them in coping with and anticipating change are potentially dramatic. Ultimately, then, people may be 'manipulating society' in its broader sense, and thereby contributing towards the further loosening of ties based on habit and routine, and the increasing level of importance that is attached to ties based on affinity and choice.

References

Alheit, P. and Dausein, B. (2002). Bildungsprozesse über die Lebensspanne und lebenslanges Lernen, pp565-85 in R. Tippelt (ed.), *Handbuch Bildungsforschung*. Leske + Budrich: Opladen

Ball, S. (2003). *Class Strategies and the Education Market: The middle classes and social advantage*. Routledge: London

Bauman, Z. (2005). *Liquid Life*. Polity: Cambridge

Beck, U. (1992). *Risk Society: Towards a new modernity*. Sage: London

Benn, R. (2000). The genesis of active citizenship in the learning society. S*tudies in the Education of Adults*. 32, 2, 241-256

Bourdieu, P. and Wacquant, L. (1992). *An Invitation to Reflexive Sociology*. Chicago: University of Chicago Press

Coleman, J. S. (1988-89). 'Social capital in the creation of human capital'. In *American Journal of Sociology*. 94, 95-120

Commission of the European Communities (1994). *Competitiveness, Employment, Growth*. Office for Official Publications: Luxembourg

Dika, S. L. and Singh, K. (2002). 'Applications of Social Capital in Educational Literature: a critical synthesis'. In *Review of Educational Research*. 72, 1, 31-60

Edwards, R. (1997). *Changing Places: Flexibility, lifelong learning and a learning society*. Routledge: London

Emler, N. and McNamara, S. (1996). 'The Social Contact Patterns of Young People: effects of participation in the social institutions of family, education and work', pp. 121-39 in H. Helve and J. Bynner (eds.) *Youth and Life Management: research perspectives*. Helsinki: Yliopistopaino

Field, J. (2005). *Social Capital and Lifelong Learning*. Policy Press: Bristol

Field, J. (2006). *Lifelong Learning and the New Educational Order*. Trentham: Stoke on Trent

Green, A. (2003). The Many Faces of Lifelong Learning: Recent education policy trends in Europe. In *Journal of Education Policy*, 17, 4, 611-26

Kim, L. and R. R. Nelson (2000). (Eds.), *Technology, Learning and Innovation: experiences of newly industrializing economies*. Cambridge University Press: Cambridge

Knoll, J. (1998). 'Lebenslanges Lernen' und internationale Bildungspolitik – Zur Genese eines Begriffs und dessen nationale Operationalisierungen, pp. 35-50 in R. Brödel (ed.), *Lebenslanges Lernen – Lebensbegleitende Bildung*. Luchterhand: Neuwied

Merriam, S. B. (1994). Learning and Life Experience: The connection in adulthood, pp. 74-89 in J. D. Sinnott (ed.), *Interdisciplinary Handbook of Adult Lifespan Learning.* Greenwood Press: Westport CT

Merrill, B. and Alheit, P. (2004). Biography and Narratives: Adult returners to learning, pp 150-62.In M. Osborne, J. Gallacher and B. Crossan (eds.), *Researching Widening Access to Lifelong Learning: Issues and approaches in international research.* RoutledgeFalmer: London

Nicoll, K. (2006). *Flexibility and Lifelong Learning: Examining the rhetoric of education.* Routledge: London

Putnam, R. D. (2000). *Bowling Alone: The collapse and revival of American community.* Simon and Schuster: New York

Rosanvallon, P. (1995). *La nouvelle question sociale: repenser l'État-providence.* Editions du Seuil: Paris

Schemmann, M. (2002). Reflexive Modernisation in Adult Education Research: the example of Anthony Giddens' theoretical approach, pp 64-80. In A. Bron and M. Schemmann (eds.), *Social Science Theories in Adult Education Research* Lit Verlag: Munster

Schemmann, M. (2007). *Internationale Weiterbildungspolitik und Globalisierung.* W. Bertelsmann Verlag: Bielefeld

Schuetze, H. G. and Casey, C. (2006). Models and Meanings of Lifelong Learning: Progress and barriers on the road to a learning society. *Compare,* 36, 2, 279-87

Schuller, T. et al (2004). *The Benefits of Learning: the impact of education on health, family life and social capital.* Routledge: London

Stauber, B., Pohl, A. and Walther, A. (2007). Ein neuer Blick auf die Übergänge junger Frauen und Männer, pp. 7-18. In B. Stauber, A. Pohl and A. Walther (eds.), *Subjektorientierte Übergangsforschung. Rekonstruktion und Unterstützung biografischer Übergänge junger Erwachsener.* Juventa: Weinheim and Munich

Strawn, C. (2003). *The Influence of Social Capital on Lifelong Learning Among Adults who did not finish High School.* National Centre for the Study of Adult Learning and Literacy: Cambridge MA

Stuart, M. (2006). 'My Friends Made all the Difference': Getting into and succeeding at university for first-generation entrants. In *Journal of Access Policy and Practice,* 3, 2, 162-84

Tett, L. and Maclachlan, K. (2007). Adult literacy and numeracy, social capital, learner identities and self-confidence. In *Studies in the Education of Adults,* 39, 2, 150-67

Walther, A., Stauber, B. and Pohl, A. (2005). Informal Networks in Youth Transitions in West Germany: Biographical resource or reproduction of social inequality? In *Journal of Youth Studies,* 8, 2, 221-40

Woolcock, M. (1998). 'Social Capital and Economic Development: toward a theoretical synthesis and policy framework'. In *Theory and Society,* 27, 2, 151-208

3 What Does it Take to Learn From One's Life? Exploring Opportunities for Biographical Learning in the Lifecourse

Michael Tedder and Gert Biesta

Introduction

If lifelong learning is to be more than the acquisition of qualifications through participation in formal education; if, in other words, an important aspect of lifelong learning has to do with the ways in which people learn *from* their lives and, through this, learn *for* their lives, then we must ask what opportunities people have to engage in processes of 'biographical learning'. We must ask further how opportunities for biographical learning and access to such opportunities are structured at different ages and stages in our lives. Between 2004 and 2007 the *Learning Lives* project[1] used repeated interviews to construct detailed biographical accounts of the lives of adults in the UK that enable us to gain insight into such issues. A particular interest was the way in which 'life' can be(come) an object of learning so that we can explore *the ways in which people learn from their lives*, and also *the significance of such learning processes*. We were able in this way to explore how people learn through their lives and how their learning relates to processes of transition and change.

An important, though unsurprising, finding of the project was that some people are more adept than others at telling stories from their lives and we found that some reveal more about the learning potential and the action potential of their stories than others (see Biesta et al, 2008). In this chapter we present a life story constructed from interviews with one articulate *Learning Lives* participant with the pseudonym Russell Jackson. We begin with a brief overview of literature on biographical learning, focusing on contributions made by Alheit

---

1 *Learning Lives: Learning, Identity and Agency* was a longitudinal study of the learning biographies of 150 adults of 25 and older during which participants were interviewed up to eight times between 2004 and 2007. The project was funded by the Economic and Social Research Council, Award Reference RES139250111, and was part of the ESRC's *Teaching and Learning Research Programme. Learning Lives* was a collaborative project involving the University of Exeter (Gert Biesta, Flora Macleod, Michael Tedder, Paul Lambe), the University of Brighton (Ivor Goodson, Norma Adair), the University of Leeds (Phil Hodkinson, Heather Hodkinson, Geoff Ford, Ruth Hawthorne), and the University of Stirling (John Field, Heather Lynch). For further information see www.learninglives.org.

and Dausien.[2] In the next section we introduce Russell Jackson through an account of his career constructed from the transcripts of seven biographical interviews undertaken between November 2004 and December 2006. We then interrogate the account with the help of five questions:

(1) What has Russell learned from his life?
(2) How has he learned?
(3) When did he learn?
(4) What has been the role of narrative in his learning?
(5) What has been the significance of this learning?

The questions are used heuristically in order to explore connections between Russell's learning and identity through the changes and transitions about which he told us stories. In the final section of the chapter we draw some conclusions to argue that biographical and life history methods of research can provide a rich and nuanced approach to understanding learning through the lifecourse.

What 'is' biographical learning?

Over the past three decades the field of research in adult education has witnessed a strong rise in the use of biographical and life history approaches (see, e.g., Alheit et al., 1995; Alheit and Hoerning 1989; Bron and West 2000; Coare and Thomson, 1996; Dominicé 2000; Erben 1998; Goodson 2001; Hoar et al., 1994; West et al., 2007). The 'turn to biographical methods' (Bron *et al.*, 2005, p.12) can be understood in part as reflecting contemporary interest in working with biography as a way of constructing 'meaning and authenticity' from people's experiences of a rapidly changing modern world. The appeal to practitioners in adult education is that it offers a means of articulating the stories of people who can be marginalised in traditional forms of research yet whose stories may enable us to develop a sophisticated understanding of learning and educational processes. The 'biographical turn' engages with a broad conception of learning, one which does not restrict the meaning of learning to institutional definitions, but which includes the cognitive and reflexive dimensions of learning as much as the emotional, embodied, pre-reflexive and non-cognitive aspects of everyday learning processes and practices.

A feature of the rise of biographical and life history approaches is an interest in *biographical learning* (e.g., Alheit 1995; Alheit and Dausien 2002; Dominicé 2000; Biesta and Tedder 2007; Tedder and Biesta, 2007, 2008) which

---

2　We are aware that Alheit and Dausien are not the only ones who have written on biographical learning. For the purpose of this paper, however, we confine ourselves to their contribution.

encompasses an interest in both the influence of biography on learning processes and practices, and an interest in biography as itself 'a field of learning' (Alheit 1995, p. 59). Alheit and Dausien define biographical learning as 'a self-willed, 'autopoietic' accomplishment on the part of active subjects, in which they reflexively 'organise' their experience in such a way that they also generate personal coherence, identity, a meaning to their life history and a communicable, socially viable lifeworld perspective for guiding their actions' (Alheit and Dausien 2002, p.17). They argue that lifelong and lifewide learning are 'tied at all times to the contexts of a specific biography' (ibid, p.15), which implies that '(w)ithout biography there can be no learning, without learning, no biography' (ibid.).

Alheit and Dausien highlight three aspects of biographical learning: the implicit dimension, the social dimension and the 'self-willed' dimension (see ibid., p.15-16). They note how learning that is implicit and tacit 'form a person's *biographical stock of knowledge'* (ibid., p.15; emphasis in original) and that we can retrieve such learning 'when we find ourselves stumbling or at crossroads' (ibid.). They emphasise that reflexive learning processes do not exclusively take place 'inside' the individual 'but depend on communication and interaction with others' (see ibid., p.16). Alheit and Dausien argue that learning within and through one's life history is interactive and socially structured, on the one hand, but also follows its own 'individual logic' generated by the specific, biographically layered structure of experience. However, it remains possible to encounter 'unexpected experiences and surprising transformations that in many cases are not foreseen by the 'learner' himself, or are not 'understood' until after the event' (ibid., p.16).

Alheit (1995) links biographical learning to emancipatory adult education. The main task of such education, he argues, is that of 'biographical coaching' (ibid., p.68), which involves 'the joint discovery by teacher and learner of biographical opportunities for shaping social, occupational and political existence more autonomously' (ibid.). Coaching also means 'exerting a particular influence on the 'social ecology' of learning - i.e., in practical terms, the framework of social conditions - in order that individuals' hidden possibilities are brought to the surface and developed, and that 'unlived' lives can be lived instead.' (ibid.) He highlights that the 'basic structure' of such educational processes is narrative (ibid., p.69). He also points at the importance of communication, since it is communication with others which 'triggers ... a new dimension of self-referentiality' (ibid.).

From this Alheit and Dausien conclude that '(i)f the biographical organisation of learning processes is to be given practical educational (and institutional) support, then *spaces* for reflection and communication, as well as interaction with 'spaces of opportunity' are at least as important as developing 'instruments for individual self-management'' (Alheit and Dausien 2002, p.16).

The implication of this observation for empirical research is that, if we seek to understand the significance of biographical learning in people's lives, we need to inquire about the 'spaces of opportunity' they have accessed and about their 'spaces for reflection and communication' and their 'instruments for individual self-management'. We need to be sensitive to their uses of narrative within educational processes. We need also to ask what else may be desirable or necessary to enable opportunities for learning from the lifecourse?

Russell Jackson: A career narrative

When Russell was first interviewed in November 2004 he held a fixed term contract as an Information and Communication Technology (ICT) Development Tutor working for a county council adult education service in a rural area of the UK. His job comprised taking a set of laptop computers to different locations in order to provide tuition in ICT skills for people in so-called 'hard to reach' groups. The first interview took place at a Job Centre after he had concluded a session with a small group of unemployed people. The second and subsequent interviews took place at his home, a substantial detached bungalow that bears witness to Russell's building and woodworking craft skills with many examples of his handiwork inside and outside the building. From the complex and at times surprising stories Russell told us in our interviews we were able to construct a narrative around his learning career that made it apparent how his skills and qualities had emerged.

Russell's career can be summarised in three stages: the first lasted nearly twenty years when he worked as an engineer in mining and quarrying; the second stage began with a conversion experience after which Russell studied to become a priest and spent nearly a decade working in the church; the third stage is Russell's most recent employment in adult education. The period covered by the interviews was one of continuing uncertainty and change: Russell was employed in a job that he enjoyed and found meaningful but he would have much preferred to be continuing his vocation as a priest.

Russell was born in 1951, the sixth of seven children in a working-class family living in a small town in the south west of England. Russell passed the eleven plus examination and went to the local grammar school (UK binary system) but his experience there was not a happy one and Russell described being a victim of bullying which he attributed to his being small in stature, being rebellious and coming from a working class background in a predominantly middle class institution. When he was asked to leave school at the age of 16, Russell followed his father's advice and applied for an apprenticeship at a local engineering company where he immediately felt more comfortable:

> *I walked through the green doors of the apprentice school and was hit by the noise and the smell and the sheer engineeringness of that place and I changed direction [laughs] like on the spot.* (Interview 1, Nov 2004)

This transition was important: not only did it mark the start of his employment career but in a subsequent interview Russell recalled that his first autonomous decision was the way he ignored his father's advice to apply for a craft apprenticeship (there were over 70 available places) and instead applied - successfully - for a technician apprenticeship (for which there were only six places).

Russell served his time as an apprentice and achieved a full technological certificate from his local college after five years in 1972. He worked as an engineer for the same company for a further six years during which time he married and became a father of two children. However, he could see few prospects for career advancement and applied for a job in Scotland where he stayed for two years and then moved to the Midlands where he worked for a succession of engineering companies. His career advanced following a trajectory in which he steadily increased his managerial responsibilities.

In the mid-1980s came the event that would lead to a major disruption in Russell's life, what he described in the interviews as a conversion experience. Although he swore, 'I was damned if I was going to get religion, you know,' *(Interview 1, Nov 2004)* he was able to describe eloquently the occasion when he underwent an epiphany:

> *In the garage doing the woodturning and ... You reflect there quietly, you're at ease with yourself. You've got a whole pile of things to - you got to sort out. ... I'm now turning away happily and minding my own business and I stop the lathe and I'm turning the big pine bowl ... I'm surrounded with chippings ... It's in the evening and I've got the light on in the garage shining on this bowl, and I just have an overwhelming sense of a presence with me really. It's really difficult to be, to describe this in rational terms. It's as real to me now as it's always been ... I had a sense of the real presence of God.* (Interview 1, Nov 2004)

Not only did Russell feel called to become a Christian but also a vocation to become a priest in the Church of England. He undertook a two year full-time course of study at a theological college. After ordination Russell was appointed to a curacy back in the south west of England and this was followed by a decade of working as a priest, not only in parishes but also in a diocesan role that involved training others to support children and young people.

In retrospect, Russell judged that he overworked and that his relationship with his wife suffered as a consequence. They undertook marriage guidance but he had started a relationship with another woman before he divorced his wife. A scandal ensued that ended with Russell's resignation as a priest and thus the end of the second stage of his career. A further career transition occurred, in that Russell still needed to earn a living but had to adjust to the loss of the role that was central to his identity, his vocation to the ministry. He needed to adjust to changed domestic circumstances when he married his second wife and gained two step children. Acting on the suggestion of a friend, he secured a fixed term contract with the adult education service to teach the computing skills he had learned during his engineering life and ventured onto the third stage.

Russell became a participant in the Learning Lives project after three years of involvement in the adult education service. Our interviews traced his changing perspective on teaching as a professional practice alongside his changing relationship with the church during the latest phase of his career.

In the second interview (December 2004), Russell said he had no inclination to return to engineering but had hoped that, at some point it would be possible to return to parish work. However, he had received an official letter stating that such a return would not be possible in the same diocese. Russell indicated a change in his attitude to being an adult education teacher, that his role as an ICT development tutor was becoming less peripheral to his life:

> *where teaching has been until very recently a stopgap measure ... I'm in the process of really coming to terms with the fact, and not quite as reluctantly as I might have supposed, that, really the teaching is my career.* (Interview 2, Dec 2004)

In the third interview, five months later, Russell's professional refocusing as a teacher of adult learners was evident when he elaborated on the ideas and values that informed his practice. He spoke of the challenge of teaching new courses and of teaching in new locations. He spoke of the growing confidence that he had in his work and of the working relationships he had established. However, he was sanguine about the prospects for the service, fearing that, in the present funding regime: '*Adult Ed I think, will just wither on the vine*' (Interview 3, May 2005).

At the start of the next academic year, in September 2005, the fourth interview found Russell still wrestling with the call of the ministry and striving to reconcile it with his occupation as an adult education tutor. In essence, Russell thought he should '*make the most of it*' (Interview 4, September 2005). He asserted that he loved teaching and recognised that the role had been a central part of his ministry as a parish priest. He expressed some resentment of what he saw as 'callous and indifferent' treatment from an institution - the church - that uses the language of compassion and forgiveness but, he felt, did not show those qualities to him. It was hardly surprising, then, to find out at the fifth interview, at the end of 2005, that Russell had stopped attending his local church. As his hopes for a return to the ministry faded, so Russell described himself as '*becoming ambitious within the context I find myself in*' (Interview 5, December 2005). He was articulate about the professional autonomy in teaching that he saw being eroded by government bureaucracy and a regime of inspection. However, he also perceived a lack of challenge in his teaching. Russell was becoming dissatisfied with holding simply a teaching role in adult education and said he was interested in strategic issues and wanted 'to make a difference'.

The sixth interview took place in July 2006, shortly after Russell had been interviewed for two Assistant Principal vacancies that had emerged as part of the re-organisation of adult education. It seems he had been a serious contender for both positions but others had been appointed; Russell was demoralised and disillusioned. The end of his ICT contract was drawing closer and he found himself in a shrinking organisation with a new line manager. His response was to meet with senior managers to secure a clearer idea of his prospects within the organisation and to ensure they were aware of his continuing commitment.

At the final interview in December 2006, it emerged that one of the two individuals appointed to Assistant Principal posts the previous summer had decided to leave after a few weeks. Russell was approached and had agreed to accept the vacant post. He found his new job a congenial one:

> *My first sort of reaction to that is I'm enormously comfortable in this role. It's like putting on a well-worn coat and just all of a sudden, just go and do the business ... There are some issues that are going to get addressed and we're going to sort them.* (Interview 7, December 2006)

Russell had formally retired from the Church of England but continued to have a sense that he had come closest to what he 'was intended to be' in the days when he was a priest and was working on youth matters for the diocese:

> *I still find it <u>really</u> hard to talk about um the things that I did as a parish priest and as a children's adviser.... we ran courses for clergy and young people on child protection issues, I did a lot of good in that role. ... I learned lots of things ... so you see, it's really close to my heart.... It's been the role um that I felt most truly mine, to what makes me most truly the person that I was intended to be.*
> (Interview 7, December 2006)

Learning from life

In this section we explore aspects of this account of Russell's life more systematically using five questions. The questions are easily stated though challenging to answer, not least because there are two perspectives: the actor-perspective and the researcher-perspective. We take into consideration not only what Russell says he has learned but also what we, as researchers, might interpret as his learning within the narrative.

(1) What has Russell learned from his life?

Russell himself summarised how his lifetime experiences of working, from the age of sixteen to his late 50s, had been a source of learning from his life that had given him the confidence and self-assurance to adapt to new circumstances. It is possible for us to infer from his stories certain identifiable 'things' that he has learned *for* his life, the knowledge he has acquired that enables him to follow a career, and the values that are revealed in his reflections on significant events within his life. However, such identifiable learning is inseparable from the understanding that Russell has developed over the years about himself, about his character and dispositions, and how that self relates to others in his family, in his workplace and in his social networks. In other words, his learning is central to his identity. Our career narrative shows how such understanding enables Russell to effect action in his life and to reflect on the outcomes of such action.

Knowledge, skills and competencies

The life stories show how Russell has learned information, skills and competencies within formal education and training that have enabled him to earn a living and pursue a career in different occupations. At times the periods of education and training had direct instrumental relevance to his work. Thus his apprenticeship and college qualifications gave Russell entry into a professional career structure as an engineer. His two years at theological college provided entry to a career structure within the church. More recently, Russell has undertaken part-time courses of teacher education that relate to his current occupation. However, having secured entry to these different fields, Russell's progress within them has depended on other forms of learning. His career trajectory within engineering moved steadily away from engineering towards more managerial responsibilities. His church career included short courses of formal learning but also extensive experience in non-formal settings. In the period covered by our interviews, our longitudinal approach enabled us to monitor the way Russell's aspirations in adult education evolved and refocused. Thus stories of formal education and training with defined or identifiable content merge within the narrative with forms of learning that have significance for the maintenance and development of the self.

Values

The biographical dimension of Russell's learning is even more evident when we look at the values that frame his approach to life. Russell's stories reveal that he has a normative and ethical stance from which he can evaluate his experiences. Such values may have come from experiences within formal education though they were not necessarily part of the formal curriculum. In his stories of grammar school life and his comments about bullying, for example, we find some of the origins of Russell's opposition to injustice. He recognises this school experience as '*one of the formative things for me*' and asserted that '*I will not be bullied, I will not be intimidated, I will not be forced into anything that I don't wish to be*' (Interview 1, Nov. 2004). In stories of later events, such as dealing with the problems of parishioners when he was a priest, Russell demonstrated a continuing determination to take a stand against perceived injustice.

The scandal occasioned by the loss of his career as a priest appears to have enhanced the empathy that Russell has with people who are disadvantaged or who have experienced disasters:

> *That is one of the hardest lessons I have ever learned about my own frailty and fallibility, really. I've sat the other side of the table on many occasions helping people who have found themselves in difficult situations .... To find myself the other side of that coin, with failure and disgrace and everything around, extraordinarily difficult ....* (Interview 1, Nov 2004)

Russell's stories reveal the sympathies and beliefs that have been learned from his experiences within life and such qualities offer a key to understanding Russell's sense of what are appropriate actions for his life. They are part of the tacit framework upon which we draw when, as Alheit and Dausien (2002) described it, '*we find ourselves stumbling or at crossroads*'.

Sense of self

In Russell's stories there were several events, such as his response to being bullied, or his becoming an engineering apprentice, that had consequences for his sense of self. The most remarkable turning point was the conversion experience which led him to the decision to become a priest. In terms of learning it resulted in the insight that the role of priest was the one that fitted him best, the role that he felt was 'most truly' his and which he saw as '*most truly the person that [he] was intended to be*'. Russell also clearly learned from the events around the end of his career as a priest and in the adoption of his new professional identity as an adult educator. A tentative conclusion here might be that Russell's accounts of the events that have led to significant learning from his life all seem to be related to his sense of self, to the person he is, the person he wants to be - in terms of his values and normative orientations - and most specifically the person he was intended to be.

(2) How has Russell learned from his life?

The opportunities that Russell has had for learning from experiences within his life are most apparent in two areas: through the periods of formal education and training that he has undertaken and through the relationships he has developed in different workplaces and in his social life. The three stages of Russell's career were each associated with a period of formal education which enabled him to make a transition to a quite different role with new sets of responsibilities and expectations. Each of those periods of formal education offered immersion in the culture of different communities and practices, and offered opportunities for interaction and communication with others as well as for reflection on his life.

In respect of Russell's relationships, he has given prominence in the interview stories to colleagues and friends who have been important at different times in his career: the colleague in the diocese with whom he worked on matters affecting children and young people; his adult education line managers; the friend in the education service who suggested that Russell consider teaching adult students.

In the final interview Russell was able to identify a range of experiences and resources from which he draws when confronting problems. In managing such challenges, he spoke of such factors as the training he received in counselling skills in a number of different courses and the importance of his own reading. Such threads have become intertwined with the accumulated experience of being a parish priest. Russell consistently emphasised the importance of reflection in learning from his life and how taking part in the Learning Lives project had required such reflection:

> *(A)ctually trying to work out what it is that you want to say in a coherent way when you're being faced with personal and piercing questions then that's a really useful reflective tool that has been of great value to me. (...) The other thing that's happened is reading the transcripts and the transcripts have been hugely moving for me on occasion to read. (...) Unless you are asked the question, unless you're pressed, unless you're asked to explain that, what is just internal, what is just accepted within yourself as being the way the world is, is not brought out, you know?* (Interview 7, December 2006)

This, then, gives an indication of how Russell has learned from his life. But it immediately raises important issues for our next question: When has Russell learned from his life?

(3) When has Russell learned from his life?

We have identified three significant transitions in our construction of Russell's life story and each were key moments for his learning. The first was a transition he shares with most people in our society, the transition from school to work. The other two transitions appear not to be structural in the same way but more individual and personal. Nevertheless, the significant learning each time depended crucially on the social context in which those transitions played out. The second transition arose from Russell's conversion experience and was narrated in his story as a personal 'calling' - a vocation - to the church. However, Russell had been made redundant not long before from his engineering post, it took place in the early 1980s, a period of decline and retrenchment in the engineering industry. Russell was dissatisfied with the lifestyle of international travel associated with his industrial career. Despite his protestations that '*I was damned if I was going to get religion*' (Interview 1, Nov 2004) there were external elements to his life that predisposed him to a life-changing experience. The third transition also would appear to be specific to Russell in that the end of his career as a priest and his transition to adult education came about as a consequence of his behaviour in his marriage. Even here, though, there are issues around the significance of relationship breakdown and how such traumas are managed within institutions like the church and perceived by public media. Within Russell's story there were continuing tensions between different perspectives on the extent to which his divorce would interfere with his ability to continue his vocation.

There are three related issues that make the answer to this question still more complicated. The first issue is that it seems reasonable to assume that what Russell has learned from his life is a mix of more implicit and more explicit learning, where things are learned but only become clear over time, as a result of later experiences or as a result of reflection. For this reason it is difficult to point to particular points in time as the moments when Russell learned something from his life. The experience of bullying was 'formative,' as he put it, but it is likely that it took time before the formative effect of this experience became 'operative' and it took presumably even longer before Russell became fully aware of how this experience and his response to it had formed him. The conversion experience has a very clear location in time and in Russell's biography but the learning that followed from this was again something that took time to emerge.

The second issue concerns life history methodology and the fact that the accounts we have of Russell's learning are all retrospective. In the stories

Russell is able to link particular events in his life to what he learned from them. Although this sometimes may give the impression that the learning happened at that particular moment in time, this is most likely an artefact of the life history approach. Retrospectively Russell is able to identify the events that turned out to be significant for his later life, which means that the learning that followed from the events gave the events their significance.

If we take these points together, there was at least one 'moment' in Russell's life where it is clear that he was learning from his life, viz., the time when he was asked to tell the stories of his life for the Learning Lives project which enabled him to become aware of life themes and 'lessons'. Taking part in the research interviews has enabled Russell to articulate how learning occurs within particular spaces. Some questions elicited a spontaneous response that suggested new insights into his life. At other times, it seems a particular understanding had taken much longer to emerge. He acknowledged that understanding the full impact of participation in the project was going to take time. *'I think I probably need to answer that question in five years time or ten years time'* (Interview 7, December 2006).

(4) What has been the role of narrative in Russell's learning?
It is clear that stories are important for Russell's learning and that storying his life for the Learning Lives interviews and subsequently reading some of the transcripts have helped Russell to become more aware of the significance of particular events in his life and of what he has learned from them. We could say that the life stories allowed Russell to 'objectify' his life - i.e., made it into an object of reflection - and it is this which can help us to understand, for example, why on occasion Russell found reading the transcripts of his own interviews a 'hugely moving' experience. Through the stories Russell experienced his life in a new and sometimes different way. In this way narratives are an important 'vehicle' for biographical learning.

For Russell the 'power of narrative' goes further than this. As he observes in the final interview:

> *(T)he one thing I've got is the power of narrative. I'm not well qualified. I'm not, you know, hugely intelligent or all those really worthwhile things, I've just got a story. And the story informs who I am and the story makes me who I am and out of that I have an ability and a confidence and the ability to deal with people in their stories.* (Interview 7, December 2006)

Such understanding suggests one of the means by which Russell achieves agency in his life and he gave examples of the way story telling about his life has given him the ability to influence others and to affect their decision-making.

What distinguishes Russell's stories from the stories of some other participants in the Learning Lives project is that Russell's stories have 'real' narrative quality in that they are organised around a 'plot.' The 'plot' of Russell's life story concerns his 'core identity' of being a priest. Although it is possible to construct a story of Russell's life in a chronological way, for Russell (or, to be more precise, in the story that Russell constructs about his life) the 'priest-position' is the centre from which the story is constructed and from which many if not all events in the story get their meaning. The priest 'position' works in an *evaluative* way, in that many of the things Russell tells about his life are presented in relation to how close or how distanced he is/was from this 'core' identity. Russell's narrative has a strong *evaluative* character in that life-events have positions and are evaluated in relation to the 'self' that is most central and most important for Russell. At least in terms of his life narrative we can say that this is the most central thing Russell has learned from his life. This became very clear in the final interview when he said: '*I'm haunted by my vocation'* (Interview 7, December 2006).

(5) What has been the significance of what Russell has learned from his life?
In our analysis we have focused mainly on what (and how) Russell has learned *from* his life. While it is interesting from a research perspective to find out how, where and when such biographical learning takes place, from an actor perspective it is much more important to ask about the relevance of this kind of biographical learning. Does learning from one's life matter? Does it make a difference *for* one's life? There is clear evidence that some experiences in Russell's life have been formative and have had an impact on Russell's agency, on the ways in which he has made decisions about his life and the ways in which he has responded to particular life events. There is also some evidence of the impact of participation in the interviews themselves, although Russell is the first to acknowledge that this itself a learning process that will take time. The most significant event - at least in the way in which Russell has storied his life - is, of course, the 'discovery' of the person he was intended to be. This discovery is clearly something that he learned from his life - through a complex process of experience, reflection, communication and interaction - and it is something that not only had significant impact on his life as an 'event;' it also had a significant impact on the perception of his life, his life narrative, and hence on the way in which he was able to make sense of his life and of himself.

Conclusion

In this chapter we have attempted to shed light on a particular dimension of biographical learning, namely, the way in which people can learn *from* their lives. The consideration of Russell's stories provides some valuable insights in the ways in which people can learn from their lives and the significance of such processes.

Our analysis shows some of the connections between change, transition and biographical learning in the life of this Learning Lives participant. The transitions we identified in Russell's life opened spaces for reflection within which he brought to bear certain instruments or strategies that enabled him to consider the exigencies of those transitions. Episodes of formal education have a role to play in providing space for people to reflect on their lives; indeed, they may be more significant as spaces for reflection and for identifying opportunities for further development than merely as opportunities to acquire knowledge and skills. (A related discussion of using a biographical approach to understanding the effects of formal education in Access courses - courses to prepare adults for higher education - can be found in Tedder 2007.)

Our career narrative shows that, through his earlier education and training, Russell acquired tools that enabled him to analyse and reflect on his experiences. Such instruments were deployed and refined through experiences at work in different organisations and in different parts of the country as the three stages of his career unfolded. At key junctures Russell was able to identify significant others, friends or relatives, who enabled him to retell his narrative and explore possible courses of action (the biographical coach, in Alheit's phrase, 1995). There is, of course, no certainty in such circumstances as Russell described that there will be others in a position to act as catalysts for change. What Russell confirmed was the centrality of narrative both as a means of communicating with others about the meanings of life course conditions and as a means of effecting change in those conditions.

Our analysis has shown that biographical learning processes are difficult to pin down and that biographical learning literally takes time. This is why biographical and life history methods are so important in trying to make sense of learning through the life course.

References

Alheit, P. (1995). 'Biographical learning: Theoretical outline, challenges and contradictions of a new approach in adult education'. In P. Alheit, A. Bron-Wojciechowska, E. Brugger, and P. Dominicé, (Eds.) *The Biographical Approach in European Adult Education,* (57-74). Wien: Verband Wiener Volksbildung.

Alheit, P., Bron-Wojciechowska, A., Brugger, E. and Dominicé, P. (1995) (Eds.) *The Biographical Approach in European Adult Education.* Wien: Verband Wiener Volksbildung.

Alheit, P. and Dausien, B. (2002). 'The double face of lifelong learning: Two analytical perspectives on a 'silent revolution'. In *Studies in the Education of Adults,* 34 (1), 3-22.

Alheit, P. and Hoerning, E.M. (Eds.) (1989). *Biographisches Wissen. Beiträge zu einer Theorie lebensgeschichtlicher.* Erfahrung. Frankfurt am Main: Campus.

Biesta, G. and Tedder, M. (2007). 'Agency and learning in the lifecourse: Towards an ecological perspective.' In *Studies in the Education of Adults,* 39 (2) 132-149.

Biesta, G. and Tedder, M. (2008). *Learning from life in the learning economy: The role of narrative,* Paper presented at the SCUTREA conference 'Whither adult education in the learning paradigm?' Edinburgh University, 2-4 July.

Biesta, G.J.J., Goodson, I., Tedder, M. and Adair, N. (2008) *Learning from life: The role of narrative,* A summative working paper for the Learning Lives project.

Bron, A. and West, L. (2000). 'Time for stories: The emergence of life history methods in the social sciences.' In *International Journal of Contemporary Sociology,* 37 (2), 158-175.

Bron, A., Kurantowicz, E., Salling Olesen, H. and West, L. (Eds.) (2005). *"Old" and "New" Worlds of Adult Learning.* Wrocław: Wydawnictwo Naukowe.

Coare, P. and Thomson, A. (1996). *Through the Joy of Learning, Diary of 1,000 Adult Learners.* Leicester: NIACE.

Dominicé, P. (2000). *Learning from our lives.* San Francisco: Jossey-Bass.

Erben, M. (Ed) (1998). *Biography and education.* London: Falmer.

Goodson, I. (2001). 'The story of life history.' In *Identity,* 1 (2) 129-142.

Hoar, M., Lea, M., Stuart, M., Swash, V., Thomson, A. and West, L. (1994). *Life Histories and Learning: Language, the Self and Education.* University of Sussex/Kent.

Tedder, M. (2007). 'Making a choice? Insights from using a life history approach to researching access students.'In *Journal of Widening Participation and Lifelong Learning,* 9 (2) 26-35.

Tedder, M. and Biesta, G. (2007). *'Learning from life and learning for life: Exploring the opportunities for biographical learning in the lives of adults',* http://www.learninglives.org/Working_papers.html#wp_7 Working Paper 7 of the Learning Lives Project.

West, L., Alheit, P., Andersen, A.S. and Merrill, B. (2007). *Using biographical and life history approaches in the study of adult and lifelong learning: European Perspectives.* Frankfurt: Peter Lang.

4   Accounting for Structure in Agency: Recursive Methodology, Social Narratives and Habitus

Simon Warren and Sue Webb

My aunty died 11 years ago with cancer and various family members helped to look after her in the last few months and it was her that actually said you ought to go into something like this and she said you're the only one in the family didn't make her feel uncomfortable. She thought I'd got a natural aptitude for it.

I was sent on a handling and lifting course. Apart from that the only other training was working with somebody else for 6 weeks, you do this, this way and if I'm totally honest I didn't agree with what they were doing anyway.   They just didn't show people dignity and compassion. And every time I wanted to go on a course, because the companies run courses themselves, like in-house training, and oh sorry this one's full, and I just got so frustrated in the end I thought right that's it, I've had it.

These quotes come from Jenny who, at the time of the interview, was a 40 year old white mother of four children, recently separated from her husband. She was enrolled on a part-time vocational GCSE (Level 2[1]) Health and Social Care course at a Further Education College in Northern England. In these two brief extracts we can detect a sense in which Jenny's employment trajectory in the social care sector and her educational trajectory are embedded in a personal biography. Importantly, for what we want to explore in this chapter, we can detect the way that Jenny's story, her narrative, is constructed through the linking of certain events in such a way that they convey a meaningful life, a life that indeed has a trajectory, has form. The central question we pose is to ask whether or not the key events that Jenny identifies in order to give form and meaning to her narrative are themselves linked to wider patterns and social organisation or structures. In other words, we ask is there structure *in* agency and if there is how has this been made meaningful in Jenny's biographical narrative. The chapter will examine these questions through the case study of Jenny in which we analyse two distinct narrative accounts produced by Jenny over a period of eighteen months and compare these with other narrative accounts from key participants drawn from the further educational context, which is pivotal to her narratives. To be more explicit, we want to suggest that

---

1   Level 2 in the English National Qualification Framework is equivalent to the level acquired at the end of compulsory schooling at age 16.

Jenny's narrative constructs the events around her Aunt's death as having a causal relationship with Jenny's subsequent 'decision' to participate in care work. Her negative experience of training opportunities while employed in this occupational sector then set the scene for her later enrolment in a Health and Social Care course. That is, her story connects disparate events in a particular temporal order, where the events have a causal relationship with subsequent events that gives a particular meaning to the account. But, we want to do more than analyse Jenny's account of herself as a narrative; we want to do more than produce an account of an account. The main task in this chapter is to examine how accounts are socially organised and saturated by social structure, and to understand how accounts can give us access to what Pierre Bourdieu calls 'habitus', that is, social structure embodied in our personal biographies. Through this examination we will demonstrate how we have analysed our interviews with Jenny in such a way that we can provide theoretical descriptions of the social conditions of the production of her account. In doing this we make one assertion, that in order to understand the particularity of Jenny's life, we have to grasp how that particularity is the product of specific interactions between history, economics, institutional cultures, education policy and individual agency – that is through the interaction between 'field' and 'habitus'.

In summary, we will outline the small-scale study, of which Jenny was a participant, situating it in relation to particular shifts in both social structure and education policy in England, but especially to a discourse of the 'responsible learner'. Following this we will present Jenny's account of herself as a narrative with a particular structure and show how this narrative analysis provides us with clues of the social organisation of the narrative. Consequently, we will provide an argument for analysing accounts as socially organised narratives, building on Bourdieu's concepts of *practice* and *habitus*. In particular we stress the methodological importance of conducting an analysis that constantly moves between field and habitus, between structure and agency. We elaborate this 'recursive methodology' through the second 'reflexive' interview with Jenny, and through our analysis of other interview data from key participants in the Further Education College[2] where Jenny has studied. In this way we deliberately situate Jenny's narratives in the context of narratives drawn from the Further Education College that locate this College in a particular space in the local education and training market.

---

2 Further Education (FE) colleges constitute the main element of the tertiary education sector, along with schools that provide post-16 qualifications. While FE is largely vocationally oriented there is an increase in the role of FE colleges provided the early stages of Higher Education.

The study

Jenny was one of three adult learners who participated in a small-scale pilot project looking at adults returning to learning. This focus of study was chosen because of the apparently ambiguous position of adults within the current reforms of the English further and higher education sectors. The position of adults as learners within these two sectors was made problematic in two ways. Firstly, Government policy in these areas, despite the rhetoric of lifelong learning, has been overwhelmingly focused on managing the transition of 16-19 year olds from compulsory schooling, through further and higher education and training, into the labour market. Secondly, recent policy reforms have created structural barriers to adult participation in further and higher education. For instance, recent Government guidance for further education accommodates adults who are in employment and do not already have a Level 2 qualification, and are therefore eligible for work-based learning. In a context where policy instruments, such as funding mechanisms, push further education institutions towards managing youth transitions, the position of unemployed adults in the further education sector remains ambiguous. Recent changes to entry qualifications for adults in higher education work to shift resources towards those without a prior degree. While this appears to address the Government's social inclusion agenda, by compelling Universities to increase the participation of lower socio-economic groups and black and minority ethnic communities, it also excludes many who are seeking what are sometimes termed 'leisure learning' opportunities, and potentially those seeking career shifts through higher education. With this in mind the pilot project was conducted in two learning sites – a part-time modern foreign languages course in a university adult education department and a full-time and a part-time vocational social care and health course in a further education college. We were also concerned to identify learners who would appear to face objective moments of reflexivity – a 40 year old woman (Jenny) returning to learning, a young woman from an asylum seeking family looking to improve her labour market position, and a young man engaged in a leisure learning course but working in an internationalised high-tech engineering industry.

The research was situated in a former industrial city, in northern England, undergoing the kinds of structural change that hegemonic policy and social theory argue is productive of reflexivity and amenable to shifts in social responsibility (for discussions of this see: Ball, 1999, Coffield, 1999, Field, 2000, Levitas, 1998, Strain & Field, 1997). This former industrial centre stands as an example of the transformative changes brought about by globalisation, moving from a situation in the 1970s where 50% of the areas economic activity was related to steel production. However, by the mid 1980s this economic base had effectively collapsed. Current projections by the regional Learning and

Skills Council (LSC)[3] is that the key growth sectors in the area will be in health, banking and insurance, communications, personal services, business services, and education. Although policy emphasises the need for people to up-skill, importantly for our discussion is that these transformations are not the product of 'natural' economic forces or the internal inadequacies of this northern city's skills-base. Rather they are the product of national and global economic restructuring on the part of national and multinational companies (Massey, 1994) and of governmental policy interventions where re-industrialisation policies were market-led, and national and local governments were left to pick up the pieces (Hudson & Sadler, 1989).

This focus on adults returning to learning in a time of change also enabled us to look at larger structural factors and how these have worked upon the agency of individuals in the form of the 'responsible learner'. The current Labour Government presents a policy narrative that is constructed around a number of related assertions that characterise the policy problem. It is argued across a range of policy texts that global processes of economic restructuring have reconfigured the relationship between national economies and global markets, refashioning the kinds of skills and knowledge perceived as necessary for economic growth and competitiveness. Local economies, once conceived of as national economies, are increasingly integrated into global markets and flows of capital and labour, with centres of production shifting geographically. Related to this, technological developments, as part of the globalisation process, are viewed as transforming the labour process, with consequent impacts upon traditional notions of career and working lives. The forward to the 2005 Skills White Paper[4] states quite clearly that one of its key objectives is 'Replacing the redundant notion of a 'job for life' with our new ambition of 'employability for life', thus helping people and communities meet the challenge of the global economy'(Department for Education and Skills, 2005, p.1). The current reform of the Further Education sector is premised upon the need to be 'focused on the employability and progression of learners' and '…to delivering the skills and qualifications which individuals, employers and the economy need' (Department for Education and Skills, 2006, p. 20). This perspective has been further underlined by the Leitch review of skills and employability (Her Majesty's

---

3   Learning and Skills Council's are government agencies responsible for co-ordinating provision of education and skills development in the post-16 education and training sector. This includes Further Education and work-based learning. Their key role is the setting of regional priorities and directing funding in line with these priorities.

4   A 'White Paper' is a document issued by the British Government outlining policy and setting out a programme of action. These are not usually consultative documents but provide a commentary on policy that is later enacted through an Act of Parliament.

Treasury, 2006)[5]. Globalisation is presented within this wider policy narrative as introducing new risks and uncertainties, disrupting traditional patterns of transition into and through employment. Learning and the 'learner' are inextricably linked to economic competitiveness, and to the risks confronting each of us in the new context of globalisation. The 'responsible learner' is situated within a wider discursive and policy move that has sought to shift the balance of social risk from a collective to an individualised responsibility; a shift from social responsibility mediated through agencies of the Welfare State to that mediated by markets and 'active citizenship' (Dean, 1999, Du Gay, 2000, Levitas, 1998, Rose, 1999, Rose & Miller, 1992). This process of 'responsibilisation'[6] has been characterised by some as being new forms of domination and control within capitalist society, arguing that post-16 education and training is constructed as a space for the moral regulation of individuals; where they are called upon to work upon themselves in order to make themselves more amenable to the demands of mobile capital (Avis, 2000, Crowther, 2004, Martin, 2003). This process of responsibilisation is related to the rise of a discourse of reflexivity or reflexive modernity (Beck-Gernsheim, 1996, Beck & Ritter, 1992, Giddens, 1991). For fear of over-simplification this area of social theory asserts that social, cultural and economic changes over the past half century have disrupted the assumed links between social identity and social structure, to such an extent that individuals are increasingly forced to make, and re-make their identities. That is, they are forced into a continual state of reflexivity.

In this section we have engaged in what Bourdieu called 'constructing the object of study'. Our immediate object of study is that of adults returning to formal learning in a policy context where the position of adults in further and higher education in England is ambiguous. While this allows us to investigate how adult learners such as Jenny negotiate this changing terrain, it also allows us to explore the notion of responsibilisation. That is, while the 'responsible learner' exists in discourse it is a matter for empirical study to see if it exists in practice. This is related to Bourdieu's argument that the object of study should allow us to examine the links between social structure, power and individual practice (Bourdieu, 1991). Our study then was as much concerned with methodological development as it was with exploring 'responsibilisation' in the context of adults returning to learning. We will now move on to meet Jenny through our account of her account of herself. This will provide an introduction to a further elaboration of what we have called a 'recursive methodology'.

---

5   Lord Leitch was commissioned by the Government to conduct a review of skills and present recommendations on the reform of post-16 education and training.

6   We have coined the phrase 'responsibilisation' in order to capture the way these shifts in the balance of social risk work to construct social subjectivities.

Meeting Jenny

Our discussion of Jenny, here, acts as a vehicle for exploring the possibilities offered by our recursive methodology. As such, we do not so much explore the social conditions of Jenny's real social practices as the capacity of the methodology to enable us to identify social structure in Jenny's practice. Our theoretical encounter with Jenny allows us to reflect on the methodology. To begin with we want to meet Jenny through an account of an account, our account of Jenny's representation of herself through the initial interview. Although Jenny was in receipt of welfare benefits at the time of the initial interview, her family background was that of self-employment in the catering and hospitality sector. At the point where we interviewed Jenny she had just completed her first of three semesters. She was close enough to her entry onto the course to reflect back on her motivations, and far enough through the course to project forward into a possible future world. As well as the interview with Jenny, we interviewed her course tutor and the course director within the FE college.

Jenny's story appears as an amazingly reflexive and rational account of a 'caring' identity being given the opportunity to be realised. Jenny's is a linear narrative with 'caring' linking different points in the story. We are aware that this is partly imposed by the fact that she was being interviewed about her participation in a 'caring' course. However, as with the women in Beverley Skeggs' study of 'respectability', caring appeared to provide Jenny with certain symbolic resources with which to construct a particular gendered identity (Skeggs, 1997). We can detect in the narrative five distinct 'caring' periods. The first period covers her post-school transition into employment. Jenny informed us that when leaving school she had wanted to work with children. This appeared to be motivated by her general sense of being good at 'caring' and good with children, something that would later be confirmed by her participation in formal adult learning. However, she was encouraged by her parents to go into the family occupation of catering. Yet, Jenny claims, she held on to the idea of working with children. Marrying and becoming pregnant offered a way out of catering and into another period where 'caring' could become predominant. Jenny provided a clear rationale for being a stay-at-home mother. While this was partly pragmatic, looking after four young children was incompatible with the work patterns of catering, it was the centrality of providing good caring that overlaid this part of her story. For Jenny, to be a 'good' mother meant being a full-time mother. There was an ethical element to this that would reappear later in her role as a care worker.

This sense of being good at caring was reinforced by her experience of looking after her dying aunt, the third period. Although caring was a shared family activity, Jenny recounted how her aunt commented that she had a natural aptitude for caring, that she cared for her aunt's dignity as much as her body, and was prepared to do things others found repulsive. Although Jenny had said earlier in the interview that there were no other 'caring' role models in her family, the family being involved in catering, she reflected on the fact that her aunt had been a nurse and that this may have influenced her sense of self as a 'carer'. There appeared to be a direct connection between caring for her aunt and Jenny taking up caring jobs working with the elderly in community care settings. In retrospect this fourth period of 'caring' appears to have set down roots that would flourish later in her decision to participate in formal adult learning. Jenny's account of working for private sector care companies was anchored around the ethical struggles she found herself engaged in. Jenny had a very strong ethical approach to caring and so disagreed with the way many people were treated in the community care settings. She conveys a strong sense that people should be treated with dignity, as with her aunt. She was not happy with the level of training provided and spoke about the way she found herself in situations she knew intuitively were wrong but did not have the relevant skills or knowledge to question them. These experiences reinforced her sense that a more appropriate form of caring was required, simultaneously reinforcing her own sense of being a 'carer'. Although she was not able to realise this 'caring' role for a number of years, the narrative sets it up as the antecedent to the fifth period. Jenny appears to have used her engagement with formal learning on the health and social care course to provide a reflective space. The part-time nature of the course fitted around her childcare commitments and her perception that she did not have the capacity to engage with the academic content and workload of a full-time course. The breadth of the course provided space to reflect on which area of care she preferred. Jenny viewed the course as a 'life-changing' experience, confirming her sense as a 'carer', and more specifically as somebody who can make a difference to children in care.

We have presented an 'account of an account', a recounting of social agents' accounts of themselves (Bourdieu, 2002, p. 483). Elsewhere, we have critiqued the emphasis given to phenomenological accounts of learners' lives in much post-compulsory education and training research (Warren & Webb, 2007). We share Bourdieu's concern that a reliance on phenomenological accounts has the danger of producing a 'naively personalist view' of social agents' practices. Instead, we adopt the approach suggested by Bourdieu that in reading interview transcripts (social agents' accounts of themselves) we need to 'read in their words the structure of the objective relations, present and past, between their trajectory and the structure of the educational establishments they attended, and through this, the whole structure and history of the teaching system expressed there' (Bourdieu, 1999, p.618). We need to look at these accounts as social narratives. The next section outlines the theoretical framework used to analyse Jenny's account.

Social narratives

The notion of agency utilised in our argument is linked to Bourdieu's concept of 'practice'. The concept of practice invokes the idea of the ordinary and mundane as saturated with the social relations they are embedded within, of what people do that both reproduces and changes social structure, '...what is done in a particular place, and what is hardened into relative permanency – a practice in the sense of a habitual way of acting' (Chouliaraki & Fairclough, 2004, p. 22). Dorothy Smith[7] similarly captures this ordinary, everyday nature of habitus when she describes the way local practices that social agents have is a taken-for-granted knowledge, a 'knowing that is the very texture of our daily/nightly living in what we know how to do, how we go about things, and what we can get done' (Smith, 1997, p. 394). Central to our analytical framework is the concept of habitus, the taken for granted knowledge that generates practice, the knowledge that is saturated with social structure. Our assertion is that we can access habitus through the narrative practices of social agents, understanding narratives as saturated with social structure.

One of the important things about practice is that it has a reflexive dimension in that 'people always generate representations of what they do as part of what they do' (Chouliakaraki & Fairclough, 2004, p. 22). Therefore research interviews can be seen as special forms of such reflexivity, producing particular kinds of representation. Our methodology views narrative as a special form of reflexive practice whereby social agents attempt to construct coherent accounts of their lives, where the temporal sequencing of events give meaning to the accounts (Elliott, 2005, Ricoeur, 1990). These narratives are simultaneously personal and social, relying upon storylines and discourses available within the public realm, in particular they rely upon hegemonic stories that connect individual accounts to the operation and circulation of power, that is with social structure (Ewick & Silbey, 1995). Narratives can therefore provide us with access to how the everydayness of life – habitus, is intimately connected to the dynamic structuring of society, mediated through accounts of our actions (Smith, 1997). As with much other work in this area we view the narratives provided by learners as enabling us to gain insight into the socially structured nature of their personal practices and therefore construct counter-hegemonic accounts of learners' lives. Following Bourdieu we see this as involving a process of interlinking individual's narratives with other stories and documentary resources, of understanding identity, whether of place (including

---

7   Dorothy Smith has critiqued Bourdieu's framework Smith, D. E. (2005) *Institutional ethnography : A sociology for people,* (Lanham, MD, AltaMira Press). However, we feel that there are conceptual affinities between Bourdieu's concept of habitus and Smith's notion of local knowledge that underpins everyday action.

institutions) and people, as being produced at the nexus of movements within the domains of economy, culture, and politics - as 'articulated moments' (Massey, 1994).

In practice we interpreted this in terms of a systematic process of iterative analyses, moving backwards and forwards between subjective account and structural context, between habitus and the social field of Jenny's practices. This process began with analysing the initial interview with Jenny in terms of its narrative qualities, producing a number of hypotheses that were tested in a second 'reflexive' interview with Jenny. The iterative process continued with situating Jenny's subjective accounts in the context of not just the further education college she attended, but the location of the college within the local education and training market, as well as in the context of national policy. The next section explores these iterations and illustrates the kinds of analyses enabled by this process.

Recursive method in practice

Jenny's account as narrative
Jenny's narrative appears to be constructed around a core 'caring' identity. Within the narrative there were a number of key motifs of caring that organised the whole narrative, such as looking after her dying aunt, being a 'good' mother. Pivotal to the narrative was her experience of looking after her dying aunt. Although caring was a shared family activity, Jenny recounted how her aunt commented that she had a natural aptitude for caring, that she cared for her aunt's dignity as much as her body, and was prepared to do things others found repulsive. Within the narrative Jenny's caring for her dying aunt appeared to have a causal relationship to Jenny subsequently taking up caring jobs working with the elderly in community care settings. In retrospect this experience of 'caring' appeared to have set down roots that would later re-appear in her decision to participate in formal adult learning. The experience of working in care settings also took on a causal property. This experience is described as two-fold. Jenny experienced a poverty of training opportunities that appeared in the narrative to lead her towards formal education. Jenny's engagement in formal education was a corrective to this poverty of training opportunity. Similarly, Jenny described the dissonance between her own intuitive ethical framework and the actual experience of care. She described being shocked at the treatment of the elderly in various care settings. Jenny's engagement with the Health and Social Care course and in particular the qualification were constructed in the narrative as equipping Jenny with the kinds of cultural capital that would allow her to challenge 'bad' practice.

Our working notion of habitus is drawn from Dorothy Smith's idea of the taken-for-granted knowledge that underpins social practice, as outlined above.

The aim of our research practice is to understand the uniqueness of Jenny's social practices through the linking of these subjective practices to the social conditions that make those practices possible, and therefore to the operation of power. We have noted, above, Bourdieu's argument that we need to read in Jenny's account of herself the whole scheme of perceptions made possible by the particular configuration of the social formation, that mix of subjective and social history and its institutionalised forms in the social relations of family, education, work, and government. In analysing Jenny's account as a narrative, we are using its narrative form as a first step into habitus, the interaction of structure and agency at the level of the subjective. The centrality of caring in the narrative led us to hypothesise that her practices are structured around a caring disposition, caring as habituated practice. Furthermore, this disposition to care was articulated in highly gendered ways in terms of care in the domestic sphere of the family. Another hypothesis concerns the translation of a caring disposition into another field of practice, the gendered field of social care work. Related to this is the question about the extent to which Jenny's caring practices represent a break with past family practices. It was these hypotheses that formed the basis for a second, reflexive interview with Jenny as a means for investigating the logic of practice of the different fields that Jenny was situated within.

Meeting Jenny again – the reflexive interview
In this interview we explicitly set out our hypotheses involving a reflexive engagement with our theoretical approximation of Jenny's 'practical knowledge' (Bourdieu, 1999, p. 614), This was done in the form of asking Jenny to respond to a series of 'narrative statements':

- 'I am a 'caring' person'.
- 'Being a caring person is very important to how I see myself'.
- 'The experience of looking after my dying aunt was an important moment – this is when I realised I wanted to work in health and social care'.
- 'Wanting to work in health and social is very different to the rest of my family'.

For the purposes of this chapter we will focus on the constitution of a 'caring self'. A 'caring self' and the desire to realise it through employment remained central to Jenny's second interview, where she talks reflexively in terms of conscious attempts to construct a different caring identity. This is conducted in the context of another caring demand, this time for her grandmother. This particular caring demand, in similar fashion to that of her dying aunt, made it possible for Jenny to articulate a different kind of caring identity based on the activation of her cultural capital. Her newly acquired knowledge of the care system, and a confidence in dealing with care professionals, using 'inside' knowledge, appeared to allow her to negotiate a care regime for her grandmother that relieved Jenny of a gendered obligation. We begin to see Jenny seeking to accrue and activate particular kinds of cultural capital (through education) in order to realise different kinds of 'caring self'. A reliance on first person narratives seems all too obvious here. In order to understand the role of cultural capital in enabling Jenny to construct a new kind of caring identity we have to go beyond the first person narrative and situate it in relation to the structural context of practice, that is situate Jenny within a field of practice. We move now to situate Jenny within both the institutional context of the further education college and the location of the College within the local education and training market.

The College in the education and training market

For adult learners the field of post-compulsory education and training is a dispersed one. Provision or opportunities to engage in forms of formal or accredited learning takes place in a range of settings. In the context of the pilot research project this included an 'old' and the 'new' university, as well as the FE College[8]. There were also the school-based sixth forms[9]. Then there were a range of extra-mural and community-based provision offered through the Workers Education Association, Sure Start and the New Deal for Communities[10]. This dispersed field of post-compulsory education and training can be conceptualised in terms of 'markets' and the hierarchical ordering of

---

8   The distinction between 'old' and 'new' Universities refers to the different status accorded pre and post-1991 Universities. Pre-1991 Universities comprise the traditional Oxbridge and 'Red Brick' institutions such as Oxford, Cambridge and Sheffield, as well as the 'green field' Universities of the 1960s Higher Education expansion such as Sussex and Warwick. Post-1991 Universities are Polytechnics and Institutes of Higher Education that were incorporated within the University sector following changes to national legislation in 1991. These 'new' Universities tend to attract the bulk of non-traditional graduates.

9   Some schools is England provide post-16 provision through 'Sixth Form' arrangements. These can be in the form of 16+ streams within existing Secondary School provision or as 'Sixth Form Colleges'. At the time of the research Sixth Form provision received higher levels of post-16 funding than Further Education Colleges. Sixth Forms also tend to concentrate on academic routes.

10 The Workers Education Association is an adult and community educational organisation that grew out of the British Labour Movement. Sure Start and the New Deal for Communities are community-level initiatives established by the Labour Government as part of its social inclusion and anti-poverty strategies. There are a range of other organisations and agencies delivering community-based learning opportunities. We have named a small number as illustrative examples.

different kinds of institution through their links with different kinds of students and the opportunities offered by those institutions to link students to positions in society via employment and social contacts.

Enrolling on the part-time course at the FE college is part of the trajectory Jenny is constructing. But Jenny's 'choices' are constrained by the location of the FE college within the local post-16 education and training market - which students the college seeks to attract, the courses it offers and how it relates to other providers in the area. In 'choosing' the FE college Jenny also chose an institution that had positioned itself within the local education and training market as a 'widening participation' institution, that is as an institution that aimed to provide opportunities for those often excluded from formal education. An example of this particular institutional ethos is that the college had always aimed to provide its full-time courses free, unlike its competitors. Similarly, the college had provided free childcare provision. However, the course tutor noted that funding for childcare for students was withdrawn by the college the previous year because this had become financially unviable as Government support decreased. The course on which Jenny had enrolled was there because of the college's institutional ethos of widening participation. The Vocational GCSE Health and Social Care was one of two L2 courses aimed at post-19 learners. Subsequent to our research the FE College rationalised its post-19 provision. The Level 3 (pre-degree) Health and Social Care 19+ course was closed, reducing options for adult learners. On the one hand Jenny has been able to construct a particular social trajectory, mediated by her re-engagement in formal education, because the college has been committed to providing opportunities for adult learners. On the other these opportunities appear to be increasingly limited as the college is required to respond to policy changes, changes that are driven locally through funding mechanisms. Jenny's potential to realise her caring identity mediated by a caring course is structured by the policy framework. This scenario is replicated nationally (Edward et al., 2005, Hodgson et al., 2006, Spours et al., 2006).

The institutional interviews allow us to reflect upon both Jenny's own narration of herself and our theoretical constructions of Jenny. The active intervention of policy and its translation within different institutional levels structures the possibility for Jenny to realise her caring self. Jenny's subjective account is therefore linked with the active political construction of the Further Education sector in the context of Government responses to global structural change. To understand the particularity of Jenny's experience, as Bourdieu argues, we need to see in her words these various links.

Conclusion

One interview gives us so much but on its own it raises as many questions as it answers. We can view the narrative as a product of a rationalising process, of imposing a linearity and rationality in retrospect (Stronach & Maclure, 1997). Ivor Goodson (1992) is critical of stopping the analysis at the production of the life story. Life stories, he argues, are a person's interpretation of her or his own life (Goodson *et al.*, 2001). These stories are the starting point for developing further understanding of subjectivity. Without this further work of putting the story in context Goodson argues the story is an individualising device that wilfully obscures collective circumstances, the social conditions of the production of the narrative. If, as Goodson (Goodson, 2005) argues, the narratives we construct are drawn from a relatively small range of possible storylines in wider society, and then embellished with the personal, we need to deconstruct these narratives. Given the power of policy discourses of responsibility and reflexive agency, we should perhaps expect stories such as Jenny's. Therefore, following Bourdieu (2002), we also need to reconstruct these narratives in order to identify the links with wider societal discourses and social structures. This involves a process of interlinking individual's narratives with other stories and documentary resources. For instance, the structural shift from an economy based on heavy industry to that of financial and personal services characterises the context Jenny lives and learns in. The possibility of realising a 'caring' identity in the form of a paid care manager is partly constituted by the rise of a care economy. The course that Jenny participates in is a product of an economisation of education, of the rise of credentialism, and the professionalisation of personal services. It is also the product of the decision by the college she attends to position itself within the local education and training market as a 'widening participation college'. That is, despite the local LSC restricting funding for post-18 adult learners, the College senior management have sought to maintain a more inclusive approach to adult learners, such as Jenny. In this chapter, then, we have sought to argue that the kind of recursive methodology employed in this small-scale study enables us to capture the richness of personal stories while also accounting for social structure. Without this structural account, we argue, research in the field of post-compulsory education and training is limited.

References

Avis, J. (2000), Policy talk: Reflexive modernization and the construction of teaching and learning within post-compulsory education and lifelong learning in England. In *Journal of Education Policy*, 15(2), 185-199.

Simon Warren and Sue Webb

Ball, S. (1999). Labour, learning and the economy: A 'policy sociology' perspective. In *Cambridge Journal of Education,* 29(2), 195-206.

Beck-Gernsheim, E. (1996). Life as a planning project, in: S. Lash, B. Szerszynski and B. Wynne (Eds.) *Risk, environment and modernity: Towards a new ecology.* London: Sage.

Beck, U. (Translated by Ritter, M). (1992). *Risk society: Towards a new modernity.* London; Thousand Oaks: Sage

Bourdieu, P. (1991). *Outline of a theory of practice,* Cambridge: Cambridge University Press.

Bourdieu, P. (1999). *The weight of the world: Social suffering in contemporary society,* (Oxford, Polity).

Bourdieu, P. (2002) *Distinction: A social critique of the judgement of taste,* (original work published 1979). London: Routledge.

Chouliakaraki, L. and Fairclough, N. (2004). *Discourse in late modernity: Rethinking critical discourse analysis,* (original work published 1999) Edinburgh: Edinburgh University Press.

Chouliaraki, L. and Fairclough, N. (2004). *Discourse in late modernity: Rethinking critical discourse analysis,* Edinburgh: Edinburgh University Press.

Coffield, F. (1999). Breaking the consensus: Lifelong learning as social control. In *British Educational Research Journal* 25(4), 479-499.

Crowther, J. (2004). 'In and against' lifelong learning: Flexibility and the corrosion of character. In *International Journal of Lifelong Education,* 23(2), 125-136.

Dean, M. (1999). *Governmentality: Power and rule in modern society,* London: Sage.

Department for Education and Skills (2005). *Skills: Getting on in business, getting on at work.* Report for HMSO. London: The Stationary Office.

Department for Education and Skills (2006). *Further education: Raising skills, improving life chances (cm 6768),* London: The Stationary Office.

Du Gay, P. (2000). Entrepreneurial governance and public management: The anti-bureaucrats. In: J. Clarke, S. Gewirtz and E. Mclaughlin (Eds.) *New managerialism new welfare?* Buckingham:Open University Press).

Edward, S., Coffield, F. and Steer, R. (2005). Coping with endless change: The impact on teaching staff in the learning and skills sector, paper presented at the *British Educational Research Association Annual Conference*, City.

Elliott, J. (2005). *Using narrative in social research: Qualitative and quantitative approaches,* London: Sage.

Ewick, P. and Silbey, S. S. (1995). Subversive stories and hegemonic tales: Towards a sociology of narrative. In *Law and Society Review,* 29(2), 197-226.

Field, J. (2000). *Lifelong learning and the new educational order,* Stoke-on-Trent: Trentham Books.

Giddens, A. (1991). *Modernity and self-identity: Self and society in the late modern age,* Cambridge: Polity.

Goodson, I. F. (1992). *Studying teachers' lives,* London: Routledge.

Goodson, I. F. (2005). *Learning, curriculum and life politics,* London: Routledge.

Goodson, I. F., Sikes, P. and (2001). *Life history research in educational settings: Learning from lives,* Buckingham: Open University Press.

Her Majesty's Treasury (2006). *Prosperity for all in the global economy - world class skills (Leitch review of skills),* Norwich: HMSO.

Hodgson, A., Edward, S. and Gregson, M. (2006). Riding the waves of policy in adult and community learning in England: The case of basic skills, paper presented at the *British Educational Research Association Annual Conference*, City.

Hudson, R. and Sadler, D. (1989). *The international steel industry: Restructuring, state policies and localities,* London: Routledge.

Levitas, R. (1998). *The inclusive society? Social exclusion and new labour,* Basingstoke: Palgrave.

Martin, I. (2003). Adult education, lifelong learning and citizenship: Some ifs and buts. In *International Journal of Lifelong Education,* 22(6), 566–579.

Massey, D. (1994). *Space, place, and gender,* Cambridge: Polity Press.

Ricoeur, P. (1990). Narrative identity. In: D. Wood (Ed.) *Paul Ricoeur: Narrative and interpretation.* London: Routledge.

Rose, N. (1999). *Powers of freedom: Reframing political thought,* Cambridge: Cambridge University Press.

Rose, N. & Miller, P. (1992). Political power beyond the state: Problematics of government. In *British Journal of Sociology,* 43(172-205.

Skeggs, B. (1997). *Formations of class and gender,* London: Sage.

Smith, D. E. (1997). Comment on Hekman's "Truth and method: Feminist standpoint theory revisited". In *Signs,* 22(2), 392-398.

Smith, D. E. (2005). *Institutional ethnograph : A sociology for people,* Lanham: MD, AltaMira Press.

Spours, K., Coffield, F. and Gregson, M. (2006). Translation problems: FE colleges, policy levers and local ecologies in the learning and skills sector paper presented at the *British Educational Research Association Annual Conference*, City.

Strain, M. & Field, J. (1997). On 'the myth of the learning society'. In *British Journal of Educational Studies,* 45(2), 141-155.

Stronach, I. and Maclure, M. (1997). *Educational research undone: The postmodern embrace,* Buckingham: Open University Press.

Warren, S. & Webb, S. (2007). Challenging lifelong learning policy discourse: Where is the structure in agency in narrative-based research? In *Studies in the Education of Adults,* 39(1), 5-21.

5 Fragments of Adult Educators' Lives: Reflecting on Informal Learning in the Workplace

Paula Guimarães and Amélia Vitória Sancho

Informal learning in workplaces

This chapter illustrates, through the stories of adult educators, the dialectical nature of informal learning in the workplace. In particular it discusses the dilemmas, conflicts, successes and failures of practice as told by adult educators participating on an international continuing education course. We focus primarily on the everyday experience at work, exploring the effects of workplace practices on learning as day-to-day events shape its nature and extent. In the workplace there are several types of learning, such as, relevant events which have an impact on the way adult educators reflect on what they do and at themselves as educators. These experiences are located in particular historical circumstances, discourses and social contexts that change practice. What is learned from work experience, (understood as informal learning), is an open, indeterminate, flexible and dynamic, but not necessarily, organised process, which presents multiple configurations. It is also subject to rapid adjustments to change. As it is not a linear process, it is frequently interrupted, resumed and/ or discontinued according to requirements, constraints, arbitrary and contingent possibilities, which depend on the existence of an opportunity to learn and the capacity of adults to seize it and to change behaviour and attitudes (Pain, 1990).

The narratives presented in this chapter express the practitioners' own ways of knowing. These are immersed in discourses, power relations and local networks as well as a range of visions about the world of practice. Knowledge acquired from practice is far from unproblematic as subjective everyday life experience contains innumerable normative interpretations of reality. Informal learning, therefore, challenges traditional knowledge bases as Dybbroe and Ollagnier argue (2003). Informal learning is supported by adult educators' theory-in-use, understood as a relatively stable element in the flow of interpretations and accounts for the identity and continuity of organisations which binds together norms, strategies, assumptions and detailed rules of action (Argyris & Schön, 1996). Learning events may act as pressures to change the theory-in-use. By this, a relevant number of events force fast reaction supported by implicit and tacit knowledge. According to Schön (1983), when trying to make sense of things, a person also reflects on the understandings which have been implicit in action. There is a need to understand the situation, when facing puzzling, troubling or interesting phenomenon with which one is dealing with.

On one hand, the theory-in-use involves knowing-in-action, that is, the types of knowledge that one uses in intended action, such as riding a bicycle or instant analysis of a balance sheet. This entails doing something without being able to explain how it is being done. Following Schön's argument:

> We reveal (knowing-in-action) by spontaneous, skilful execution of the performance; and we are characteristically unable to make it verbally explicit (1987, p.25).

Reflection-in-action is, therefore, very much tied to knowledge which is acquired through experience, repeated trials, failing, succeeding, and wasting time and effort, getting a feel for a problem, and knowing when to go by the book and when to break the rules.

On the other hand, knowing-on-action occurs when people consciously try to learn from experience. This may involve individual or group reflection and discussion. Schön (1983) states that one may reflect on action, thinking back on what was done in order to discover how our knowing-in-action may have contributed to an unexpected outcome. Reflection-on-action may be done after the event, in tranquillity, or in the midst of the action, in a kind of 'stop-and-think' (Schön 1983, p.26). As it is not classroom-based or highly structured such as formal instruction, control of learning rests primarily in the hands of the learner (cf. Marsick & Watkins 1990, p.12).

As informal learning is predominantly experiential, it is never neutral nor independent of social interaction and of personal positioning in the division of work which influences the access to and experience of learning opportunities. Rather it is constrained by the social, organisational and emotional context in which it occurs. Informal learning shapes one's identity, leading to different knowledges of reality (Garrick, 1998). Everyday life at work is, in this text, is presented by adult educators' interpretations of a coherent world. This world is not only taken for granted as reality in the subjectively meaningful conduct of practitioners' lives; it is a world that originates in their thoughts and actions and it is maintained as real by these (Berger & Luckman, 1979).

Reality is socially constructed. The stories discussed in this chapter reflect secondary socialisation by the internalisation of institutional or institution-based sub-worlds, resulting from relevant knowledge that arises from the division of labour. According to Berger and Luckman (1979) the acquisition of role-specific knowledge and vocabularies, based on the internalisation of semantic fields structuring routine interpretation and conduct within an institutional area, tacit understanding, evaluations and affective coloration of these semantic fields were expressed by the ways adult educators looked at their practice and at themselves.

Collecting and analysing narratives

Experience is a foundation of and a stimulus for learning. Thus, learning takes place through an ongoing dialectical process of action and reflection. To use reflection for learning one must consciously become aware that one is actually learning. The narratives collected during the Good Adult Educator in Europe project (AGADE) reflect on experience and its impact on learning (cf. Jääger, Irons & Varga 2006). Discourse analysis was used to analyse the stories in order to understand the meaning of adult educators' work worlds.

The decision to collect and analyse life stories was due to the need to develop a more innovative and reflexive continuing education course and training for adult educators. This type of programme does not fit into a school-based curriculum supported by theoretical contents, transmission and reproduction of specific knowledge, or into a work-based curriculum, focused specifically on practice and competence. The decision to change the course rested on the belief that adult educators have to be listened to in continuing education. This type of approach to training establishes a place and a space where their voices can be heard and gives them the opportunity to tell about their world as practitioners.

The narratives discussed in this chapter were the outcomes of a first course task on a distance education programme. The exercise undertaken by the adult educators was entitled 'Sharing relevant learning - life stories' (Module 1 - Sharing Experiences, Knowledge and Perspectives: Building a training map). They were asked to share relevant learning events. The challenge was to write three texts (maximum of 4000 words each) in which three different learning situations were told. These were stories and experiences that occurred after their initial education and ones that were relevant to understanding how adult educators became practitioners.

Some examples and suggestions were given to them. Narratives could be related to: a) the moment in which learners experienced the most relevant learning for becoming adult educators; b) the colleague, the tutor, the friend, etc. with whom learners learned; c) the mistake that made learners learn; d) the problem that learners faced that made them learn; d) the example with which learners learned; e) what learners learned with a trainee, a student, etc; f) new information and communication technologies that made learners learn; g) new rules that made learners learn; h) new tasks that learners had to perform that made them learn; i) an occasional event that made learners learn; j) the right question at the right time that made learners learn; k) the situation in which learners have learned with their colleagues; l) the moment in which learners learned by their or somebody else's mistake.

Stories were provided by twelve adult educators from eight countries in the European Union. This generated thirty different narratives regarding informal learning. This chapter looks at the most meaningful stories in relation to the purpose of our analysis. The narratives were written in English although for many this was not their mother tongue. However we believe that writing in English did not change their meaning.

The narrative data which is critically examined in this chapter was the result of a process that included apprehending experience, reasoning or logically thinking through direct experience while also giving interpretation of the facts. Due to the nature of the narratives in this chapter they are seen as being 'detachment fragments' of professional lives as told by a 'constellation of voices' (Clarke, 2003, p. 42). The first stage of the learning task focused on the individualisation of a narrative by the self-reflection on a relevant learning event. In the second stage writing the story led to its detachment by setting a distance between experience and reflection upon what had been learned. For this purpose, stories were analysed as pieces of a life-patchwork, an interpretation on learning that would frame quite distinct experiences.

From the data collected, a learning map was drawn including the most referred to events such as: i) critical incidents, new tasks, problem-solving and misunderstanding; ii) interpersonal relations such as with a mentor; iii) confrontation between formal knowledge and practice. Apart from these, specificities of workplaces and the impact of these on practitioners' ways of learning are also discussed.

The main argument of this chapter is that adult educators' informal learning is the outcome of events that are diverse in themselves. This diversity is owed to the nature of experience but also to adult education as a field of practice, built upon several heterogeneous domains of intervention that are developed by organisations   which are state dependant, private and profit-making or civil society organisations. These different adult education contexts have different aims, modes of actions and implement distinct initiatives involving different social groups.

Learning by reflecting-in-action

Incidents, new tasks, problem-solving and misunderstanding
Incidental learning happens at specific times, occasional or not, involving events that are not expected but yet relevant to learners because of the kind of impact they have on practice. In this sense incidental learning is a by-product of some activity, such as a task accomplishment, interpersonal interaction, sensing the organisation, its norms and rules and trial-and-error experimentation (cf. Marsick & Watkins, 1990, p.12). It takes place while one performs something and something happens, often tacit and not seen as learning, at least not at the time of its occurrence. Therefore, incidental learning occurs almost coincidentally with action; it is something for which there can be no pre-

planning. It is also reactive to and reflective on - an 'unintended experience' as defined by Jarvis (1992).

Some of the collected narratives were about situations in which things came about without being expected and were also surprisingly puzzling. For practitioners, these were occasions for feeling confused and facing difficulties in overcoming problems or finding adequate solutions:

> *The first problem was during my first formal job as a teacher in Mexico with one of my evening classes. It was an intermediate class of learners but each learner had very different needs and expectations about the class - it was difficult to manage all of these expectations in preparing class materials and working in groups and I found myself using psychology tools a lot!* (Story 1 E).

Learning by doing was emphasised frequently by learners, particularly those in new professional situations. This group felt the need to create quick and appropriate ways for achieving tasks for a job or a work context that was new or not well known. Some stories expressed anxiety, for instance, when new professional situations were encountered. These situations were both simultaneously challenging and stressing:

> *Ten years ago when I started my career at the institute I had neither experience nor knowledge in adult education. But I had to work and face this problem everyday. Very often I used to hear complaints from adult learners who were taught like children and felt like they were pupils of a school. And I got interested in the problem of how adults should be taught.* (Story 9 Z).

Some narratives were also related to experiences based on observation of, or participation in problematic situations. In these contexts learning occurred when practitioners were involved in problem-solving and realised that the invented solution was an interesting one (or not):

> *In another job I had, in a cultural organisation, we once arranged an annual meeting that included a complex and slightly chaotic development process. We wanted all the representatives to be present at the meeting, approximately 150, and to take part in this process, but in such a way that they were both heard as individuals and as representatives of a group. A couple of consultants who used to work in organisational development were in charge of the process. I was quite impressed by their ability to lead the process without anarchy being the final result.* (Story 2 L).

Other stories were about the confrontation of expectations, owing to conflict situations which occurred as a result of a misunderstanding. Sometimes this resulted when practitioners realised the failure of a choice or a decision they had made:

> *When I was doing my apprenticeship I had to organise an afternoon meal for children of a poor neighbourhood in Porto. I decided to give these children food that I wanted them to have (milk with chocolate, nice scones) and not what they were used to eating (they hardly eat twice a day and when they had some food it was bread without butter and milk without chocolate). The fact was that they didn't eat at all what I prepared for them. I was astonished. They were not used to the kind of food I was used to.* (Story 7 A).

Trials and errors were relevant learning events particularly when experience was the re-creation of a practice which was more appropriate for a specific context. As Schön (1987, p.27) states, during action, one invents procedures to solve the problem, discover further unpleasant surprises, and make further corrective inventions. Some of the collected stories described unexpected events, such as errors. Many mentioned that this is one of the most efficient means of learning. A few of these narratives were described as very unpleasant. Solutions created (or re-created) were on some occasions the opportunity for adult educators to look at their practice from a new point of view:

> *In the early years of my professional life as a trainer I had to develop a module on adult education pedagogy. There were several trainers; we had previously agreed on the contents and pedagogic strategies. I worked hard on my content, the methods I would work with in training sessions and I was quite happy about the result. I started the course and afterwards the trainees asked me several questions related to the structure of the course, the aims, the other trainers, etc. They were not pleased with what was going on in the course ... I thought about something different and tried to have some work done with trainees. Of course, as I didn't have enough time to think about it and how to do it, I believe that it was a total disaster. I wanted to say things which were not previously prepared, thought, agreed upon by my other colleagues and which were not even in the programme. Trainees were not really interested in what I was saying because it didn't make sense with the rest of the content. And I had to change the strategy again.* (Story 6 T).

Incidents, new tasks, problem-solving, misunderstanding and errors were the subjects of many of the stories told by practitioners involving reflection-in-action and informal learning. Sometimes the narratives included sayings of disconfirmation, especially when a major discrepancy between expectations and experience was felt. This was often when a period of intense disorientation and confusion was accompanied by a crisis of confidence and withdrawal from other people who were associated with the source of confusion. By naming the problem, by thinking about an unresolved issue, through an intuitively guided, collaborative and open-ended exploration with gathering of insights, confidence and satisfaction, a private reflective review may be made and reorientation could be established by the means of a new insight or synthesis experience involving a different approach in practice (cf. Jarvis & Gibson, 1997, p. 11-12). This is when informal learning had occurred.

Learning by reflecting-on-action

Learning with others: the importance of a mentor
A significant number of narratives referred to learning with colleagues, by sharing experience, asking for support or by telling something relevant that had happened. Some stories were about mentoring - not a very common issue in domains such as adult education (Jarvis & Gibson, 1997) - but quite significant for the adult educators. Mentoring is concerned with personal and professional development through developing dialogue and sharing practice. Distinct from teaching, the mentor relationship is one by which people relate to each other with the explicit purpose of assisting the other to learn. For this reason, a mentor can be a facilitator of reflective practice or an opener of doors that leads someone to learning opportunities, by advising, coaching, counselling, guiding, being a role model, a sponsor, a teacher and/or a resource facilitator as referred by Jarvis and Gibson (1997, p.30-33):

> *Since I started to work at the Unit for Adult Education I have been working with a professor of Sociology of Education, someone that was for a long time the Head of the Unit. I learned my work here with him (with Vitoria as well), the way I deal with things, the way I look upon subjects and problems but also relevant issues in adult education namely whose side I am on, who gets profit from education and who loses with it, etc. I believe that in most decisions I have to take I always think about what he would do before deciding anything. Even if I decide differently, his words are relevant to me because I believe that he is direct, objective, fair and usually sees things that are 'behind the curtain' in terms of who is going to get*

something good from an event or initiative and who is going to be harmed. (Story 6 U).

As illustrated in the above narrative, sharing experience and knowledge is emphasised in mentoring. Telling the best way of doing something or seeing someone doing something in relationships that involves support (listening, providing structure, expressing positive expectations), challenge (setting tasks, engaging in discussion, promoting a debate, constructing hypotheses and setting high standards) and vision (modelling, keeping tradition, offering a map, suggesting a new language, providing a mirror) formed the basis for reflection-on-action. Sharing discoveries and testing out the new understanding with others, namely with the mentor, could even provide equilibrium; a new perspective and approach would then be elaborated, refined and applied (cf. Jarvis & Gibson, 1997, p.12).

Confronting different worlds
Adult education is not a domain in which one finds professionals according to Etzioni's (1974) definition. In many countries adult educators become practitioners through their own choice. This is often through attending a higher education course in the social sciences, such as education, psychology, sociology, etc., on teaching or on specialised fields of knowledge - or just by chance without having joined a specific initial or continuing education path. There are few specific courses available for training people to become adult educators. During their working life they may or may not join professional associations related to adult education. Generally they do not share a common social and professional recognition. This situation has created the existence of several worlds of practice (and of knowledge) amongst adult educators.

Some teachers joined the AGADE test-course. Their collected stories talked about the confrontation between formal knowledge and conditions of everyday practice. This confrontation in many cases resulted from a conflict between theory and practice. This gave rise to moments of analysis and critical reflection - events which are important for reflective practitioners (see Argyris & Schön 1996; Schön 1983). A few narratives mentioned the relevance and importance of working in initial education in order to work with adult students. Formal knowledge was essential to deal with everyday life at work:

I have to say that it was my training to be an English teacher (teaching English as a foreign language - TEFL) that helped me to understand group work, group dynamics and working with adult learners. (Story 1A).

Even if formal education was referred to as being significant for understanding the work they achieved and to be better prepared for solving dilemmas and finding solutions to problems, some stories expressed some disenchantment towards practice by including the description of something that was distinct than what was learned in formal education settings or what was taken for granted:

> *Looking back on the starting moment of my profession, I can see clearly the importance given to the participation of adults in each task and decision we take, the relevance of their active participation in exercises and subjects discussed. In fact I thought that it was enough to arrive and say we all agree that they were the most important part of this course, so it was up to them to decide and make the most important decisions. This perspective made me feel that I had the key to the success of an adult education course. What I've discovered quickly was that it wasn't sufficient to agree with it or to defend this point of view theoretically. I had a long way to run.*
> (Story 3 O).

Disenchantment was in many situations associated with 'the real world', a world usually seen as a difficult scenario for practice, in which what was proposed theoretically and in abstract terms did not reflect the work achieved by practitioners. This gap between the content of discourses professed and what happened in practice sometimes resulted in critical reactions from adult educators, some of which were based on resistance, others on a passive acceptance of the strangeness of reality.

As we have seen informal learning was intimately connected with a constant defining and redefining of informal theories that were applied to practitioners' organisations, roles and purposes within them and their required performance levels. Reflection-on-action, by means of sharing knowledge or confronting visions of the world of practice, was essential for the meaning given to knowledge itself and to its appliance within work organisations. It was also one of the main basis for informal learning.

Learning in the workplace

Specificities of organisational settings

Work settings are characterised by specificities and offer relevant potential learning situations. In this sense, workplaces as an arena for secondary socialisation involve the reproduction of rules and norms but also new ways of acting created and re-created according to adult educators' aims and strategies performed more coherently with their representations of the world of practice (Berger & Luckman, 1979).

There are significant links between the modes by which work is organised, its content and the opportunities adult educators have for informal learning. We should also be aware that the manifest curriculum is always accompanied by the hidden curriculum of work that socialises and shapes workers. The modelling of workers' identities requires compliance with organisational objectives and directions, but a compliance that also involves active subjects making choices and decisions about their place in the culture of the institution practitioners are working in (Garrick, 1998).

The collected stories showed the plurality of adult education as a field of practice, as events told occurred in different settings, such as schools, non-governmental organisations, enterprises, and state-funded institutions as well as in fluid contexts such as research projects or activities that somehow were related to adult education. As a result, the workplace curriculum resulted in narratives about different experiences which involved actors being engaged in quite distinct situations. Owing to this, practitioners seemed to perform several roles, which expressed a wide range of jobs and tasks. The stories were about teachers teaching and trainers training adults, and coordinators of education departments which offer many activities. They also focused on animators in social and educational projects, mediators of adult education and training initiatives, managers responsible for large programmes and researchers of adult education in higher education institutions:

The first story was during my first formal job as a teacher in Mexico with one of my evening classes ... (Story 1 E).

The second was when I was working for a pharmaceutical company and I had to train groups of pharmacists in the working of a new IT system ... (Story 1 J).

When I started my career at the teaching institute I had neither experience nor knowledge in adult education ... (Story 9 Z).

In another of the jobs I had, in a cultural organisation, we once arranged an annual meeting that included a complex and slightly chaotic development process ... (Story 2 L).

At one time I worked in a school for psychiatric patients ... (Story 2 M).

When I was starting my career I was a teacher and coordinator of teaching in a school of social workers ... (Story 7 Z).

I join teams that are engaged in projects and do seminars with adult educators ... (Story 9Z2).

The most recent situation is in my current role as an administrator in the Department ... (Story 1 H).

Being a mediator of an Adult Education and Training Course I was asked to perform some logistic tasks ... (Story 5 S).

This plurality of tasks and roles was expressed by descriptions of jobs and workplaces framed by distinct rules and norms. All of these narratives involved specific knowledge about doing a particular job, resulting in the internalisation of a certain vocabulary that structured the interpretation of work to be accomplished and a tacit understanding of professional behaviour and attitudes required. Some stories described workplaces characterised by structured, hierarchical organisations as well as asymmetric power relations, in which practitioners had to achieve tasks according to one best way of doing things and without asking for support or sharing knowledge:

As a young and inexperienced teacher, I worked in a school in the far North of Norway. We were three newly graduated teachers who started to work at the same time, joining the staff of three: the director, his wife and one more teacher. I remember very well asking the more experienced teacher for advice, but just getting a cold shoulder: if you have problems teaching, you should solve them yourself! This attitude was something that all we newcomers had to learn to live with. (Story 2 N).

Other narratives were about work organisations in which the division of labour was less evident, in certain contexts of practice amongst a specific group of teachers:

There are a few situations where I have learned a lot from my colleagues. The first was when I was working in the Language Department of a third level college in Northern Spain. All the teachers were from different countries and were teaching different languages and used different methods. All we had in common was that we were all teaching adults - it was a great experience as we all taught and helped each other with our work (Story 1 F).

Other stories focused on events that happened in networks, projects and groups of practitioners in which the division of labour was negotiated and power relations were quite symmetric:

> *I had the chance to work with a Swedish team of adult educators in the late 1970s and beginning of 1980s. With these people I learned the importance of establishing a horizontal relationship among trainers and between trainer and trainee; the relevance of acquiring systematically my practice within a critical attitude; and the need of avoiding taken for granted solutions* (Story 7 Y).

These different patterns of power relations within work organisations suggest that informal learning was dependent upon work itself and practitioners' behaviour and attitudes were constrained by workplace specificities, depending on the social, cultural, economic and political contexts in which adult educators and organisations were engaged. Narratives showed a diversity of workplaces, a range of job differentiation, different work patterns and a variety of power relations which had a relevant impact on informal learning and in adult educators' professional identity construction. Due to this fact there was a hidden curriculum of learning at work having as a main outcome the shaping of several professional identities according to languages influenced by professional, functionalist, humanistic, radical, etc. approaches to adult education. This in turn depended upon the type of organisational settings in which practitioners were involved in and their ethics. As several trends could be identified, not a single adult educator's identity could be found but instead multiple identities (cf. Jarvis 1992, p. 187-189; Dubar, 1997). Some of these identities were more willing to reproduce the teachers' ways of looking at their job and practice, while others evidenced the impact of humanistic or radical thinking. Others still were closer to the renovated languages and approaches in adult education of (lifelong) learning, self-direction, competency-based, etc:

> *Some other type of learning was for instance the participation in an adult educator's project - Grundtvig 3 - with international partners from France and Italy. This experience made me develop myself as an adult educator because I dealt with different realities and experience concerning the same subject, the main topic of the project - a competences portfolio* (Story 3 Q1).

By expressing so many different languages, practitioners seemed to be involved in different organisational contexts and perform several roles in a field of practice characterised by heterogeneity and a lack of congruence among its main domains of practice.

Some concluding remarks

The analysis presented in this paper stresses the relevance of biographical narratives in the continuing education of practitioners. The AGADE test-course was an opportunity for reflecting upon access to the dynamics between their own lives and experience, opening the way to a better understanding of the conditions for learning in adult life (Dominicé, 2000). This is something which is rarely discussed and looked at in relation to the engagement of adult educators in continuing education. This was, therefore, the reason for including this approach in the development of the AGADE test-course. It thus enabled practitioners to share life stories and use them as vehicles through which they could reflect upon the nature of informal learning.

These stories were small parts of a larger piece: they were fragments of learning in life. The analytical patchwork which we have developed in this chapter is based on two assumptions. Firstly, the environment in workplaces is often uncertain and unpredictable. Moreover, practice can be quite distant from more normative patterns which are common in formal education and in certain measures in the workplace. The second assumption is related to the ambivalence of practice. In some stories the knowledge known was enough to solve the problems faced. Other practitioners experienced limitations in reproducing formal knowledge in daily practice and invented new ways of acting. These two assumptions were expressed by the diversity of informal learning in the workplace.

Making sense of what to do in the face of conflict and problems at work can highlight how problematic meaning giving can be. It is sometimes completely unclear as to what one ought to do, which in turn illustrates the importance of self-reflexivity in making sense of informal learning. Therefore, the workplace embraced a learning dimension that emphasised the development of several skills and forms of knowledge in accordance or in disagreement to what was learned before in formal education and in practice.

The narratives discussed in this paper evidenced continuity between formal knowledge, theory-in-use and practice. However, many other narratives stressed discontinuity or contradictions between explicit knowledge and knowledge resulting from practice. These tensions were clear through critical incidents, new tasks, problem-solving and misunderstanding as well as when learning with others and when the confrontation between formal knowledge and practice occurred.

As stated, informal learning is characterised by diversity owing to the specificities of organisational settings, times, spaces and contexts in which it happens as well as having a meaningful influence on experiences that seem to be quite distinct when we listen to each practitioner. This heterogeneity shows that informal learning happens in many situations and occasions, highlighting individual patterns of learning as well as social and collective ones. Underlying tensions that characterise workplaces and work are personal and professional beliefs, convictions and values. These are influential factors on individuals, and have to be considered as strategies to deal with everyday problems and dilemmas.

To a certain extent, continuity and discontinuity, tensions and problems faced in workplaces seem to be the cause and the result of the heterogeneity of adult education as a field of practice, or as a moorland as Edwards (1997) claims, due to the variety of domains of intervention, resulting in job differentiation, distinct patterns of power relations within organisations and multiple identity forms.

The existence of multiple identity forms raises the following issues: the recognition by adult educators of their specific practice and of adult education as a field of practice; the recognition of adult educators as performers of an educational area which is becoming more important in the building of knowledge-based societies, as according to many educational policy discourses. The need for working on a professionalisation process has been emphasised on several occasions, namely regarding a core curriculum in initial education, the establishment of organisations that represent practitioners' interests and the social and political acknowledgement of adult education (as a field of practice and a field of educational policy). In spite of discussion, research projects and recommendations made on this issue and the lack of a semi-professional status (Etzioni, 1974) weakens the roles of adult educators in work organisations. The consequences of this situation are a fragile recognition of individual competences, emergent reference frames of occupational skills and irregular working conditions. Even if one may agree that late modernity does not allow the emergence of new professions such as an adult educator. However, the Lisbon agreement emphasises the importance of lifelong learning as a means of achieving its goals. At the same time competitive work organisations require adult educators. Problems which many adults face today require practitioners to be aware of the challenges as well as of the impact of individual and collective decisions upon learning, work and wider social and political issues. To avoid incoherence, these practitioners will have to be socially and professionally recognised due to the fundamental role they are playing within the strategy of building the European Union as a learning society and work organisations as environments in which learning occurs.

References

Argyris, C. & Schön, D., (1996). *Organizational Learning II. Theory, Method, and Practice.* Massachusetts: Addison-Wesley Publishing Company.
Berger, P. & Luckman, T., (1979). *The Social Construction of Reality. A Treatise in the Sociology of Knowledge.* Harmondsworth: Penguin

Clarke, J., (2003). Being there - where are women returners returning from? In B. Dybbroe & E. Ollagnier, eds. *Challenging Gender in Lifelong Learning: European Perspectives.* Roskilde: Adult Education Research Group/Roskilde University & ESREA, p.29-45.

Dominicé, P., (2000). *Learning from our Lives. Using Educational Biographies with Adults.* San Francisco: Jossey-Bass.

Dubar, C., (1997). Formação, trabalho e identidades profissionais. In R. Canário, org. *Formação e Situações de Trabalho.* Porto: Porto Editora, pp.43-52.

Dybbroe, B. & Ollagnier, E., eds., (2003). *Challenging Gender in Lifelong Learning: European Perspectives.* Roskilde: Adult Education Research Group/Roskilde University and ESREA.

Edwards, R., (1997). *Changing Places? Flexibility, Lifelong Learning and the Learning Society.* London: Routledge.

Etzioni, A., (1974). *Análise Comparativa das Organizações Complexas. Sobre o Poder, o Engajamento e os Correlatos.* Rio de Janeiro: Edições Afrontamento.

Garrick, J., (1998). *Informal Learning in the Workplace. Unmasking Human Resource Development.* London: Routledge.

Jääger, T., Irons, J. & Varga, K. (2006). (Eds.). *Agade. Towards Becoming a Good Adult Educator. Resource Book.* Riga: Latvijas Pieauguso Izglitibas Apvieniba.

Jarvis, P., (1992). *Paradoxes of Learning. On Becoming an Individual in Society.* San Francisco: Jossey-Bass Publishers.

Jarvis, P. & Gibson, S., (1997).*The Teacher Practitioner and Mentor in Nursing, Midwifery, Health Visiting and the Social Services.* London: Stanley Thornes Ltd.

Marsick, V. J. & Watkins, K., (1990). *Informal and Incidental Learning in the Workplace.* London: Routledge.

Pain, Abraham (1990). *Éducation Informelle. Les Effets Formateurs dans le Quotidien.* Paris: Éditions L'Harmattan.

Schön, D. A., (1983). *The Reflective Practitioner.* New York: Basic Books.

Schön, D. A., (1987). *Educating the Reflective Practitioner. Toward a New Design for Teaching and Learning in the Profession.* San Francisco: Jossey-Bass Publishers.

6 Talking of Learning …
Auto/biographical Narratives of Learning and Computer-assisted Analysis of the Language of Professional Discourse(s) in Interviews

Rob Evans

Adult learners' experiences in different learning contexts across the life-course have a significant impact on identity formation. In the world of work, in particular, professional knowledge management and organisational learning processes within business organisations have in recent years increasingly been played out within the context of ostensibly globalising tendencies in which gargantuan mergers and 'fusion' processes as a result of trans-national acquisitions have played a prominent part. The ambiguities involved in such changes to the work-place may be experienced as problematic learning processes (Risberg, 2001, Very & Schweiger, 2001). The learning experiences both of individual employees and of employees company-wide are played out, too, between conflicting demands for tacit/informal and/or explicit/formal knowledge. Tacit knowledge, strongly experiential, subjective and acquired often over years, is ranged against market-oriented knowledge, which is highly dependent on specific (and changing) work-place profiles (Evans, 2001, p. 63). This paper seeks to examine precisely organisational discourse(s) of learning (and *unlearning*) elicited in talk with employees of an international corporation. In this context of organisational change, auto/biographical narratives, elicited in open depth interviews, can start an important critique of deficits in organisational communication and intercultural learning as well as of dominant business agendas of 'flexibility' and 'entrepreneurialism' .(Avis, 2002).

Organisational auto/biographies of change: methodology and methods

The language of the auto/biographical narratives used here was collected in 20 in-depth interviews to construct a language corpus (see Bauer 7 Aarts, 2000 and below)[1]. The investigation of learning experiences, using a combination of narrative and biographical approaches, with detailed analysis of linguistic phenomena, seeks to provide evidence of learners' discourse practices in relation to their experiences of the organisational learning environment. Close attention to the language resources employed by company employees is achieved by

---

1   At the time of writing, the construction of this corpus is only in its initial stage. Remarks made in the following pages about the capabilities of corpus-based research are based on my use of corpora in previous research.

employing the related methods of conversational and discourse analysis (for recent useful overviews see Peräkylä, 2004, Hepburn & Potter, 2004). Conversation analytical methods, in particular, are employed in order to make visible the sequential unfolding of shared interaction in interview talk. Talk is understood as action. The sequential construction of meaning in talk is constitutive of shared social realities (Peräkylä, 2004). Further, this understanding of talk as action seeks to show that the deployment of a range of discourses is a significant characteristic of individuals' negotiation of the intricacies of asymmetrical institutional talk (Drew & Sorjonen, 1997).

A biographical approach to learning and 'biographization'

Narratives of change to ideas of professionalism, to professional identity, to subjective participation in specific institutional relationships, and subjective reactions to change, are not merely individual case stories. There are gender, generation and cultural systems interacting with (the) educational system and labour market structures in which they are played out (Mason, 2004, Salling Olesen, 2003). The narratives, too, are laden with the individual's relationship to the professional discourses of their job, of their relationship to their professional-personal codes of expression and their most personal language resources. All of these resources are intrinsically bound up with the subject's sense of their life and with the autobiographical accounts they construct of that life.

The auto/biographies narrated across encounters are discrete sequences of talk. This talk is 'biographized' in that it is structured both temporally and sequentially, drawing on the subjects' life stories. With Hoerning we can see biographized talk and the biographic knowledge that arises from it and through it as "not merely the laying down of a stratum of things experienced but also the continuous re-working of all that is experienced"[2] (Hoerning, 1989, p.153-154). In addition, through the interaction of interviewer and respondent and through the wider out-of-frame interaction of both with their respective social worlds, strong elements of interdiscursivity enrich the work of meaning-making that these learning biographies represent.

The importance of interdiscursivity and levels of meaning

A significant element of the development within the talk of respondents' discourses of learning is that they are embedded in interdiscursive sequences

---

2   ["Biographische Erfahrungen und das daraus entstandene biographische Wissen ist nach dieser Vorstellung also nicht nur die Ablagerung des Erfahrenen, sondern die fortlaufende Überarbeitung des Erfahrenen ..."]

which can be described as 'micro-narratives'. These discrete narrative units - themselves embedded within longer sequences of narration or suspended within brief turn-exchanges - act as interactive 'wooden horses' which transport interviewee discourses into the stream of discourse upheld by the respective institutional context. These heteroglossic elements of the biographized narrative, together with a whole range of linguistic options deployed by respondents (Capps & Ochs, 1995) enhance the 'tellability' of the narratives exchanged in the interaction and 'ground' the talk in 'own' contexts of doing-being-an-employee or a professional which are relatively resistant to the institutional context and the challenge of the interview encounter. (Akerström et al, 2004).

An interplay of contexts: the 'local' and the 'wider' environment in auto/biographical talk

The accomplishment of meaning in the interplay of interactive contexts (social, institutional, physical, or emotional, and so on) is achieved through the sequential unfolding of the interactive resources of members of such diverse settings. Sequence of action in talk and context are inextricably bound together in the process of meaning-making because "social context is a dynamically created thing that is expressed in and through the sequential organization of interaction". Thus context is built in and through talk and is radically local in its construction (Heritage, 1997, p 162-3).

The wider contexts in which participants are active are understood here as, in Gale Miller's words, interconnected 'ecologies of knowledge' in which situation-specific interactional meanings are organised (Miller, 1997, p. 168). According to this view of things, subjects are able to make use of the resources of different, socially organised settings to which they belong (or to which they are *positioned* as belonging, for example) in order to discursively constitute and reconstitute themselves *and* the institutional settings in which they interact.

At the level of the auto/biographical interview itself - the 90 to 150 minutes of 'talk' - the context is acutely interactive, and encompasses the physical setting and the joint accomplishment of understanding in interactive talk. Gender, age, ethnic origin, class, educational and linguistic resources flood the micro setting. At a further remove, the interview is embedded in a wider interactive context, including the institutional character of the research interview and its organisation, 'longer' sequences of interaction between researcher and respondents (involving questions of access, diverse discourses of learning and knowledge) and, put simply, the 'long sequences' of experience narrated in the interview and which have evaluative and interpretive significance within the interactive construction of understanding. Finally, at what we can see as the 'macro' level, we have the context of social-political-ideological discourses, the

social context in which the participants and the institutions involved interpret
their roles and positions.

Computer-assisted analysis of auto/biographical talk
Creation of electronic corpora for data analysis

From the beginning, the method I have used for the management and
presentation of the qualitative data collected here is that of the electronic corpus
investigation (see Bauer & Aarts, 2000, Evans, 2004). A collection of texts - a
corpus - is stored electronically in order that it may be analysed with textual
analysis software capable of creating word-counts, listing word-fields,
establishing concordances (i.e. numerical and statistical recurrences) or
establishing repeated collocations. The literature on the potential application of
computer-assisted qualitative data analysis software (or CAQDAS for short as it
is now universally known) is already considerable. The pre-history and rise of
CAQDAS and discussion of the theoretical and methodological aspects of this
research tool can be found in Kelle (Kelle, 1995, 2000a, 2000b, 2004), Fielding
and Fielding and Lee (Fielding, 2001, Fielding & Lee, 1998), Seale (2002), and
Lewins (2001). Much of the literature is concerned to combat still widespread
fears that CAQDAS means the end of ethnographic and qualitative research as
practiced since the grand old days of doing street corner work. The bias of many
CAQDAS products towards one direction in qualitative analysis - e.g. grounded
theory - is not in question (Dey, 2004, p. 84-6). ATLASti, for example, which I
opted to use in this study and others previously, is quite clearly based on the
methods of grounded theory research (Muhr, 1997). The ability to code and
retrieve data pertaining to a code is central to the grounded theory method of
'constant comparison'. Likewise, the analytic memo facility that CAQDAS tools
like ATLASti possess are, too, important for grounded theory (Seale, 2002, p.
657, 666). The value of these facilities for *interrogating* the data corpus cannot
be ignored. They do represent, however, a pre-determination of the analytical
process which needs to be taken account of at every step in the process of
theory-building. As Kelle rightly points out, there are:

> ... in fact, quite considerable risks of creating [research] artefacts
> above all if the user overlooks the difference between the indexing
> function and the representational function of coding categories.   The
> researcher should be clear about the significance of the complex
> algorithms which can be carried out by pressing one single key (Kelle,
> 2000b, p. 501)[3].

---

3   ["Tatsächlich bestehen vor allem dann, wenn der Nutzer die Unterscheidung zwischen der
    Indizierungsfunktion und der Repräsentierungsfunktion von Codierkategorien vernachläs-

At the same time, surveys of recent CAQDAS use have shown that the danger of the software galloping away with the researcher, so to speak, has been exaggerated (Kelle, 2000b, p. 500-501). In this research, the emphasis is essentially on the close detail of sequences of interview talk and thus represents a compromise between the data management and selection possibilities of CAQDAS tools, with all the potential for in-vivo and open coding during the process of comparison and selection of significant extracts for analysis, and the 'craft' work of linguistic analysis of the transcripts and the audio tapes themselves. I remain convinced that caution and a critical approach to the hidden, technological 'traps' or 'snags' of CAQDAS (Kelle, 2000b, p. 501) are the common-sense reaction of careful qualitative research. In this perspective, CAQDAS clearly is itself "no more than a craft skill, a new tool to make an old craft more itself" (Fielding, 2001, p. 454), and should be rather understood as a presentation and storage method than as a method of data *analysis*. After all, no one expects index card systems to perform theory-building (Udo Kelle cited in Fielding, 2001, p. 466).

Use of CAQDAS and analysing auto/biographical language data

Textual analysis software such as TACT 2.1 of the University of Toronto (see Lancashire, 1996), MonoConc Pro 2.0 (Barlow, 2000) as well as a qualitative research application like ATLASti (Muhr, 1997) may be employed for word-counts, KWIK (key-word-in-context)-concordancing, search and retrieval and to code the corpus. The first step in *analysis* is already contained in the theoretical agenda brought to bear on and during the unstructured depth-interview, i.e. the constant critical questioning of question-selection between interviews (Seale, 2002). The theoretical requirements of the analysis - i.e. conversation analytical approach to turns, sequences, repair work, etc., and its basis in a constructivist theory of language use - dictate the level of detail included in the transcript (Kowal and O'Connell, 2000, and the essential Ochs, 1979). Careful, repeated listening to the audio-taped and digitally stored talk determines the shape of the transcript and the selection of codes, but, equally, the revisiting of the audio record brings to the surface, often quite unexpectedly, new hearings, new questions regarding the co-construction within the frame of the interview talk (Akerström et al., 2004).

Topics arising from the recorded interview narratives, likewise interactive turns in talk, are coded in order to manage data retrieval. Straightforward word counts, concordances of specific language phenomena (e.g. employment of

---

sigt, nicht unerhebliche Risiken, Artefakte zu produzieren. ... erfordert, daß der Forscher bzw. die Forscherin sich beständig Rechenschaft gibt über die Bedeutung der komplexen Algorithmen, die mit manchmal nur einem einzelnen Knopfdruck durchgeführt werden"]

modal particles, topic-setting by gender, collocations and co-occurrences of key concepts, deixis) are among the most important categories coded. This is an essentially iterative process, and is the stage in the research process arguably most facilitated by the archiving and coordinating potential of qualitative data storage and presentation applications (Kelle, 2004).

The analysis of the talk-in-interaction remains firmly the 'craft' element, the supposed imminent disappearance of which is lamented by those most sceptical of the value of CAQDAS methods. The "tedious restrictions of pen and ink" (Dey, 2004, p. 86), and the laborious cut-and-paste methods so sedulously described by Ball (1991) and so tellingly and so dramatically evoked in Nias' reminiscences of her longitudinal qualitative study of trainee teachers and of the peripatetic adventures of her shoe-boxed index cards erroneously thrown out and recovered from the local refuse dump (Nias, 1991), are replaced by the "tireless capacity of the computer to confront the analyst with all coded instances" (Seale, 2002, p. 653) which ultimately enhances enormously that attention to detail - that "fine-grained sequential analysis" (Silverman, 2005, August [16]) - quite rightly called for.

Voicing change: Organisational biography work

I turn now to Herr K and his narrative from within a company in the grip of confusing change. Change, for many employees in organisations undergoing a seemingly perennial process of definition and redefinition as a result of mergers, fusions and radical 'down-sizing exercises' (Very & Schweiger, 2001), means that their position within the familiar work environment is rendered strange, is turned inside out, and becomes hostile. Relationships at work and in the wider community also undergo radical transformations as local, regional and national relationships (inter-departmental, customer-client) built up over years in many cases are re-defined and re-positioned in the company hierarchy, and re-valued in terms of expected employee-input, required skills, and performance demanded. Further, as new types of management appear, increasingly independent of the organisation, loyal to a version of virtual glocality rather than any particular locality, and foreign to its traditions and practices (Very and Schweiger, 2001, Castells, 1998), years of company service and collective discourses of belonging are re-translated to become mere vestiges of a conservative, outdated personnel regime that can no longer pay its way. According to the logic of an environment increasingly unhinged from the ties of the local and long-term stability of socially-based agreements, the enterprise is no longer the place where a 'rational' person would wish to deposit their rights for safe-keeping. Nor, as Bauman continues, would a "rational person ... expect to spend their whole working life, or even a chunk of it, in one company" (Bauman, 2001, p. 28). The erstwhile 'centre' or 'middle point' of collective experience and of employees' individual work biographies - is transformed into a de-valued periphery. This "degradation of locality rubs off on the locals" (Bauman, 2001, p. 38) and the learning and work biographies of those 'trapped' in the local periphery are blighted by exclusion within the organisation and exclusion from educational, career-related chances. The organisations and their local networks of communities, relationships and lives face a loss of experience and knowledge as peoples' skills are classed en masse as 'incompetent' by the new accounting standards of the enterprise society (Bourdieu, 1998, p. 99).

Herr K: loss of expert status and the new style of management[4]

In 2001 the company in which I collected the data was sold to an Anglo-Iranian company which installed its London-based, UK/US-educated and English-speaking management team in the German concern headquarters. The extract below, the narrative of Herr K, a specialist in currency hedging deals within the Finance Department, in his late fifties and with 24 years of work in this company to his credit, deals with salient aspects of the increase in uncertainty and disorientation referred to earlier. The rough tone of business in the company after the foreign takeover is the prompt for Herr K's narrative. Taken simply as a relatively natural 'chunk' of personal narrative, the 'facts' evoked by Herr K, here in translation, seem to speak for themselves.

Extract 1
"A rough tone"

K: it was often like that before (1.0) when when the (new owners) brought their people here a head of Finance was put put in place here (.) whose situation and position wasn't clear to anyone as well as who had put him there? but he spoke to me (.) in a strange way and you didn't really know (1.5)

---

[4] The following markup is used in the interview transcript extracts produced here:

xx:: =	Word-lengthening
(.)	Pauses (audible breaks in flow of speech)
(1.0)	Pause timed in seconds (to nearest second)
hh	Out-breaths/laughter
.hh	In-breaths
°xxx°°	Quiet speech
+xxx++	Rapid speech
(ESp)	Embedded speech – speech of others
(xxx)	Indistinct speech
xxx:::	Drawn-out utterance, drawl

> what he was talking about for example he himself gave me the possibility to use a large sum as a (.) currency investment (.) and I earned a bit wodge of money (.) for the company (.) and then when it came to pay me out a bonus or a dividend he said I hadn't done anything? I didn't have a book you talk about having a book when in some business or other you can invest something whether it's bonds or foreign currency we talk about having the option to do something or not to do it (1.0) and? I could prove that he had said "you can do that or that" and I'd done that successfully? and for this success he didn't want to give me my due (1.5) then I went with this zu Herr B (the CEO) and I said "Herr B. the bonus I've been paid is not (.) as it should be (2.0) and then Herr B had to pay me a top up payment because he agreed that it was unacceptable (4.0)

This first part of Herr K's narrative expresses a strong sense of disgruntlement and disdain for the new bosses. Herr K's own professionalism and the initial trust placed in him to do the currency deal is emphasised in juxtaposition to the new boss, who is scarcely intelligible let alone honest and correct in his dealings. His punctilious use of insider slang ("wodge" = "Batzen"), plus the professional aside to the interviewer explaining insider discourse, capped with the status-defining account of his (custom-sanctioned) access to the highest in the company, can all be heard as defensively arrayed professional discourse, and his particular professional knowledge is what he is defending. The specific contribution through discursive elements to the construction of meaning (his boss' denials and K's own words to the CEO) connect the context of narration to multiple contexts of K's professional world.

If we consider the original German talk as it was coded using in-vivo free coding, it is possible to render some of the micro-detail of this passage of Herr K's narrative more visible[5.] The recurrent recourse to organisational discourse ('OD') is clearly present throughout the telling, playing as it does on the insider's familiarity with the knowledge of the organisation,

1	K: es war oft schon (1.0) als als die X6 ihre Leute	*Narrative / self-repair / Evaluative discourse*
2	mitgebracht haben da war ja ein Leiter	*Narrative / Organisational discourse*
3	Finanzen von X hier eingesetzt (.) ueber)	*OD lexis / Alternative OD*
4	dessen Situation und Position man auch nicht	*Generalizing alignment / Modality*

---

5 OD = Organisational Discourse; Modality; ESp= Embedded Speech; MCD = Membership Category Device; LBC = Location-Bound Category; PD = Prosodic Device

6 X stands for the foreign company

5	so im Klaren war wer ihn ueberhaupt	*Alternative OD / Modality*
6	eingesetzt hatte? aber der hatte sich schon mir	*Evaluative discourse*
7	gegenueber (.) etwas komisch geaeussert (.)	*Alternative OD / Prosodic discourse*
8	ohne also (1.5) genauer zu wissen was er da	*Hedging*
9	ueberhaupt gesagt hat zum Beispiel selber	*Alignment to researcher*
10	hatte er mir die Moe::glichkeit gegeben einen	*Narrative / PD*
11	sehr grossen Betrag als (.) Waehrungsposition	*OD*
12	zu nehmen (.) da hab ich dann einen schoenen	*Colloquial lexis / Insider discourse / MCD*
13	Batzen mit verdienen koennen (.) fuer die	
14	Firma (.) und als es dann darum ging die eine	*PD / stylistic cohesion*
15	Tantieme oder die eine Dividende fuer mich	*PD*
16	auszuschuetten hatte er gesagt <ESp> ich	*Embedded speech begin*
17	haette gar nichts getan? ich haette kein Bu::ch <ESpE>	*Reported OD /Embedded speech end*
18	man spricht von einem Buch wenn man in	*Alignment to researcher/Insider discourse/MCD*
19	irgendeiner Sache eine Position nehmen kann	*OD*
20	ob es Wertpapiere sind oder Fremdwaehrung	*OD*
21	spricht man von der Moeglichkeit etwas zu	*LBC*
22	tun oder zu lassen (1.0) und? ich hatte ihm ja	*Colloquial lexis /PD/Deixis*
23	bewiesen indem er mir gesagt hat <ESp> sie	*Embedded speech begin*
24	koennen das und das tun (.) <EspE> hab ich das auch	*Embedded speech end*
25	mit Erfolg getan? und fuer diesen Erfolg	
26	wollte er mich nich honorieren (1.5) dann bin	*Narrative development*

27 ich damit zu Herr M gegangen und hab gesagt	*Membership category device*
28 <ESp> Herr M die Tantieme die man mir	*Embedded speech begin*
29 zahlt ist nicht (.) so wie sie sein muesste	*Self-repair?*
30 <ESpE> (2.0) und dann hat Herr M mir dann	*Embedded speech end / narrative*
31 einen Nachschlag geben muessen weil er	*Own evaluative coda of narrative*
32 eingesehen hat dass es eben eben nicht	
33 annehmbar war (4.0) und (3.0)	*Alignment to researcher*
34	

its people, its positions, its processes and secrets and his communication of these essential categories as anchor marks in the narrative, creating meaning, signalling emphasis now on his sense of belonging (lines 3, 11, 12-13, 19-20), now on his sense of alienation from an organisation environment of which his whole way of speaking, his physical appearance and his authoritative ease showed him to be an organic part (ll. 1,3,5,6, 17). Organisational discourse - chains of technical and semi-technical jargon and insider talk - is constructed through the pointed use of professional-organisational lexis (Heritage, 1997, Drew & Sorjonen, 1997, Munby & Clair, 1997). These lexical choices are flanked by talk which is coded as membership category devices (MCD) or location-bound categories (LCB), for example, where the language reinforces the identity construction of the speaker as member of a (professional) group or active in a specific (interactional) location context (Baker, 1997, Peräkylä, 2004). The identification with, acceptance of, or resistance to, events in the told career biography are heard in the sequential employment of these discourse elements (ll. 12, 18, 21 and 27), differently weighted as they are with subtly dosed charges of emotion, irony, self-deprecation and so on. Prosodic effects in speech refer specifically to those 'staging' devices used to heighten the dramatic significance of utterances (here at ll. 7, 10, 14-15 and 22). Thus Herr K moves in the extract above between pride, boasting even, to the almost vulgar denigration of his own prized professional work, when he slips between professional/organisational lexis on the one hand (the money made as a 'Position') and street language ('Batzen') or between explanations aligned to the outsider-interviewer (nevertheless entrusted with insider secrets) and strands of embedded speech (ESp), imbued with the physical setting and conjured up through prosodic and paralinguistic devices expressing the whole gamut of emotions and sensations the speaker wishes to convey about his encounters with a hostile professional ethos, foreign to his experience and beyond his understanding. The exact meaning of the layered accounts may not be entirely clear to the listener, but their discoursal aim is broadly tailored syntactically, semantically and pragmatically for comprehension: it is an act of communicative 'ritualization' (Schiffrin, 1993, p. 258).

Extract 2

"Fixed costs start with staff"

> K: and (3.0) on account of the situation we've got here now they are trying to reduce fixed costs? (3.0) and fixed costs begin of course with personnel (2.0) so I've been told that what I have always done up to now for example when the trading department was still with us (1.0) this business they say is no longer relevant (1.5) and for that reason I am not needed (1.5) without the (1.0) normal (1.0) readiness to talk to me or to ask anything see? or to take some kind of decision on social grounds or whatever I was told I am the one who has to go and that was done with a rough attempt at a letter of dismissal (6.0) but of course I have a handful of proofs that show what I did here all the time (1.0) and (1.5) and which can prove precisely the opposite of what they accuse me namely that I couldn't do anything more for the company see? and when you see that and (1.0) negative things are said about me (1.5) to dismiss me then I don't see why I should do anything now that I don't have to do and in the past I did th- things that I didn't have to do? namely I made a lot of money for the company ...

1	K: und auf der Situation die wir getzt hier haben wird	Colloquial lexis / Alternative OD
2	versucht unter fixe Kosten einzusparen? (3.0) und fixe	OD
3	Kosten ja erst mal beim Personal beginnen (2.0) hat man	OD
4	mir jetzt gesagt <ESp> dass das was ich bisher getan hatte	Embedded speech begin
5	als meinetwegen noch Trade[7] da war (1.0) dieses Geschaeft	*Modality /Alignment to researcher*
6	nicht mehr anfiele (1.5) und ich aufgrund dessen	*OD / Modality*
7	ueberfluessig waere <ESpE> (1.5) ohne die (1.0) normale	*PD/Modality /Embedded speech end*

---

7   "Trade" stands for a division of the company for which Herr K was active.

8	(1.0) Gespraechsbereitschaft irgendwo zu finden oder	*OD / LBC*
9	nachzufragen [uhmmm] na? eine gewisse soziale Auswahl	*OD / Concessive hedging*
10	zu treffen oder was auch immer hat man mir gesagt \<ESp>	*Embedded speech begin*
11	ich waere derjenige welche da zu gehen haette \<ESpE>	*PD / Embedded speech end*
12	und dann eben mit dem Entwurf einer Kuendigungsschrift	*Modality / OD*
13	manifestiert (6.0) aber ich hab natuerlich ein Handvoll	*6-second pause / PD*
14	Beweise die eben aufweisen was ich hier eher getan habe	*Modality /PD*
15	(1.0) und (1.5) die auch genau das Gegenteil beweisen	Consecutive pauses
16	koennen was man mir hier vorwirft naemlich dass ich	Modality /PD-Modality
17	nichts haette tun mehr fuer die Firma na? wenn man sich	*Alignment to researcher*
18	ueber dessen bewusst ist und (1.0) mir negativ etwas (1.5)	*Dispreferred / PD*
19	nachsagen will indem man mir kuendigt sehe ich natuerlich	*PD*
20	auch nicht ein dass ich jetzt was tue was ich nicht tun muss	*Own discoursal rationalisation / PD*
21	und ich hab in der Vergangenheit et etwas getan was ich	*Face-saving move / Self-repair*
22	nicht musste? naemlich Geld verdient fuer die Firma	*Modality / PD*

In this second part, apart from the massed pauses which become denser and longer the more difficult the narrative gets, organisational discourse is brought to bear to define someone as a 'superfluous cost' (l.7). There is clearly a strong element of dismay, shock and perhaps pain in this stretch of narrative. Yet Herr K keeps it under control. His defence mechanisms search out each instance in which he sees himself as being the victim of a loss of correctness, the target of a management style which discards knowledge, skills and proficiency (lines 7-9, 11, 14-15, 17, 20-22). Herr K can be heard to experience the sense of loss of status as well as exclusion within the organisation, and to effectively expect nothing more from the professional environment he has worked in so long, least of all further learning chances.

Reference is made in the data extracts above to 'Modality' and 'Hedging'. Herr K layers his narrative, in fact, with approximations, hesitations, hedging qualifications and silences. This active negotiation of meaning through circumlocution is the site where the speakers' mutual relationship is established and where positions of certainty, necessity, opinion, belief and factuality are adopted. Stubbs defines modality as

> the ways in which language is used to encode meanings such as degrees of certainty and commitment, or alternatively vagueness and lack of commitment, personal beliefs versus generally accepted or taken for granted knowledge. Such language functions to express group membership, as speakers adopt positions, express agreement or disagreement with others ... (Stubbs, 1996, p. 202).

Emotion, too, is a central element in this interview. The emotion is charged with professional jargon, justified with facts, numbers, specialist details, formulated in a narrative only dimly comprehensible to an 'outsider' and sufficiently understood at its face level by this researcher only after years of shared presence in the same building, observing the same events and dramas. It is a mark of Herr K's trust and willingness to employ a narrative that allows the researcher behind and beyond his professional-linguistic defences to hear his deep anxiety. The interview was physically conducted in a tract of office space emptied of employees as a result of cost-cutting over a period of years, a kind of symbolic space in which this narrative received its fitting embodiment. Both researcher and interviewee were acutely aware of this consonance between a narrative of destitution and a physical example thereof.

Conclusion

We have seen that the difficulties met with in radically and rapidly changing work/professional environments can be observed and heard in auto/biographical depth interviews. The superficial script of the interview which starts from routine interactions, assumed behaviours and relatively stable expectations is expressive enough of conflict and points to the difficult learning process that may be taking place. I have tried to show how closer analysis of the language resources employed in the interview, however, is able to enhance the analysis. The "grammar" of change, disorientation or resistance as the resources of experience are brought to bear on the narrative is seen to be a complex play of discourse elements. Professional scripts and frames of self-identification are brought into play with the theorising process of accounting for self in change. Gendered coping strategies, resulting in differences in the type of auto/biographical narrative created can be plausibly expected, though confirmation could only come from other interviews within the corpus. Herr K aligns his talk to the other - here the interviewer - yet remains almost helpless, locked into his own version, and thereby remains at half-way house to, and from, his distress and his attempt to make social and interactive sense of his loss of status and the challenge to his professional knowledge.

An important criticism to which the procedure of extracting pieces of data from a corpus for detailed analysis is potentially open, is the risk of authorial inscription and serious de-contextualization of the research subjects. Rhetorical inscription of meanings can so easily usurp the 'intended' meanings of the respondents as they selected language tentatively, moving around their own, rarely narrated, biographies. Close attention to the development of narrated auto/biographic 'data', attention to the dialogic, interactive context in which the 'stories' unfold (themselves) and to the considerable lacunae and failings in our comprehension of much of that which takes place, can, I feel, serve as a cautious basis for the analysis of individuals' talk in connection with the talk of others.

The electronic corpus, and interrogation and investigation of the corpus of transcribed talk, then, is no more than the sum of the listening, writing, transcribing work of the researcher. Computer-assisted collection of auto/biographical talk does not 'close the book' on the research. Managing the comparison and presentation of the co-construction in context, and the interdiscursive creation of meaning over sequences of talk rather than in individual instances alone permits analysis of auto/biographical narratives in talk which "pays close attention to the local embeddedness of interaction" (Silverman, 2005, August [5-7]). Moreover, as Seale writes, "by forcing researchers to become explicit about the underlying operations of data analysis, CAQDAS creates an auditable trail that ought to enhance the credibility of findings" (Seale, 2002, p.656). These can be made available for secondary analysis by other researchers, thereby encouraging, rather than preventing, attention to the theoretical care that is important at each stage of the research experience.

References

Akerström, M., Jacobsson, K. and Wästerfors, D. (2004). Reanalysis of previously collected material. In C. Seale, G. Gobo, J. F. Gubrium, and D. Silverman, (Eds.) *Qualitative Research Practice*. London/Thousand Oaks: Sage.

Avis, J. (2002). Imaginary Friends: managerialism, globalisation and post-compulsory education and training in Britain. *Discourse,* 23, 75-90.

Baker, C. (1997). Membership Categorization and Interview Accounts. In D. Silverman, (Ed.) *Qualitative Research. Theory, Method and Practice.* London: Sage.

Ball, S. J. (1991). Power, Conflict, Micropolitics And All That! In G. Walford, (Ed.) *Doing Educational Research.* London/New York: Routledge/The Open University.

Barlow, M. (2000). *Concordancing with MonoConc Pro 2.0,* Houston: Athelstan.

Bauer, M. W. & Aarts, B. (2000). Corpus construction: a principle for qualitative data collection. In M. W. Bauer, and G. Gaskell,. (Eds.) *Qualitative Researching with Text, Image and Sound. A Practical Handbook.* London: Sage.

Bauman, Z. (2001). *The Individualized Society.* Cambridge: Polity Press.

Bourdieu, P. (1998). *Acts of Resistance. Against the Tyranny of the Market.* New York: The New Press and Polity Press.

Capps, L. & Ochs, E. (1995).*Constructing Panic. The discourse of agoraphobia.* Cambridge (MA): Harvard University Press.

Castells, M. (1998). *The information age: economy, society and culture: 3. End of Millenium.* Cambridge, Mass: Blackwell.

Dey, I. (2004). Grounded Theory. In C. Seale, G. Gobo, J. F. Gubrium, and D. Silverman, (Eds.) *Qualitative Research Practice.* London: Sage.

Drew, P. and Sorjonen, M. L. (1997). Institutional Dialogue. In Van Dijk, T. A. (Ed.) *Discourse as Social Interaction. Discourse Studies: A Multidisciplinary Introduction.* London: Sage.

Evans, K. (2001).Tacit Skills and Work Inequalities. A UK Perspective on Tacit Forms of Key Competences, and Issues for Future Research. *ECER.* Lille.

Evans, R. (2004). *Learning discourse. Learning Biographies, Embedded speech and Discourse Identity in Students' Talk.* Frankfurt / Main: Peter Lang.

Fielding, N. G. (2001) Computer Applications in Qualitative Research. In P. Atkinson, A. Coffey, S. Delamont, J. Lofland, and L. Lofland, (Eds.) *Handbook of Ethnography.* London: Sage.

Fielding, N. G. and Lee, R. M. (1998). *Computer Analysis and Qualitative Research.* London: Sage.

Hepburn, A. and Potter, J. (2004). Discourse Analytic Practice. In C. Seale, G. Gobo, J. F. Gubrium, and D. Silverman, D. (Eds.) *Qualitative Research Practice.* London/Thousand Oaks/New Delhi: Sage

Heritage, J. (1997). Conversation Analysis and Institutional Talk. Analysing Data. In D. Silverman, (Ed.) *Qualitative Research. Theory, Method and Practice.* London: Sage.

Hoerning, E. M. (1989). Erfahrungen als biographische Ressourcen. In P. Alheit, and E. M. Hoerning, (Eds.) *Biographisches Wissen. Beiträge zu einer Theorie lebensgeschichtlicher Erfahrung.* Frankfurt/New York: Campus Verlag.

Kelle, U. (Ed.) (1995). *Computer-Aided Qualitative Data Analysis. Theory, Methods and Practice.* London: Sage.

Kelle, U. (2000a). Computer-Assisted Analysis: Coding and Indexing. In m. w. Bauer, and G. Gaskell, (Eds.) *Qualitative Researching with Text, Image and Sound. A Practical Handbook.* London: Sage.

Kelle, U. (2000b). Computergestützte Analyse Qualitativer Daten. In U. Flick, E.Von Kardorff, and I. Steinke, I. (Eds.) *Qualitative Forschung. Ein Handbuch.* Reinbek bei Hamburg: Rowohlt.

Kelle, U. (2004). Computer-Assisted Qualitative Data Analysis. In C. Seale, G. Gobo, J. F. Gubrium, and D. Silverman, D. (Eds.) *Qualitative Research Practice.* London/Thousand Oaks/New Delhi: Sage.

Kowal, S. & O'connell, D. C. (2000). Zur Transkription von Gesprächen. In U. Flick, E. Von Kardoff, and I. Steinke, I. (Eds.) *Qualitative Forschung. Ein Handbuch.* Reinbek bei Hamburg: Rowohlt.

Lancashire, I. (1996). *Using TACT with Electronic Texts.A Guide to Text-Analysis Computing Tools, Version 2.1 for MS-DOS and PC-DOS.* New York: MLA.

Lewins, A. (2001). Computer Assisted Qualitative Data Analysis. In N. Gilbert, (Ed.) *Researching Social Life.* London: Sage.

Mason, J. (2004). Personal narratives, relational selves: residential histories in the living and telling. *The Sociological Review.* 52, 162-179.

Miller, G. (1997). Toward Ethnographies of Institutional Discourse: Proposals and Suggestions. In G. Miller, and R. Dingwall,. (Eds.) *Context and Method in Qualitative Research.* London: Sage.

Muhr, T. (1997). *ATLASti, The Knowledge Workbench. Short User's Manual.* Berlin: Scientific Software Development.

Munby, D. K. & Clair, R. P. (1997). Organizational Discourse. In T. A. Van Dijk,. (Ed.) *Discourse as Social Interaction.* London: Sage.

Nias, J. (1991). Primary Teachers Talking: A Reflexive Account of Longitudinal Research. In G. Walford, (Ed.) *Doing Educational Research.* London/New York: Routledge/The Open University.

Ochs, E. (1979). Transcription as Theory. In E. Ochs, and B. B. Schieffelin, (Eds.) *Developmental Pragmatics.* New York: Academic Press.

Peräkylä, A. (2004). Conversation Analysis. In C. Seale, G. Gobo, J. F. Gubrium, and D. Silverman, (Eds.) *Qualitative Research Practice.* London/Thousand Oaks/New Delhi: Sage.

Risberg, A. (2001). Employee Experiences of Acquisition Processes. *Journal of World Business,* 36, 58-84.

Salling Olesen, H. (2003). Work, Identity and Learning. *Life History Project Roskilde University.* 16, 1-25.

Schiffrin, D. (1993). 'Speaking for another'. Sociolinguistic Interviews: Alignments, Identities and Frames. In D. Tannen, (Ed.) *Framing in Discourse.* Oxford: Oxford University Press.

Seale, C. F. (2002). Computer-assisted analysis of qualitative interview data. In J. F. Gubrium, and J. A. Holstein, (Eds.) *Handbook of Interview Research. Context & Method.* Thousand Oaks - London - New Delhi: Sage.

Silverman, D. (2005). Instances or Sequences? Improving the State of the Art of Qualitative Research [71 Paragraphs]. *Forum Qualitative Sozialforschung / Forum: Qualitative Social Research [On-line Journal].* August ed.

Stubbs, M. (1996). *Text and Corpus Analysis. Computer-assisted studies of language and culture.* Oxford: Blackwell.

Very, P. and Schweiger, D. M. (2001). The Acquisition Process as a Learning Process: Evidence from a Study of Critical Problems and Solutions in Cross-Border Deals. *Journal of World Business.* 36, 11-31.

7 Understanding Women's Learning Trajectories: Examining Life Histories of Women Learners in Canada

Patricia A Gouthro

The current neo-liberal context that is shaping discourses and policy frameworks in lifelong learning is characterised by its emphasis on individualism and competition. Within this context, gender differences in life experiences and socially assigned responsibilities are ignored, minimalized, or treated as independent problems that do not need to be taken up as a matter of public debate. Using a critical feminist theoretical framework for analysis, this chapter discusses some of the results of a research study conducted within Canada that explores concerns of mature women students in adult and higher education contexts. It is argued that policies and practices in the field of lifelong learning need to take into account that women's learning trajectories are frequently different from those of their male counterparts. While women make decisions around their educational commitments as individuals, they do so within a broader social context that exerts far more pressure on women than it does on men to defer, modify, or alter their learning trajectories to meet the needs of other people. A competitive and individualised model of learning consistently and systematically places women at a disadvantage. A more equitable and holistic approach towards lifelong learning is needed to create inclusive and supportive policies and practices in adult and higher education to benefit women learners.

The research study overviewed in this chapter was funded by the Social Sciences and Humanities Research Council of Canada (SSHRC). Forty mature women university students were asked to trace their lifelong learning trajectories and discuss concerns they faced in continuing their formal education. In addition, twenty interviews were conducted with 'key informants' – individuals in either administrative positions in universities or in the government and/or policy sector to find out more about their insights and perspectives around the barriers, supports and programmes that impact on women's participation in lifelong learning.

This chapter begins with some background information on the evolving discourses of lifelong learning, and then overviews the methodological approach using life histories. Some of the findings from the life histories are presented by examining factors that affect decision making around learning trajectories, and exploring the supports and barriers that impact on women's learning experiences. The chapter concludes by developing a critical feminist analysis of the implications of this research for policies and practices in adult and higher education contexts.

Lifelong Learning Discourses

In the early 1970's, the discourses of lifelong learning were enthusiastic in enjoining all people to participate in learning throughout their lifespan. The well-known UNESCO Faure Report *Learning to Be* (1972) argued that education was a basic human right, and could be used to eradicate inequalities between disparate nation-states. Lifelong education would provide radical and innovative approaches to address global problems of poverty, hunger, and literacy. Emerging technologies were heralded as providing opportunities for access to educational programmes that had previously been hindered by lack of localised resources. The emphasis on adult learning presented education as a lifelong process, rather than just as career preparation for children and youth. The authors argued that "for far too long education had the task of preparing for stereotyped functions, stable situations, for one moment in existence, for a particular trade or a given job" (Faure et. al. 1972: 69). Instead education should address the need for ongoing change and continuous growth so that people could become engaged with learning at different stages in their lives. In addition, learning was not limited to workplace objectives, but was connected to a broader sense of 'learning to be' that incorporated a social justice orientation and the ability to think freely and critically.

In the 1990's, a resurgence in interest in the concept of lifelong learning emerged, but this time the emphasis was more on the need for lifelong learning to meet the needs of the marketplace (Gouthro, 2002). Learning was situated not as a social equaliser, but rather as a high stakes commodity. The individuals, regions, and countries that invested in ongoing educational opportunities were more likely to be successful in economic competition, which would lead to a higher standard of living. The UNESCO Delors (1996) report pointed out that the gap between North and South was widening in part because of the disparity in opportunities and support for education.

Edwards (1997) argues that the resurgence in support for lifelong learning is linked to continuous change. Technology is evolving rapidly, altering the way we communicate with one another, participate in the workplace, and socialise. Populations are in a state of flux, with constant migration and movement as well as changes in structures of nation-states. The paid workplace is affected by the shifting and frequently unpredictable currents of globalised capitalism, as jobs move to sites where the most lucrative profits can be made (Klein, 2000; Friedman, 2005).

Lifelong learning is increasingly defined within an individualised context as learners are expected to craft their unique learning biographies (Dyke, 1997), within what Beck (1992) has called a 'risk society'. Beck explains that the current neo-liberal context has created a competitive environment for living and learning, in which:

a universally valid and applicable policy mix is being propagated: political reforms are to be geared to the standard of economic goals – low inflation; balanced budgets; the dismantling of trade barriers and currency controls; maximum freedom for capital; minimum regulation of the national labour market; and a lean, adaptable welfare state that pushes its citizens into work (2001, p. 85).

The implementation of these policies creates numerous tensions and 'risks' around environmental sustainability, employment, poverty, and democratic rights (Beck, 2001). Within the 'risk society' individuals assume responsibility for locating themselves in the most advantageous position. This means determining one's learning trajectory is an individual responsibility. Each person must assess the opportunities and the challenges of participating in different educational programmes, and determine his/her participation accordingly.

Yet not all people are equally positioned to access learning opportunities. Women frequently have different lifelong learning trajectories than men (Gorard, Rees, & Fevre, 1999). Women are more likely to modify or abandon educational opportunities because they often put the needs of other family members ahead of their career interests. Women's responsibilities for unpaid labour often creates challenges in continuing their education (Stalker, 2001; Gouthro, 2005). Rather than addressing gendered differences in learning experience, however, policies and practices in adult and higher education frequently reinforce structural barriers that perpetuate women's inequality in the 'learning society'. Rising tuition and cutbacks in supports to higher education institutions mean that the government is assuming less responsibility for ensuring equitable access to higher education. Increasingly, individuals are expected to finance their own costs to participate in adult and higher education programmes.

At the same time, governments trumpet the need to have a highly educated workforce in order to compete effectively in the globalised marketplace. Current policy papers, such as the *Canadian Delegation Report of the OECD Education Chief Executives* (2005) and the Council of Ministers of Education International Report on *Education in Canada* (2005) both emphasise the importance of adult education with regards to employment and connections to the paid workforce, rather than focusing attention on a broader learning mandate.

The individualist approach to lifelong learning and concern with creating connections between education and the paid workforce are indicators of the increasingly pervasive influence of the marketplace in lifelong learning discourses (Gouthro, 2002). In a marketplace context, learners are reframed as educational consumers (Collins, 1998), and broader philosophical and social democratic concerns are less central to the educational agenda (Welton, 1998). The marketplace reflects a masculine framework of values that disadvantages women by privileging competition over cooperation, individual hierarchical success over cooperation, and learning for profit over learning for life (Gouthro, 2005; Hart, 1997). Recent policy discussions about the 'Third Way' suggest strategies that are intended to soften some of the effects of globalised capitalism, but they still emphasise individual responsibility for charting one's course through a lifetime of learning. The primary emphasis in education is still to be on learning for the marketplace. This can be seen in Canada's Innovation Strategy that "reduces adult education to an instrument for the development of an appropriately skilled workforce" (Rubenson & Walker, 2006, p. 181).

Policy development in lifelong learning in Canada acknowledges some need to address issues around equity and inclusion, but the continuing emphasis on learning connected to paid work marginalises and devalues unpaid labour contributions. Full citizenship in the broader society becomes linked with participation in the paid labour market. This has gendered implications, since women's lives are frequently shaped by their unpaid socially assigned commitments and responsibilities in the homeplace (Gouthro, 2005). Even within policy discussions that address the need to consider inequality of access, gender is not a central issue. The focus is more on targeted groups such as youth, Aboriginals, or New Canadians. The implicit assumption seems to be that overall women are doing just fine, and that there do not need to be any considerations as to whether current policies and practices in adult and higher education address and support women's learning experiences adequately.

Life History Methodology

Decisions around learning trajectories may be considered an individual responsibility, but these decisions are shaped by social contexts. Life history methodology enables a deeper understanding of the complexity of women's lives and the responsibilities and commitments that impact upon their decision-making processes. In bringing a critical feminist lens to develop an analysis of women's lifelong learning experiences, life history methodology works well because it is a truism that individual experiences are inherently political and deeply embedded in power (Dhunpath, 2000, p. 544). Detailed interviews provide thick, descriptive accounts, providing extensive amounts of data for analysis (Yow, 1994). Life histories provide a means for educators and learners to share their stories and raise significant concerns that impact upon learning experiences (Keats Whelan, Huber, Rose, Davies, & Clandinin, 2001; Taylor, 2000).

Life histories are also beneficial because they provide insights into concerns that are often left out of the official policy discourses. They reveal the multitude of factors that work together to influence individual decisions and learning pathways. Dhunpath argues that life history methodology is valuable in "providing a means of understanding how motives and practices reflect the intimate intersection of institutional and individual experience" (2000, p. 544). By examining a number of different life histories, and comparing this data to the literature, certain commonalities and themes begin to emerge.

For this study, a purposive sampling method was used to attain as much diversity as possible amongst the potential participants. The research design included life history interviews with forty mature women learners in higher education from four different geographically and culturally dispersed Canadian provinces; Nova Scotia, Ontario, Alberta, and British Columbia. Participants were recruited by sending out notices on listserves and bulletin boards on university campuses in different parts of the country, asking for participants who self-identified as lifelong learners. This study was limited to women over the age of forty since some oral life history research (see Yow, 1994) argues that once people reach this stage in life (or older) they begin more of a reflecting back process in examining their lives. In addition, these individuals have longer learning trajectories.

Women were very generous in offering to share their stories, and there was a high response rate. As a consequence, initial, brief biographies were compiled from a group of twenty to thirty individuals who responded in each location, and then out of these ten were selected as potential participants. Selection was made by trying to obtain as much diversity as possible within this limited sample, taking into accounts variables such as age, ethnicity, marital status, sexual orientation, and ability. Numerous other factors were taken into consideration to obtain as wide a range of experience as possible. These included differences in careers, types of educational programmes, levels of current education (ranging from undergraduate to graduate), whether or not women had children (and of different ages), where they had lived, and whether they were New Canadians/international students.

During the life history interviews, participants were asked to trace their lifelong learning trajectories and discuss concerns they faced in continuing their formal education. The interview schedule was semi-structured, to enable more conversational responses. Participants were asked to describe significant learning experiences in their lives in a chronological order, challenges that they have had to overcome, motivators that have affected their desire to learn, and issues that have impacted upon their learning experiences. Snick, Wildemeersch, & Celis argue that the development of a life history (and its learning processes) is situated in a personal, social and societal context (2000, p. 3).

In addition, interviews with twenty 'key informants' provide insights into higher educational institutional operations and the government policy sector around supports or programmes that exist for women learners. The individuals were also asked to share their understanding and insights into the challenges and barriers that exist for women who intend to continue on informal post-secondary education.

The findings of this research study draw on both content analyses of literature and related documents, as well as analysis from the interview transcripts. Atlas-ti is a qualitative software programme that assists with organising data as it is coded according to categories determined by the researcher. It is based upon the premise of grounded theory (Glaser & Strauss, 1967; Kirby & McKenna, 1989) whereby understanding emerges from the data, as themes emerge after the data has been repeatedly reviewed. In addition, the lens of critical feminism is brought to the analysis, to search for indicators that reflect not only individual concerns and circumstances, but structural issues that need to be assessed.

Decision Making and Learning Trajectories

Women who continue on with higher learning opportunities later in adulthood are juggling multiple responsibilities as mothers, partners, employees, and caregivers for the elderly. In some cases male partners support women's decisions to return to schooling by providing assistance in the homeplace and sharing financial resources. Some women spoke about the ways that their partners had made it possible for them to continue on and be successful in schooling. For example, one participant had been discouraged from going to university by a high school teacher who said she did not have the academic ability. A few years later as a young wife, her husband said to her, *"We live across the road from the university – Why don't you go?"*. With his continued encouragement she applied and found that contrary to that teacher's predictions, she was able to excel in university. In another instance an ESL (English-as-Second-Language) student spoke about her partner's practical help and support in reviewing and editing her research papers because he had greater fluency in English.

In some cases, however, male partners were not very supportive. Women worried that there might be some resentment about the time that their studies took away from family life. They frequently felt that they had to negotiate different educational goals so that it would create less inconvenience for their families, ie. selecting a local programme or a distance course that would not have been their first choice but was be less disruptive to the family's schedule.

The majority of women interviewed had very non-linear work/life trajectories. Many, if not all, had experienced some sort of life crises that had helped shape their life trajectory, including dealing with major health problems, coping with divorce, having a family member who suffered from mental illness, or surviving sexual abuse. To my surprise, almost a quarter of all the participants spoke of problems with alcoholism in their family, and the effect that it had on them. One woman explained, *"My mother was an alcoholic and so I was the perfect rescuer child"*. Many of these women were learners who were driven to excel in their studies.

Minority women, particularly those who grew up in Canada, often faced additional burdens of discrimination. One participant talked about the overt racism she faced as a child in the community and school system: *"I just accepted that we were inferior and that made me feel very ashamed of who I was"*. Many of the women in the study spoke about the struggles that they experienced with issues around self-esteem and confidence in various aspects of their lives that impacted on their decisions around education and career paths. Sometimes this was linked with systemic issues, such as racism or poverty, while in other cases it was connected more to their particular family circumstances.

In many instances, it was clear that women worried about prioritising their individual educational aspirations because of the need to take care of responsibilities in the homeplace. Many of the women in the study had made career and educational decisions to accommodate the needs of their husband and/or children. Their learning trajectories had numerous breaks as they took time out to have children, move because of their husband's career, or work to support their partner while he went to school. For example, one woman talked about a competitive programme that she was accepted onto, but decided to withdraw her application from: *"I actually got accepted there, but...we decided it would be better for him [her ex-husband] to finish his degree"*. A number of other women gave similar examples, where they either deferred or altered their educational and/or career choices to accommodate what they believed were the best interests of either their husband/partner or children.

Several of the women who waited until their children were grown before returning to university worried that by the time they graduated they would face age discrimination when seeking employment. These women had doubts about how much opportunity they would get to actually use their education in the workforce, yet the decision to return to school was generally a very positive life learning experience. They felt they had a lot of potential to contribute to the workplace, but were afraid that others would view them as too old.

Barriers and Supports

Returning to higher education created a number of challenges for many of the women. Juggling time to accommodate responsibilities around the homeplace, paid workplace, and academia was frequently an issue. With rising tuition rates, and high costs of living in some of the university city centres, financial concerns were often one of the main issues raised by participants. A few of the women were fortunate in that they had sufficiently high family incomes that their tuition rates posed little concern, and a couple of women were funded by the government or employers. While there were scholarships available to some students, as well as subsidised student housing in a couple of instances, the majority of students did not have access to these kinds of financial supports. Many students reported racking up large amounts of student debt. This was especially worrisome to older students. As one participant bluntly stated when asked about her job prospects, *"I'm not overly optimistic. I'm old"*. A number of women also raised concerns about having sufficient funds for their retirement.

The high cost of post-secondary education means that learners are often caught between the competing demands of workplace, homeplace, and academia. One of the participants expressed her disappointment in going back to do her doctorate because she had assumed that during her residency she would have this collegial experience, where *"great, everyone's going to be there."* Instead she found:

> *It doesn't work like that. People still have full-time jobs and just take their courses. Very few people can position themselves to actually do full-time residency and not have other commitments.*

Certainly for most of the women who were interviewed (including this participant) returning to school as a mature student generally meant juggling a wide range of commitments and responsibilities. Even amongst students who talked about supportive partners, there was often inequity around household labour and childcare. As one participant explained, my husband *"will do anything I ask him to do, but that always the rub. I have to ask"*.

Many of the women combined paid work with domestic and caregiving responsibilities in addition to attending university. Therefore, they were often appreciative of opportunities for flexibility, either from an employer who would give them time off to attend class, or from a university that offered either night/weekend courses and/or distance delivery options. As one participant explained about her choice to take her programme via the internet:

> *I drive all day long and when I get home, I don't want to drive anywhere. So having the option of doing something on-line, and doing it whenever I have the time to do it, and whenever I fell like doing it, is huge. I cannot stress how much I love that.*

For many women it seemed that while higher learning contexts often provided a different sort of stress, the actual chance of being able to learn, think, and explore ideas at a more abstract and complicated level was actually a very freeing and rewarding experience. Being successful in going back to university helped increase self esteem and personal confidence, and they often surprised themselves with how well they did. One woman described the way she felt when she first returned to university: *"I was terrified. I won't understand it. It'll be over my head"*. But now she states, *"I'm getting the highest marks in the class."* Despite the concerns around finding employment upon graduation, most of the women had a strong sense that they had something important that they could contribute to society. They also often felt that by continuing their education they set a good role model for their children.

In terms of faculty support, there did not seem to be a significant gender difference in terms of mentorship or assistance. There were complaints that some women and some male faculty members were difficult and non-supportive, and there was also glowing praise for both male and female faculty members who served as mentors. One student described one of her female advisors as *"absolutely wonderful"*. However, another student said of her supervisor who was a woman; *"If your family is important to you it takes several hours a week to show how important they are to you, and she just didn't get that at all".* Eventually, she ended up switching supervisors to someone she felt was more empathetic.

The relationship with faculty is not only important in terms of supervision for the students' own academic work, but also for opportunities to do research and obtain scholarships. Some of the foreign students, particularly those who spoke English as a second language, mentioned that they felt that they were disadvantaged in that faculty as they often did not select them to be assistants. This meant that they lost out on both the practical research experience and financial support that role would bring.

For students in graduate studies, particularly at the doctoral level, competition between students seemed to be quite intense. Although there was some discussion of camaraderie and support, there were even more stories about the competitive nature of academe at this level.

Participants raised a number of concerns about the need for additional supports for women in continuing on in higher education. Not surprisingly, with rising tuition and living costs, improved financial assistance was key for many women. ESL students raised concerns that while universities were anxious to recruit foreign students because of the higher differential tuition fees that they could charge, they were not as willing to provide adequate resources to help them write at the required advanced level of their studies.

Many of the women seemed anxious to stress that although their learning pathways may have had numerous breaks and interruptions, they were still very committed to their studies. Most of the women became most excited and engaged when they were talking about their particular research projects, courses that they enjoyed, or faculty who had supported or inspired them. For many of the women, this learning also impacted on different aspects of their lives, causing them to reassess their own opinions of themselves, to think about the important relationships in their lives, and to consider what their long-term goals might be in a different light. Even the women who wryly acknowledged that they could not devote as much time to their studies as some of their colleagues because of extensive demands from other commitments still indicated that they valued the opportunity to continue learning. The majority of the women expressed a sense of confidence that they had a lot to offer – even if some of them were concerned that others may not recognise or give them opportunities to prove themselves within the paid workplace.

Critical Feminist Approach

As discussed earlier in the chapter, since the 1970's, when lifelong learning first received widespread popular attention (Faure, 1970), the discourses in lifelong learning have changed to reflect shifting educational values. Instead of using adult education as a means of addressing world problems and enhancing human potentiality, increasingly, lifelong learning is being defined as an important means to secure a competitive advantage within a global marketplace (Gouthro, 2002). A critical feminist perspective draws upon both critical and feminist theories to examine the underlying values that shape existing policy and institutional structures in adult and higher education and assess the implications of this for women's learning experiences. From a critical feminist perspective, it is clear that differences in lifelong learning trajectories may not only be ascribed to *individual* experiences and decisions, but are linked to social contexts such as how unpaid labour is allocated. While women might make personal decisions about when to enter the workforce, take university programmes, or spend time in the unpaid activities of providing full-time care for children or elderly parents, these decisions are influenced by broader social contexts that shape gendered expectations in behaviour and responsibilities.

Critical theories in lifelong learning, particularly those drawing upon the work of Jürgen Habermas (1987; 1996) provide insights into how the *system* (political economy) delineates educational discourses from an individualistic and competitive marketplace agenda. The overarching influence of the system shapes and distorts our everyday learning contexts, thus undermining opportunities for more emancipatory and communicative forms of learning that may be generated from the *lifeworld* (everyday world of homeplace/community). Newman explains that "the lifeworld denotes those myriad shared understandings upon which we construct our lives and upon which we base our interactions with others" (1999, p. 143). As Brookfield (2005) explains, according to Habermas (1987) we are so immersed in the lifeword it is impossible to fully comprehend how it shapes the way we think and interact with one another. Yet as phenomenologists such as Schutz & Luckmann (1973) argue, by attempting to 'bracket out' our assumptions, we can create a sense of distance from which we are then able to view our everyday world and thus gain insights into the social factors that shape the way we interact with one another. Therefore it is only by pulling back from our common, taken-for-granted assumptions about how the world is supposed to work that we can begin to question the underlying values that influence our belief systems and everyday behaviours.

Critical Habermasian discourses in adult education help reveal the social power structures that impede certain kinds of learning while supporting others, and address the essential *social* and *communicative* aspect of learning that values democratic processes (Welton, 1998; Brookfield, 2005). In his work, Habermas (1987) points to the detrimental ways in which the system has gradually encroached and impinged upon the lifeworld, thus undermining traditional social forms of interaction and decision-making. Newman notes that Habermas understands that "the system would include all transnational economic systems, institutions and enterprises, and include such bodies as major churches, military alliances, and other kinds of political, cultural and industrial associations" (1999, p. 153). Critical educators note the detrimental effect of the system in educational contexts when we observe a market-driven agenda that overrides more holistic or emancipatory approaches towards lifelong learning. Brookfield states that:

> The explanation Habermas proposes as to why adults are not continually and conspicuously learning is that contemporary political and economic systems, and their various steering media, attempt to foreclose the possibility of learning that challenges systemic imperatives. Since learning involves asking "why?" it is potentially very threatening to the system and must be controlled. (2005, p. 248).

Therefore, critical educators point out the many ways in which challenging questions are often discouraged in many learning contexts. Arguments for 'accountability', 'professionalism', and attention to the 'bottom-line' are all couched in the language of the marketplace, thus narrowing the scope for radical or alternative frameworks or perspectives (Gouthro, 2002). Brookfield continues his explanation of Habermas's analysis, noting that "If learning to ask why cannot be stopped at the outset, then the system tries to divert the energy generated by learning into channels that confirm the legitimacy of the existing order" (Brookfield, 2005, p. 248).

In this context, it seems 'common sense' to assume that the rationale for continuing with formal education should be linked primarily with employment opportunities. At the same time, our assumptions around the best career and learning trajectories are determined by what employers (or those who have the most control in a capitalist system) would benefit the most from. Therefore, people who can commit to a linear work/learning trajectory that has few, if any interruptions, those who can give their primary commitment of time and energy to their work (studies), and those who are flexible (in terms of being able to meet employer (supervisor needs and expectations) are perceived to be the most valuable employees (learners).

The current individualistic focus in lifelong learning policies fosters a sense of competition as each person is expected to navigate within an increasingly volatile and insecure marketplace. Rising tuition rates and uncertainty about employment opportunities undermines support for more collaborative approaches to learning. The uncertainty created by constant changes in technology, erosion of support from the welfare state, and rising costs of formal education, all serve to keep learners focused on short-term goals of obtaining credentials and getting jobs rather than reflecting upon or challenging broader system structures.

A critical *feminist* framework draws attention to the inherent masculine bias in critical theoretical discourses that tends to overlook or diminish the unique concerns that women face in continuing their education. Women are still the primary caregivers in all societies. Mothers bear a disproportionate cost for childbearing, since there are significant gendered differences in the detrimental impact having children has upon income earning opportunities (Budig & England, 2001).

Women are more likely to have interrupted career and educational trajectories because they take breaks to attend to caregiving responsibilities. Women returners often use education as a strategy to re-enter the paid labour force (Bird, 1999). As noted in my earlier research on the homeplace (Gouthro, 2005) Hart's work around motherwork (1995; 1997) the learning that takes place in unpaid, caregiving contexts is rarely acknowledged or valued informal learning or paid work spaces.

In the workplace, since women and minorities are often located on peripheral rather than in core positions, they are less likely to be provided with financial support from their employers in continuing their education (Forrester, Payne & Ward, 1995). This is also seen in academic workplaces, where women are more likely to be in part-time and/or contract positions that do not provide opportunities for professional development, advancement, or support for research (Hannah, Paul, & Vethamany-Globus, 2002). Stalker and Prentice (1998) note women in universities continue to have problems with sexual harassment, worries around personal safety, access to affordable childcare, and lack of flexibility in course expectations and delivery. While women are outpacing men now in many undergraduate degrees and are fairly well represented at the Masters' level, their participation drops off at the highest levels of academe. As Leonard (2001) points out, women still only obtain a third of all doctoral degrees.

Women's decisions around learning pathways are frequently affected by gendered differences in responsibilities and commitments outside of academe (Stalker, 2001; Hayes & Flannery, 2000). Minority women often face additional challenges in post-secondary contexts, such as discrimination from other students or faculty, fewer financial resources, and exclusionary curriculum and teaching practices (Johnson-Bailey & Cervero, 1996; Tisdell, 1998). Unfortunately, a number of women learners encounter resistance from male partners that may range from a subtle undermining of effort to verbal or physical violence (Stalker, 2001; Horseman, 1999).

Implications for Lifelong Learning

Combining critical theory with feminist insights provides opportunities into the challenges, barriers and supports that impact on women's learning trajectories. Learning should not be perceived only as a means to an end, or as a prerequisite for the paid workforce, but as a process that engages the whole person and is influenced by the individual's connections to the homeplace, workplace, and community. A better understanding of gendered differences in experience can inform the development of policies and institutional supports for women in adult and higher education programmes. The poor representation of women in higher levels of academia, business, and government may be linked to similar challenges and obstacles women face in continuing their education.

Duke argues that lifelong learning has come of age as a popular and commercially viable proposition. It would be difficult to find a nation in which educational policy is not committed rhetorically to enabling lifelong learning. Its practical attainment is a central policy dilemma (2002, p. 25). Given this context, how is it possible to assess whether policies that purport to support a learning culture adequately address women's experiences? Drawing upon critical and feminist analyses, we need to challenge lifelong learning policies and practices that give primacy to marketplace values and individualistic concerns. As Burke & Jackson note, "'Lifelong learning' continues to speak to us of individualised lives, moving hierarchically and/or in a linear fashion through the processes of (formal) learning" (2007, p. 213). Yet it is clear this is not the case for many learners, particularly women. A broader notion and conceptualisation of lifelong learning is required, to create more inclusive and holistic policies and practices within adult and higher education contexts.

References

Beck, U. (1992). *Risk Society,* London: Sage.

Beck, U. (2001). Redefining Power in the Global Age: Eight Theses. *Dissent.* 48 (4), 83-89.

Bird, E. (1999). Lifelines and life lines: re-training for women returning to higher level occupations - policy and practice in the UK. In *International Journal of Lifelong Education.* Vol. 18 (3), 203-216.

Brookfield, S.D. (2005). *The Power of Critical Theory: Liberating Adult Learning and Teaching,* San Francisco, California: Jossey-Bass.

Budig, M.J. & England, P. (2001). The Wage Penalty for Motherhood. *American Sociological Review.* Vol. 66, 204-225.

Burke, P.J. & Jackson, S. (2007). *Reconceptualising Lifelong Learning: Feminist interventions,* London: Routledge.

Collins, M. (1998). *Critical Crosscurrents in Education.* Malabar, Florida: Krieger

Council of Ministers of Education, Canada. (November 2005). *Education in Canada.* Retrieved November 14, 2007 from the Council of Ministers of Education website: http://www.cmec.ca/international/educationcanada.en.pdf

Council of Ministers of Education, Canada. (September 2005). OECD Education Chief Executives. Retrieved November 14, 2007 from the Council of Ministers of Education website: http://www.cmec.ca/international.oecd/CanDel_EducationCEs_2005.en.pdf

Davies, P. (1999). A new learning culture? Possibilities and contradictions in accreditation. In *Studies in the Education of Adults.* Vol. 31 (1), 10-20.

Delors, J. (chair) (1996). *Learning: The Treasure Within – Report to UNESCO of the International Commission on Education for the Twenty-First Century.* Paris, France:UNESO Publishing.

Dhunpath, R. (2000). Life history methodology: Anarradigm@ regained. *Qualitative Studies in Education.* 13, 5, pp. 543-551.

Duke, C. (2002). The morning after the millenium: building the long-haul learning university. *International Journal of Lifelong Learning.* Vol. 21 (1), 24-36.

Dyke, M. (1997). Reflective learning as reflexive education in a risk society: empowerment and control? *International Journal of Lifelong Learning.* Vol. 16 (1), 2-17.

Edwards, R. (1997). *Changing Places? flexibility, lifelong learning and a learning society.* London: Routledge

Faure, E. Herrera, F., Kaddoura, A.R.Lopes, H., Pretroksky, A.V., Rahnema, M. & Ward, F.C. (1972) *Learning to be: the world of education today and tomorrow.* France: UNESCO

Forrester, K., Payne, J., & Ward, K. (1995). Lifelong education and the workplace: a critical analysis. *International Journal of Lifelong Education.* Vol. 14 (4), 292-305.

Friedman, T.L. (2005). *The World is Flat: A Brief History of the Twenty-First Century.* New York: Farrar, Straus & Giroux.

Glaser, B. G. & Strauss. A.L. (1967). *The Discovery of Grounded Theory: Strategies for Qualitative Research.* Chicago, Ill.: Aldine Publishing Co.

Gorard, S., Rees, G., & Fevre, R. (1999). Two dimensions of time: The changing social context of lifelong learning. *Studies in the Education of Adults.* 31(1), 35-48.

Gouthro, P.A. (2002). Education for sale: at what cost? Lifelong learning and the marketplace. *International Journal of Lifelong Education.* 21, 4, pp. 334-346.

Gouthro, P.A. (2005) Examining the homeplace as learning site: creating a more gender inclusive perspective for adult learners. *International Journal of Lifelong Education.* 24, (4), 334-346.

Habermas, J. (1987). *The Theory of Communicative Action, Vol. 2.* McCartney, T. (trans.). Boston: Mass.: Beacon Press.

Habermas, J. (1996). *Between Facts and Norms: Contributions to a Discourse Theory of Democracy.* In W. Rehg, (trans.) Cambridge, MA: MIT Press.

Hannah, E., Paul, L., & Vethamnay-Globus, S. (2002). *Women in the Canadian Academic Tundra: Challenging the Chill.* Montreal & Kingston: McGill-Queens University Press.

Hart, M. (1995). Motherwork: A Radical Proposal to Rethink Work and Education. In Welton, M.R. (Ed.) *In Defense of the Lifeworld: Critical Perspectives on Adult Learning.* Albany, New York: State University of New York Press.

Hart, M. (1997) Life-Affirming Work, Raising Children, and Education, *Convergence.* XXX, 2/3, pp. 128-135.

Home, A.M. (1998). Predicting Role Conflict, Overload and Contagion In Adult Women University Students with Families and Jobs. *Adult Education Quarterly,* Vol. 48 (2), 85-97.

Horsman, J. (1999). *Too Scared to Learn: Women, Violence and Education.* Toronto, Ontario: McGilligan Books.

Johnson-Bailey, J. & Cervero, R.M. (1996). An Analysis of the Educational Narratives of Black Reentry Women. *Adult Education Quarterly.* 46, 3.

Keats Whelan, K., Huber, J., Rose, C. Davies, A. & Clandinin, D.J. (2001). Telling and Retelling Our Stories on the Professional Knowledge Landscape. *Teachers and Teaching: theory and practice.* 7, 2, pp. 143-156.

Kirby, S.L. & McKenna, K. (1989). *Experience, Research, Social Change: Methods from the Margins.* Toronto, Ontario: Garamond Press.

Klein, N. (2000). *No Logo: Taking Aim At The Brand Bullies.* Toronto, Ontario: Random House.

Leonard, D. (2001). *A Women's Guide to Doctoral Studies.* Open University Press: Buckingham, UK.

Newman, M. (1999). *Maeler's Regard: Images of Adult Learning.* Sydney: Stuart Victor Publishing.

Rubenson, K. & Walker, J. (2006). The Political Economy of Adult Learning in Canada. In Fenwick, T., Nesbit, T. & Spencer, B. (Eds) *Contexts of Adult Education: Canadian Perspectives.* (pp. 173-186). Toronto, Ontario: Thompson Publishers.

Schutz, A. & Luckmann, T. (1973) *The Structures of the Life-world.* Zaner, R.M. & Engelhardt, H.T. (trans). Evanstown, Ill.: Northwest University Press.

Snick, A., Wildemeersch, D. & Celis, R. (2000). Life History Method Paper. Helsinki Meeting, October 2000. Leuven-Belgium. (pp. 1-17).

Stalker, J. (2001). Misogyny, women, and obstacles to teritary education: a vile situation. *Adult Education Quarterly.* 46 (2) 98-113.

Stalker, J. & Prentice, S. (Eds) (1998). *The Illusion of Inclusion: Women in Post-Secondary Education.* Halifax, Nova Scotia: Fernwood Publishing.

Taylor, A.M. (2000). (Auto)biography and Drama: life history work with adult returners to education. *Research in Drama Education.* 5, 2, pp. 249-261.

Tisdell, E. Poststructural Feminist Pedagogies: The Possibilities and Limitations of a Feminist Emancipatory Adult Learning Theory and Practice, *Adult Education Quarterly.* 48, 3, pp. 139-156.

Welton, M.R. (1998) Educating for a Deliberative Democracy. In Scott, S.M., Spencer, B. & Thomas, A.M. (eds.) *Learning for Life: Canadian Readings in Adult Education.* Toronto, Ontario: Thompson Educational Publishing. (pp. 365-372).

Yow, V.R. (1994). *Recording Oral History: A Practical Guide for Social Scientists.* Sage Publications: Thousand Oaks, California

8 Lone Parents as HE Students: A Qualitative Email Study

Tamsin Hinton-Smith

The research project

Within the international context of persistently high numbers of lone parents, policy emphasis on economic self-sufficiency as a response to overburdened welfare states, and drives toward widening participation in higher education (HE), exploring the meanings and motives of lone parents is of central relevance.

The research comprised of 79 participants, all lone parents and UK HE students. Inclusion rested on self definition of lone parenthood, though some participants moved in and out of non-cohabiting and cohabiting relationships over the research period. The sample included individuals studying non-degree courses at Higher Education Institutions (HEIs) as well as those studying for HE qualifications at tertiary colleges as it was anticipated that meeting the sampling requirements would prove challenging and that applying too strict criteria would exacerbate this. An unanticipated outcome of this was demonstration of the extent of the diversification and intersection of the HE and further education (FE) sectors. Undergraduate and postgraduate students at all ages and stages of parenthood and study were included, studying any HE qualifications and disciplines, including full-time, part-time, and distance learning students. It was anticipated that even given this breadth, snowballing would be necessary to achieve the proposed sample of 80 participants. Networking through personal contacts, students encountered through teaching, and childcare facilities at the two local universities was planned. However, provision of a hyperlink requesting participants from the website of Gingerbread, a high profile national organisation for one parent families, to the research website, quickly yielded an overload of offers. It was soon necessary to update the research website that no more participants were required, further sampling techniques therefore becoming unnecessary.

It was unfortunate that only three of the sample of 118 participants were male, given that men represent approximately 1 in 10 lone parents. It was recognised that this figure may be skewed by men's lesser willingness to take part in research. Though skewed also toward able-bodied, British, white, heterosexual participants, the sample did include participants with a range of disabilities, nationalities, ethnicities and sexual identities. Most participants were also in their late twenties to early forties, though there were some older and younger.

Participants were emailed fortnightly prompts over twelve months, totalling 24 prompts. Prompts were usually 200-300 words long, each covering a specific topic, including transition to university, finances, childcare, support, and stress. Informed by prompts used by the Mass observation archive, housed at the University of Sussex, the aim of prompts was to stimulate detailed qualitative responses directed by participants' interests. An extract from prompt 16 on Assessment follows below:

> I'd like to hear about your experiences of managing university assessment. How are you assessed in terms of exams and coursework, and do you find one mode of assessment preferable and why? Are you currently undertaking or preparing for assessment, and have you found the timings of any assessments problematic for any reason?
> How confident do you feel about assessment? Do you think you get more or less nervous than other students - perhaps your other responsibilities keep your studies in perspective or perhaps you feel there's more hinging on your academic success than for other students?

Of 118 volunteers, 39 never replied, resulting in the final sample of 79. While some responded to all prompts, many did not. Responses varied from 10-2,500 words. While some researchers propound computer mediated contact (CMC) to be generally inferior for qualitative research to that conducted face-to-face (FTF) (see Mann & Stewart, 2000, p.3; Sudweeks & Simoff 1999, p. 42), this research illuminated CMC as beneficial in the candidness of responses and consequent richness of data produced by the unique relationship of intimacy (as reported by Sudweeks & Simoff 1999, p.43) and simultaneous anonymity (as reported by Mann and Stewart, 2000, p.5).

Participants often responded to prompts weeks or months after they were sent, many 'catching up' with missed prompts at the close of data collection. Reminder emails were sent throughout the data collection. Based on email research by the research supervisor (Woodfield, 2005) and other researchers (for example, Mann and Stewart, 2000), it was conjectured that email would be suitable for researching the target group. As HE students they were anticipated to be internet users, and email enables individuals with busy schedules and stretched childcare to respond from home in their own time, without prior arrangement (Mann & Stewart, 2000, p. 17, 24; Kendall, 1999, p.60), as was affirmed by feedback:

> *It was also good that it didn't matter if I took a while to reply (as often I did!). That was really good as it meant there was no pressure*

or additional deadlines (Andrea, 23, Development. Studies, full-time).

Feedback also relayed the internet to represent valued accessible social contact for many with limited social interaction and childcare:

most of my friends I speak to via the computer, it is a life line for me
as I don't get to have face to face relationships with many people
(Danielle,33, BA History & American Studies, Full-time).

Atlas.ti qualitative data analysis software was chosen for a number of coding and graphic presentation considerations (Weitzman 2003, p.326-333). It features fast and powerful search and retrieval, easy coding and revision, and good text and graphic display, recommended for predominantly exploratory research, as well as the strong theory building features necessary for hypotheses testing (Weitzman, 2003, p.328). As the research incorporated hypotheses testing and grounded theorising, Atlas.ti was seen as an appropriate choice.

The research is at the data analysis stage. Funding from the European Social Fund has enabled development of the research framework to explore the experiences of lone parents studying as adult learners at all educational levels.

Findings from the data

What can the HE access routes, processes and experiences of this group illuminate about the uncertainties and complexities of modern life? While the data analysis is incomplete, preliminary observations are used below to address key themes.

1. How does the data illustrate the non-linear nature of learning careers?
Narratives documented diverse experiences of education through the adult life course. While some had dipped in and out of education, others kept the thread running throughout their lives, even if sometimes much thinner than others. Still more returned to education after a total and often long break. For these, the return was often tentative and fraught with fear of failure. This was compounded by the motivation for such drastic life change often being a major life event like relationship breakdown. Alongside low intellectual confidence from years out of education, many spoke of confidence knocked by partners. Returning to education for these represented both an instrumental decision to enhance employability and so make independence from partners achievable, and an expressive motivation to build self-esteem, embark on personal development and do something for themselves rather than for others. Relative balance of motivations varied according to factors like current level of financial resources.

Long term studiers were frequently also long-term lone parents, often with relatively limited financial resources and career paths compared to others. In the absence of other distractions or available avenues, studying (often through distance learning) became a lifeline providing an affordable interest beyond childrearing, that nevertheless fitted in around children and limited childcare. Meaning and motivation for HE could change throughout the process, so that for example, a one off Open University module to provide mental stimulation slowly developed into a long term career strategy. The determination and long term view participants took of HE was often humbling. Even those aware of the implications of their advancing age in an unforgiving labour market were nevertheless engaged in elaborate long term strategies to advance in chosen directions of career development, whilst fitting studies in around employment, children and other responsibilities. For example, one participant finally received her MA fifteen years after leaving school. During that time she studied continuously toward her BA then MA through evening classes whilst working and bringing up her children (Juliette, 45, Graduate Diploma in Psychology, Distance Learning).

The third category of participants dipped in and out of HE through the years as circumstances permitted in terms of factors like employment, childcare and health. Though they had not stayed in HE consistently it tended to be a more comfortable, familiar experience for them than for those who took long unbroken gaps out of education. These were predominantly confident learners, enjoying learning and returning periodically to pick up additional work and life skills and qualifications. Some undertook additional learning in modern languages, GCSE subjects, Business Studies or information technology alongside their HE course.

Previous HE episodes for these had resulted in either successful completion or non-completion. The subsequent strategies of those who failed to complete HE courses demonstrated determination to succeed. When financial hardship or illness of self or children prohibited continuing, individuals retreated from HE always intending to return when circumstances permitted. Narratives from participants who returned to HE after non-completed episodes suggested that such determination often comes to fruition. Participants often reported coming to distance learning after unsatisfactory experiences in conventional HE.

One recurring factor in narratives of those with long educational gaps was unhappy secondary school experiences. A notable body reported having been happy and academically successful at primary school, while secondary school ended this. For many the transition marked the beginning of unhappy teenage years that knocked self-esteem, destroyed earlier promise, limited employment possibilities and put them off education for many years until they regained confidence to return.

The following lengthy quote encapsulates a range of the experiences, considerations and landmarks experienced along the educational journey by many:

> *I picked up a flyer from the staffroom table one day advertising a BA (Hons) in Learning Support. ... (It) was scheduled to take five years!! However, I managed to complete nearly three years and earned 120 Level 1 and 80 Level 2 credits before the burden of trying to be a housewife, mother, worker and student without any physical or emotional support finally crushed my spirit and I gave in! During this period I also had to deal with my dad slowly dying from Motor Neurone Disease, then breaking up my own family by asking my ex husband to leave (there were other problems apart from the lack of support) and the subsequent attempt at reconciliation. It was a few months after this (whilst professing support for what I was trying to achieve but surreptitiously sabotaging my efforts to study) that I realised I just didn't have enough strength to fight it any more and dropped out of the course just before the end of Level 2. When my ex husband finally made his own decision to leave us I put together the things I needed to do with the thing that I really had wanted to do at some point (but thought I probably wasn't good enough) and applied for a place on the BA (Hons) Primary Education and Teaching course at Chichester (Bognor Regis campus actually) - out of desperation really. I think if it hadn't been for the fact that I needed to try and compensate for the £30,000 a year the ex took with him, I wouldn't have had the courage to apply.* (Josephine, 40, BSc Social Sciences & Social Policy, Distance Learning).

2. How does the data illustrate the impact of adult learning upon identity of self?

Participants reported adult learning to have many negative effects on themselves and their families, including demands on time and finances, and consequent stress and guilt. However in terms of impact upon self-identity, the reported effect was unanimously positive, with increased confidence frequently mentioned. While failed or failing relationships could be catalysts for returning to study, this also worked in reverse, with return to HE and ensuing developing independence and confidence often signalling the end for unsatisfactory relationships:

> *I can say that me becoming a student was a catalyst in the break down of my marriage. He encouraged me to study but didn't like that I became confident again and more like the person I was before he*

> *controlled me...[...]... Oddly enough, going to university really*
> *helped. For the first time in years I had a voice, confidence and*
> *friends. He hated that and even banned them all from*
> *phoning/emailing etc.* (Rita, 36, B Ed, Full-time).

Increased confidence came from different sources. For some it was proving to themselves and others - partners ex and present, parents and wider family, and the memories of former teachers who had dismissed their younger selves' potential, that they were academically capable. For others it was the increased status of being a university student, training for a career to support their families, leaving stereotypes of dole scrounging single parents. Though still publicly financed, the change from welfare benefits to student grant, and the ensuing feeling of a transition from being paid to do nothing to being paid for doing something worthwhile (the perception that being a student is a more worthwhile activity than bringing up children is notable) played an important part in this:

> *after six years of full time single motherhood it's fantastic to be in a*
> *new and stimulating environment. I feel very supported in the*
> *education system and am relieved to not be on benefits anymore. I*
> *would say my self esteem is much higher being a 'psychology*
> *undergraduate' rather than a single mum on the social.* (Anne-Marie,
> Psychology Undergraduate).

The language in which participants described the impact of their studies upon self-identity was unequivocally powerful. Participants reported feeling 'capable', 'fulfilled', 'enormous confidence', 'self-esteem' and 'a new kind of respect.' This had repercussions not only in terms of informing exits from unsatisfactory relationships, but also in shaping the future. Participants talked about new self-identity developed through returning to education significantly altering their own and their children's futures: *"I feel like a new person - with renewed confidence and an exciting future ahead"*. (Lucy, 34. LL.B Law, evening class). For most this went beyond instrumental advantages of increased education, manifesting in qualitative benefits engendered by developing self-identity and esteem. *"Because of increased confidence, I would be a lot less likely to settle for a relationship which does not give what I need, or what my children needed"*. (Rosa, MBA, Distance Learning).

3. How does the data illustrate the juggling of multiple identities?
As highlighted, 'balancing' and 'juggling' emerged as central themes, participants often explicitly applying the terms to their own lives:

There is just so much to juggle and it's coming from all angles,
University, teaching, home life, my organisation skills have really
improved!! (Gloria, 39, MSc Research, and PG Dip Higher Ed.,
Full-time).

Participants discussed juggling combinations of study, children, paid
employment, voluntary work, new relationships and challenging ex-partners
who were often seen to present deliberate obstacles to the smooth running of
life. Also high on the juggling list were care responsibilities for ageing parents
and other family members and friends - for example caring for the children of a
terminally ill sister and providing moral support for a mentally ill friend.
Relationships added most stress to the juggling load in their early stage. At this
time participants expressed a need to devote time and attention to new partners.
The early stage was crucial for new relationships, when they were often
abandoned because they were seen as too big a drain on precious time or the
new partner felt dissatisfied with the amount of attention received. A significant
number of participants reported satisfaction at single status, allowing more time
to be devoted to study. This reinforces existing work, for example Gina
Wisker's findings of married women students reporting hostility to their studies
from husbands (1996, p.8), sometimes amounting to 'domestic sabotage' (1996,
p.5).

Demand to fulfil the range of roles and be different things to different people
could be a heavy burden. Being an employee and student alongside what many
lone parents report seeing as taking on the roles of both mother and father could
be exhausting:

There's no-one to share this with, whether it's visits to the dentist to
have a brace checked, or the AWFUL and time-consuming job of
buying new school shoes/clothes (Gillian, 48, BA Education, Full-
time).

Central to this juggling of multiple identities are analyses of the conflicting
demands of the family and HE as two 'greedy institutions' (Acker, 1980), each
making insatiable demands upon the individual's time and energies. Individuals
never come fully 'off duty' from either role, and however much attention is
devoted to either, guilt invariably remains that more attention would have been
better:

Yes I feel guilt. Constant guilt. Isn't that the joy of being a woman
today? We supposedly have it all, but I think someone forgot to give
us the time we needed to do everything! - I often think my situation is

magnified by being a single-parent, as being a parent is in itself difficult, but trying to be both is near impossible! I also feel that the added burden of being the sole breadwinner is often overwhelming - how do you balance the commitment of a good career, with being a good mum? (Shelby, 33, PGCE, Full-time).

Guilt was a recurring theme, and though the number of men in the study was too small to be significant, it was interesting that men balancing the multiple identities of lone parent, employee and student also discussed feeling guilty that none of these roles were being accomplished adequately. This challenges common notions of 'maternal guilt', suggesting that it is the role of primary carer for children that is salient, rather than being a gendered experience.

Juggling the conflicting and greedy identities of student and sole parent was for many compounded by the demands of paid employment. Participants repeatedly reported juggling near impossible conflicting loads of study, children and paid employment, often because within the current UK context the financial advantages of working at least 16 hours per week in order to qualify for Working Families Tax Credit (WFTC) makes continued employment alongside studies the most attractive option for many. Because of additional benefits this conveyed including substantial help with childcare fees, it was often central to lone parents' ability to study in HE, despite also hindering their studies time wise.

Though as reported previously, participants valued the focus HE participation provided for themselves outside the family, the negotiation and juggling of multiple conflicting roles that this necessitated was reported by and large a negative. Far from the liberating potential that postmodern theory attributes to the possibility for multiple identities, these individuals felt exhausted by being torn in many directions.

4. How does the data illustrate the fragmented lives often present in modern life?

Much of what participants reported illustrated lives fragmented in simultaneous pursuit of studentship, parenthood and employment, alongside other responsibilities as previously documented. This fragmentation could be geographical, with individuals often making substantial journeys several times a week in order to attend their nearest HEI. For most, these journeys constituted road trips by car between provincial towns, but for others it meant journeys short in distance but lengthy in time by public transport through major city centre rush hour traffic - usually whilst worrying about being late to arrive at lectures, or the other end of the day, to collect children from daycare or check on older children left unattended. Guilt at not being there for children was often mentioned in these contexts. Travelling to and from childcarers added to this journeying for many as childcare was frequently located in a further separate location, away from home, HEI and place of employment. A recurring theme relating to the fragmentation of participants' lives was that managing the combination of responsibilities would be easier were there greater availability of on-site childcare provided by HEIs. Participants reported that their HEI either did not make childcare provision, or that provision was oversubscribed and/or prioritised children of university staff.

Parents facilitating contact between children and absent parents encountered more cross-country car journeys, adding to the fragmented life experience of both individuals and families. Many experienced the Christmas break as something of a mixed blessing, being a rare time when children visited absent parents for a prolonged period. This allowed participants a much needed opportunity to rest, socialise and study, yet it was a time of loneliness for many being alone over the festive period and unused to solitude. Sometimes present children of new partners as well as the sometimes presentness of new partners themselves, many of whom lived separately to participants, represented further fragmentation. Juggling different elements of these separate areas of fragmented lives could be a complicated and stressful task:

The course is difficult in that I am learning 'on the job', so juggling motherhood, a relationship with a partner (who does not live with me) and running a home and work makes it not altogether an easy experience. (Zeena, 36, PGCE, In-service).

I have a relationship with a guy who I see when my ex has the boys. Now he isn't having them I have to work out how we will get together, so stressed is my middle name at the moment!!! (Emily, Nursing, Part-time).

Fragmentation of experience often exceeded being challenging in terms of time management. Many participants perceived an inability to fully engage with the university experience. Childcare limitations rendered it seldom possible to attend university activities beyond the essential. Thus induction activities, social events, postgraduate seminars and Open University tutorials and summer schools were frequently bypassed, and even exchanging library books before or after classes could be challenging to fit in. Participants were acutely aware of the detrimental impact on studies and often felt isolated without friends amongst their university peers:

The weekly or bi-monthly schlep down the M11 and M25 (motorways) was difficult, expensive and more importantly, made things difficult in terms of providing a fully rounded life experience in [my University town] (Beth, 33, MPhil Archaeology, Full-time).

The following comment summarises key recurring themes around fragmentation of university experience:

All the welcome meetings, staff drinks parties and induction talks were in the evenings after 5pm so I felt excluded and although the staff were very understanding, I felt at a social disadvantage as a result of not meeting the others. The only time I see my fellow students is either in the library (not the most conducive venue for chatting) or in lectures (ditto) and then I have to run off home to be back for my son. Whether in the pub or the monthly department party the standard communal get-togethers are centred around evening drinking so I (and Muslim students) feel excluded... my son is in the house for about half an hour on his own before I get in (he is 11 years old and comes home from secondary school on the bus) which is not excessive but is still not ideal. I never have the chance to go to the library after a lecture which would be the most beneficial approach for my studies. (Michelle, 35, MSc History of Science, Full-time).

5. How does the data illustrate the risk and individualisation of life in late modernity?

Evidence of the individualisation of modern life was most present in participants' narratives of living arrangements and family relationships. Apart from having separated from one or more co-parents of children, many reported geographical separation from their own parents and wider families, often contributing to the loneliness and care burden experienced by participants. Many reported that it would make life easier if ex-partners, maternal and paternal grandparents and wider families lived close enough to help more with childcare.

In many participants' narratives of intimate relationships, the relevance of contemporary discourses of individualisation and risk in modern society met. The research included a large proportion of participants who either were or had been in stable non-cohabiting relationships, 'living alone together,' or 'LATs' (Haskey, 2005). This is unsurprising given that relationships involving children are a key category contributing to the increase in LATs. Though one participant dropped out of the study when she met and had a baby with a new partner, for many, past experience made intimate relationships a risky area to be kept at arms length. Although many participants had partners, no one talked of working toward building a shared future with this partner. Emphasis was on independently providing a secure future for oneself and children, and as previously mentioned, new relationships often came under threat if they were perceived as compromising study time.

However important, this goal of achieving economic security through education was far from being unproblematic. The path was fraught with fears of unknown quantities. While studying created an avenue of hope for the future for many, it also generated a range of risks. Financially secure jobs had sometimes been sacrificed in order to study, often with participants perceiving no guarantee that studies would pay off with a job at the end. Many were acutely aware of the potential impact of their advancing age upon their labour market opportunities, particularly as for many qualification through part-time study was such a long-term project. Participants reported unsureness about whether they had made the best decisions and were doing the right thing, whether their desired goals would be realised and whether too much had been sacrificed in the process:

> *I see my future as a bit uncertain as of where we will live and where I would be able to find a job.* (Carys, 31, DPhil Sociology, Full-time).

> *Am I striving down this career path at the expense of my son? Will I ever actually get my foot on the property ladder?* (Law, 34, LL.B, evening class).

Studying also meant debts for many, in the forms of student loans, credit cards and overdrafts. Many struggled to single-handedly meet monthly mortgage payments as students, borrowed as half of a dual-earning couple. In addition, when relationships broke down some were left to repay substantial debts accumulated by ex-partners. Managing debt repayments on diminished incomes caused many substantial stress and worry:

> *This is causing me a lot of stress at the moment and yes, it is affecting my sleep. It takes me ages to drop off and then when I do, I'm plagued by nightmares of one description or another... Because the current account is looking quite sick, I've had to use my credit cards again which has resulted in me owing around £1000 but I'm only able to make minimum payments so the debt isn't being reduced* (Gloria, 39, MSc Research and PG Dip Higher Ed, Full-time).

6. How does the data illustrate the impact of factors such as institutional cultures, class, gender, ethnicity, age and disability in determining learning careers, identities, individualisation and risk?

Both demographic variables and institutional factors impacted upon learning experiences. Participants discussed the importance of how supportive, knowledgeable, friendly and helpful university teaching, administrative and support staff were. Issues of particular importance included whether children were welcome on university premises (in some cases this was not allowed at all while in others participants were able to take children into lectures with them). Also important were whether staff were flexible over seminar group allocation according to childcare constraints and whether assignment extensions were permitted on grounds of care responsibilities for sick children. At the extreme end of the effect of institutional culture, one participant felt alienated by an article by a senior member of staff published in the magazine of the top university she attended, arguing that: "*Funds for student childcare was not money well spent and that those with children should consider options other than (this University)*". (Beth, 33, MPhil Archaeology, Full-time).

In terms of individual demographic variables, a large proportion of participants identified as working-class, and for many this impacted upon learning identities. For these participants gender and class identities intersected to inform expectations that HE was not for people like them. Parental disinterest or pressure at school leaving age had resulted in educational careers cut short in academically able and motivated individuals, who, frequently going on to have unsupportive partners, had often taken many years to regain the confidence to return to education:

> *My class has affected my experiences of being a single parent and a student, because I come from a working class background where it is normal for a women to get married and have children and have no other life or work outside the marital home.* (Francesca, 34, BA History, Full-time).

For others, ethnicity added to the effects of gender and class upon student identity. The combination of joining such an overtly hierarchical institution as a university, alongside learning ideas around inequalities, contributed to awareness of effects of such variables upon determining identities:

> *I've noticed that being female, Black and single, I appear to be somewhere near the bottom of the rung in society. At the top of the hierarchy are white, middle-class men. White women come below that, and black women even lower.* (Beatrice, 31, BA Primary Ed, Full-time).

A recurring theme was planning and time management. Participants frequently explained that they only managed hectic schedules through meticulous planning of exactly when each activity would take place. Several participants with disabilities or debilitating illness described the frustration of disruption of this schedule by unpredictable flares ups of illness. These often coincided with times of stress when there was a lot to manage, compromising meeting of assessment deadlines. There was often no one to help with children at these times, leaving no choice but for limited conserves of energy to be directed away from studies toward family:

> *I am in pain every day with this, some days are worse than others. It impacts terribly upon family life, and mine. I never know how I shall feel from one day to the next, it limits my ability to work, study (got my study pack this morning from the O.U-start next week!), play with the girls, cook, clean, walk distances, etc. Daily routine is dictated by how I feel, obviously, and so I have to plan my days accordingly. It has an effect on studies and employment* (Nicky, 37, BA Health and Social Care, Distance Learning).

Other participants described how children's disabilities and chronic illness affected both ability to study in the present and career hopes for the future. A further consideration affecting hopes for the future, as previously mentioned, was participants' awareness of their own advancing age. As one woman explained who had been struggling over many years to achieve HE qualifications in order to realise career goals, with several false starts and major obstacles along the way:

> *In 5 years time I do hope to be working and in a job I enjoy and making ends meet. I don't have any hopes that I will get out of social housing. I just hope that I can give my kids the help they will need to make a future for themselves. In a sense I have given up on my life. That is partly due to (my son's) disability and as I am an older mother (47) it feels as though I am running out of time.* (Ruth, BA Social Policy & Criminology, Distance Learning).

Conclusion

Despite the diversity of experiences documented in the narratives of this group of lone parent HE students, the data gathered also attests to some key strands of shared experience, illustrating important similarities in terms of motivations, lifestyles and   challenges. It is clear that there are many areas of common ground echoed throughout participants' narratives that are unique to their specific set of experiences as lone parents studying in HE. In the context of the governments' drives to increase HE participation, including amongst non-traditional groups like lone parents, and given the high proportions of children now spending at least some part of their childhoods in single headed households, shedding light of the experiences and obstacles facing lone parents as HE students holds value in its own right. But do the testimonies of HE access routes, processes and experiences amongst lone parents presented above have wider relevance in illuminating some of the uncertainties and complexities faced by us all in modern life? I would suggest that this is indeed the case in many ways. A broad range of key issues in late modernity are represented in the narratives of these individuals, including those relating to intimate relationships, paid work, informal care responsibilities, and the extended life course.

The narratives attest to the widespread experience of multiple breakdowns of significant intimate relationships throughout the life course, often including children, and the complex patterns of family and contact that develop within these contexts. The relevance to this area of notions of the risk society (Beck, 1992, Giddens, 1991) is embedded in the testimonials provided by individuals, with relationships often being approached as calculated risks. Lives are kept fundamentally separate in a range of ways, often living separately, or, as some participants did, continuing to self-define as a lone parent in the presence of a new co-habiting partner, rather than redefining the household as a new family unit. Implicit in participants' guarding of their own space, securities and fruits of their achievements, refusing to risk submerging all of this in relationships, is recognition of the irrationality of assuming that current relationships will last permanently. Intertwined with this perspective is the seeking of current and long-term financial stability, personal fulfilment and leisure individualistically, manifested in participants' explanations of their motivations for HE study.

Discussion of children, including participants' current motivations and priorities, as well as future hopes for offspring, revealed consciousness that children will need to be well tooled with skills and education to compete in an insecure labour market. Alongside supervising children's leisure, homework and educational paths, many participants were also involved in caring for ageing parents, being 'squeezed at both ends' by dual care responsibilities, a result, particularly for women, of declining mortality and delayed childbearing. As discussed, further care responsibilities resulted from extended family members' dependency needs around ageing, disability, and physical and mental illness, representing the increasing informal care burden resulting from the decrease in institutionalised care provision.

Further trends resulting from the lengthening of the life course relate to perceptions of the necessity to ensure economic self-sufficiency through employment late into life. Many participants reported a primary motivation for HE participation being orientated toward career progression or change of direction, representing broader trends in the necessity for workers to retrain to continue to compete in the labour market into later life. Although not directly researched, the modern pensions crisis can be seen as relevant to participants' motivation to equip themselves with educational training to promote secure employment into advancing age. Participants' perceptions of ageism in the labour market as already discussed have broader social relevance, as does preoccupation with housing, with the heavy burden of achieving secure, affordable, adequate housing in a climate of shortage featuring frequently in participants' responses. As mentioned, debts accumulated through loans, overdrafts and credit cards formed a major source of stress, reflecting another malady of modern life. In light of all these factors, it seems that the narratives of these lone parent students offer much insight beyond their specific experiences. Encapsulated in their stories of everyday lives are many of the key features, motivations and concerns of our age, highlighting some of the major complexities and uncertainties facing individuals' constructions of identities and learning careers, as well as experiences of fragmentation, risk and individualisation.

References

Acker, S. (1980). 'Women in HE: What is the problem?', in Acker, S. & Warren Piper, D. (Eds) *Is HE fair to women?* London: SRHE/NFER-Nelson

Arksey, H., Marchant, I., & Simmil, C. (Eds) 1994 *Juggling for a Degree: Mature students' experience of university life* Lancaster: Unit for Innovation in HE

Beck, U. (1992). *Risk society: Towards a new modernity* London: Sage

Edwards, R. (1993) *Mature women students: Separating or connecting family and education* London: Taylor & Francis

Giddens, A. (1991). *Modernity and self-identity* Cambridge: Polity

Haskey, J. (2005). 'Living arrangements in contemporary Britain: Having a partner who usually lives elsewhere and Living Apart Together (LAT)', Population Trends 122, Winter, pp35-46. Available at: http://www.statistics.gov.uk/downloads/theme_population/PopTrends122v1.pdf

Kendall, L. (1999). 'Recontextualizing "cyberspace": Methodological considerations for on-line research', in Jones, S. (Ed.) *Doing internet research: Critical issues and methods for examining the ne.t* London: Sage

Mann, C. & Stewart, F. (2000). *Internet communication and qualitative research: A handbook for researching online.* London: Sage

Sudweeks, F., & Simoff, S. J. (1999). 'Complementary exploration data analysis: The reconciliation of quantitative and qualitative principles', in Jones, C. (Ed.) *Doing internet research: Critical issues and methods for examining the net.* London: Sage

Weitzman, E. (2003). 'Software and qualitative research' in Denzin, N. and Lincoln, Y. (Eds.) *Collecting and interpreting qualitative materials.* Thousand Oaks: Sage

Wisker, G. (1996). *Empowering women in HE.* London: Kogan Page

Woodfield, R., Earl-Novell, S., & Solomon, L., (2005). 'Gender and mode of assessment at university: Should we assume female students are better suited to coursework and males to unseen examinations?' In *Assessment and Evaluation in HE*, 30 (1): 33-48

9 Developing Learning Identities for Working Class Adult Students in Higher Education

Rennie Johnston and Barbara Merrill

Introduction

Higher education (HE) institutions across Europe are transforming, albeit reluctantly in some cases, as a result of changing state/university relationships, economic and social changes and globalisation. Externally universities are now engaging with other knowledge producers while internally new student groups are entering through the doors. As Barnett points out, "institutional boundaries become less tight as interrelationships with the wider society grow" (2003: p.27). This change process in the UK has enabled working class adults to re-engage with learning and enter the world of academia. Such students bring with them to the learning process in higher education their life experiences and their biographical and cultural baggage or, to draw on Bourdieu, a particular habitus, a set of dispositions which incline agents to react in certain ways. During their university career adult students develop and (re) construct a learning identity in a learning environment, culture and structure which is largely geared towards meeting the needs of younger, 'traditional' undergraduates.

This paper explores the changing 'learning identities' of non-traditional adult students through focusing on two UK case studies arising from a Socrates Grundtvig European research project on 'Learning in Higher Education'. This project involved seven European countries (England, Finland, Germany, Ireland, Portugal, Spain, and Sweden) and used biographical approaches to explore the experiences and attitudes of non-traditional adult undergraduate students in relation to learning and teaching approaches in higher education. This paper focuses on how the biographies of these learners reveal a range of learning experiences which influence the construction of new learning identities.

Researching Learning Identities

In recent years there has been an increasing interest in understanding learning processes and experiences from the viewpoint and perspective of the learner through the use of biographical methods. This type of approach is useful as it enables a person's attitudes and experiences of learning to be understood across the lifespan. The terms 'learning career', 'learning trajectory' and 'learning identity' have been employed to describe such processes. The term learning career was utilised by Bloomer and Hodkinson (2000) in their study of 16-19 year olds in further education colleges and later further developed by Crossan, Field, Gallacher and Merrill (2003) in their study of marginalised groups of adult learners in further education (FE) in Scotland. In the latter study, learning career was defined as "a concept that facilitates an understanding of the biographical processes experienced by adult learners in returning to learn and their subsequent engagement in learning over a period of time" (Merrill, 2001: p. 1). Like symbolic interactionists the study veered away from the assumption that a learning career has to occur in a linear fashion. This paper takes one step further in considering this non-linear dimension. It uses the term 'learning identity' as a way of acknowledging the irregular and complex interrelationship of learning and identity and the fact that particularly for non-traditional adult students, learning identities co-exist with and influence and are in turn influenced by other adult identities (Johnston and Merrill 2004: p.154).

A non-linear learning identity reflects the fragmented, risky and sometimes unstable experiences of the lifeworld in postmodernity. For Bauman the constant changing of identities is now characteristic: "The hub of postmodern life strategy is not making identity stand – but the avoidance of being fixed" (1997: p. 89). Biographical methods enabled us to discern how learning identities change and develop over time, explore these processes and examine the meaning of learning throughout the lifecourse. Learning is experienced subjectively. Learning in higher education is a new biographical experience for working class adults which brings with it expectations and risk but also a possibility that the self and identity will be changed. It provides as Alheit and Dausien describe it "a biographical opportunity" (2002: p.17). In such situations, individuals have to draw on their biographicity (Alheit and Dausien, 2000) - a knowledge resource for coping with the modern world. There has been a growing interest in linking biography, identity and learning (West, 1996, Antikainen et al, 1996, Merrill, 1999, 2007). For Antikainen, "the telling of a life-story is one way of identifying one's self, and researching life-stories is one way of studying identity" (1996: p. 18).

Linking Learning and Identities

Identity is a problematic word yet it is used frequently in both academic and everyday language. Sociologically, identity has been the subject of discussion by key theorists such as Goffman, Giddens, Castells, Bauman. Recent discourses on identity reflect a growing concern about the uncertainty and risk of life in late modernity as the individualisation of society makes the maintenance of identity problematic (Giddens, 1991, Castells, 1997). Discussions also inter-relate identity with biography. For Giddens, identity is defined as "the self as reflexively understood by the individual in terms of his or her biography" (1991: 18). Côté and Levine usefully link structure and agency/ the macro and the micro as they define identity as "a function of both external (social) and internal (agentic) factors" (2002: p. 9). Identity is, therefore shaped by social, institutional and personal experiences. Identity, however, is also the product of our historical and biographical experiences. Although identity often remains a nebulous concept, at the same time it is core to sociological understanding of human behaviour as identities cut across the boundaries of public and private lives while changing learning identities highlight the dialectics between structure and agency.

The adult students in our study live the postmodern condition of having to cope with multiple identities. Their learning identity interfaces with their other identities as worker, parent, carer, housewife, trade unionist, working class, female/male etc. Identity, as Castells (1997) argues is an active process of construction shaped by cultural factors, participation in social institutions and through interaction with others providing individuals with sources of meaning. Many participants in our study were actively seeking to construct new and different identities through learning while still holding on to their working class identity. As Scott points out:

> ...reflexivity in terms of individual experience as higher education provides a key arena for the construction of personal biographies in place of inherited and involuntary, identities (1998: p.10).

Looking at Structure and Agency

The role that structure and agency play in influencing human behaviour has always been fundamental in sociological theory. The structure-agency debate, according to Emirbayer and Mische, has its origins in "the Enlightenment debate over whether instrumental rationality or moral and norm-based action is the truest expression of human freedom" (1998: p. 968). The humanistic writings of Marx on historical materialism, for example, attempted to inter-relate structure and agency in recognising that men (and women): "make their own history, but not...under conditions they have chosen for themselves; rather on terms immediately existing, given and handed down to them" (1852/1983:287). In recent years some sociologists have attempted theoretically to relate what Dawe (1970) calls the 'sociology of systems' and the sociology of action'. However, there are two main distinct but opposite approaches to this. Archer's (2003) work promotes the notion of dualism whereby structure and agency remain logically exclusive of each other. In contrast Gidden's structuration theory argues for the interdependence of the objective and subjective – what he calls duality.

Bourdieu's structuration approach is different to that of Giddens. Bourdieu's approach is a more collective one as he looks at how a person is positioned and constrained by habitus or class and institutionalised power structures. The use of agency is always, therefore, restricted by one's position in society. Bourdieu draws on Marx but combines this with phenomenology as experience and practice are central to his structuralisation approach. Theoretical perspectives on structuration are useful for breaking down the structure/action divide as behaviour is never fully agentic or structurally determined but an interaction between the two. At particular points in people's lives one may be more dominant than the other as the lives of participants in our study illustrate. However, the theories remain largely abstract. Using biographies enables us to understand more fully the process of and interaction between structure and agency/objectivity and subjectivity through the lives of actors.

Our study draws on Bourdieu's (1977) work on habitus and identity as this enables us to examine how learning identities are constructed in relation to different educational biographies. Using Bourdieu may appear to be contradictory as he was critical of what he calls the 'illusion of biography' (2000). However, habitus is a valuable concept as it allowed us to explore how the social and cultural capital of working class students copes and adjusts or not to the symbolic and intellectual capital of universities:

> Adults construct and make sense of their learning experiences in higher education within a framework of a particular habitus which can either constrain and/ or empower their learning and change identities (Johnston & Merrill, 2004: p.157).

Using Bourdieu's concepts of habitus, capital and field also enables us to link class and identity. Habitus and the levels of capital (cultural, social, symbolic and economic) locate a person's position or "a sense of one's place" (Bourdieu, 1990:131) in relation to others and the wider social space. While habitus reproduces and determines an individual's class and social trajectory Bourdieu also recognises that this can be transformed through the use of agency:

> Habitus is not the fate that some people read into it. Being the product of history, it is an open system of dispositions that is constantly subjected to experiences, and therefore constantly affected by them in a way that either reinforces or modifies its structures (Bourdieu in Bourdieu & Wacquant, 1992: p.133).

Class and Learner Identity

The biographies of the students identified in this paper reveal the centrality of class, (as well as issues of gender and race) in their lives and biographical research provides a useful tool for highlighting this:

Biographical research may at first sight appear to be too much of an individualistic approach for engaging with class and adult learning as biographies are largely analysed as an individualistic way of understanding the social world. Yet in constructing a biography a person relates to significant others and social contexts: a biography is, therefore, never fully individual (Merrill, 2007: p.71).

Social class, once dominant in UK sociological theory, has lost its popularity with the emergence of postmodernism and the 'cultural turn' (Abbott, 2001). For many sociologists class became an out-of-date concept as it is no longer viewed as being useful in categorising people's lives (Pahl, 1989). Yet there are signs that some sociologists are re-engaging and re-asserting, albeit in different ways to earlier UK sociological approaches, the importance of class in UK society (Devine et al, 2005, Savage, 2000, Skeggs, 1997). For as Skeggs argues:

To abandon class as a theoretical tool does not mean that it does not exist any more; only that some theorists do not value it...Retreatists either ignore class or argue that class is 'an increasingly redundant issue' (Skeggs, 1997: p.6-7).

The use of biographical approaches enables us to look at class in terms of past and present actions and the interaction between structure and agency for as E.P.Thompson emphasised:

By class I understand a historical phenomenon, unifying a number of disparate and seemingly unconnected events both in the raw material of experience and in consciousness. I do not see class as a structure, nor even as a category, but as something which in fact happens (and can be shown to happen) in human relationships (1963: p.9).

Social class, however, cannot be looked at in isolation. We, therefore, agree with the assertion by Anthias that:

Within societies and nations, within so-called communities, there are divisions and conflicts around class, around ethnicity and racialisation, and around gender as well as other social categories and positions (2005: p.24).

The intersectionality of inequalities means that "classes are always gendered and racialised and gender is always classed and racialised and so on" (Anthias, 2005: p.33). Social scientists are increasingly linking gender and race into an understanding of social stratification through three main models: the reductionist model, the intersectionality model and the identity model (Anthias, 2005). We draw on the identity model as it introduces the notion of consciousness and questions of 'where do I belong?' in relation to class, gender and ethnicity. The concept of identity thus raises issues of social positions and positionality (by the self and others) both in the past and present which are illuminated through life histories.

Many of the adult students in our research identified themselves as working class and this remained a strong aspect of their identity both during and after their studies. However, it was at times problematic for them dealing with both a working class identity and an academic identity. For some it distanced them from family and friends although they wanted to cling to their working class roots in a similar way to the adult students in Brookfield's (1994) study. For some their self-image and identity felt fragile in the public world of elite, middle class universities resulting in a feeling that they are a fraud to be there or not good enough to be there. Agency, in some cases, was employed in order to cope with learning at degree level to overcome what were perceived as the constraints of culture, class and structure. The transitional space of the university provided a social space through learning for the working out and re-constructing of identities, dispositions and habitus. As Devine and Savage argue: "Identities are not labels of your position, but 'claims for recognition' which are both contested and fraught" (2005: p.12).

By drawing on biographies, identity and habitus the individual's subjectivity can be linked to the external social world thus helping to make sense of the dialectics of structure and agency. In previous papers (Johnston and Merrill 2004, 2004a) we have explored the way that learning identities are affected by personal, interactional and institutional factors and how universities need to adapt in order to support adult students in developing positive learning identities at university and beyond. The rest of this paper will focus on two case studies of working class adult students in HE as a way of illustrating and exploring the above issues in greater depth. In particular it will investigate the inter-relationship of learning identity, working-class habitus and other identities as students develop their learning career in higher education.

Peter

Peter is a trade unionist in his early 40s, just finishing a degree in Applied Social Sciences (Labour Studies) at New College, University of Southampton where he studies part-time on a block release basis alongside trade union colleagues. He was interviewed twice over two years, halfway through and near the end of his part-time degree. Peter identifies himself as working class, an environmentalist, a vegan, an anarchist, a surrealist and a trade unionist. Learning has always been an important part of his life. This factor was shaped by his early family experiences:

> *My mother was sort of hands on with education from quite early on you know sort of like educational games and all that sort of stuff ... she used to talk to me a lot and involve me in whatever she was doing.*

His mother's approach was complemented by his father's:

> *The other side of that also as I was growing up my dad was a union activist, always had the news on. Always shouting at the news because he had an opinion and that sort of stuff. So you got that sort of education.*

He wasn't particularly successful or comfortable at school, disliking routine and conventional authority. In terms of learning, he always had a strong need to get to grips with basic ideas before he could move on:

> *I was told, my parents told me that when I was young I always used to end up getting into trouble for sort of like you know when you are kids its always WHY, sort of thing. I never stopped with the WHYs and as I got older I argued it further and further.*

So, sometimes at school he fell behind, a situation, which was repeated when, he started an apprenticeship in electronics and communications:

> *Once again we come to one of these situations where I didn't quite get my head around something to start with. Electronics, ... the electronics teacher said basically, this is how a transistor works, accept it, don't try and understand it. I couldn't, in my head I had to understand it and I lost me self there and from that moment on, electronics was a foreign language to me. Whereas other people were telling me it was dead easy.*

Peter's real learning impetus came well away from formal learning. His learning identity was shaped in the worlds of science fiction, punk, anarchism and surrealism:

> *Yes I ... got involved with Punk and all that and the anarchist stuff that got me into anarchist theory and those sort of things ... They sort of lived their life ... they were getting away from hypocrisy. If*

you bought a single it tended to be this great big sort of fold out thing full of various ideas, contacts for various things. I mean animal rights, CND, the whole thing.

As a result of his gradual immersion into this type of cultural learning, Peter was able to complement his strong family and working class identity with a new agency and learning identity, which engaged actively with challenging ideas and complex language. Later when, as a trade union representative, he was sent on a training course, he did not have high expectations:

I had in my mind, I suppose that the trade union's training school would be sort of like an old flat cap stereotype of thing if you like or a sort of New Labour brainwashing.

To his surprise, the course combined practical trade union training with a high level of debate. One tutor particularly impressed him because he was:

clearly from a working background but also very open to ideas ... When we went on to equality and diversity some of the brainstorming sort of stuff involved talking about paedophiles and all that sort of thing.

The course helped him make stronger connections between his punk/surrealist learning identity and his working class trade unionist habitus and to link his idealism to a more pragmatic approach. Apart from the stimulus of debate:

It had a really practical use because I went back from that course as a (trade union) rep and I started achieving things out of the disagreements with managers whereas before I was just being an awkward bastard.

This first feeling of achievement in more formal education led Peter on to HE where he found his earlier cultural learning experiences:

regularly tied in and provided a good framework for what I am doing here. I think ... some people when they come here they are quite surprised by the challenging of the context. I wasn't so much because I had already gone through that process ... I have always enjoyed sort of kicking around some of the theoretical stuff.

In this process, Peter was well aware of the role language can play in excluding working class people from university learning and the intimidating effect it had on some of his fellow trade unionists coming into HE. But, in his own attitude to and use of language, he made an important distinction:

> *between not speaking down to people and not patronizing them by simplifying your language to the lowest common denominator, tabloid style communication.*

He had already put this into practice in editing a trade union branch magazine which he felt should be about expressing and exchanging people's ideas as much as about practicalities of pay and terms and conditions of work. What higher education gave him was self-confidence and discipline:

> *I have always been able to string an argument together and all that ... but tidying it up and making sure you hit all the key points and presentations skills, all that came out of it (HE).*

This discipline even extended towards imbuing within him a new pragmatism, instrumentalism and conformity, completely at odds with his past learning identity:

> *Yes, I mean for, example, I think exams are a total waste of time in as much as I think it's just from memory. But I will revise and do all the things I need to do to try and get the best mark possible. You know because it's quite possible I want to carry on my education here and you know so you have got to play the game in that respect and you have got to show them that you are capable of doing it on their terms.*

It appears that from the outset, Peter had a strong individual learning identity which had its roots in parental support and was developed through his engagement with the sub-cultures and ideas of punk, anarchism and surrealism. At a later stage, his growing commitment to trade union work and his gradual exposure to HE study helped him complement his love of ideas and debate with a new discipline and instrumentalism which had been missing in his earlier encounters with formal learning. As a successful student he was able to draw on his social capital as a trade unionist as well as his cultural capital derived from the punk/surrealist movement. Because learning had always been a strong part of his identity, he was able to use both his agency and structural position positively in his development as a good and successful HE student.

Paula

Peter's learning identity and experience in HE was different from Paula's. Paula is in her late 30s and is a mother with two boys. She was interviewed first in her final year of a BSc in Applied Social Sciences at the University of Southampton, New College and then two years later when she was a teacher in a secondary school in a working class neighbourhood. Paula has a strong working class identity, at one time referring to herself in her role as teacher as a 'defender of her class'. She feels very strongly about not patronizing or making unjustified assumptions about working class kids:

> *... I think I will stay in a school that I work in because I can say to them, I do say to them: 'I was the same as you and there is no reason if you want other things you can't get them. Whatever it is doesn't matter, whether you want to be a teacher, whatever it is, you can get there.*

This class identity is closely connected with a learning identity that was initially shaped by her mother's wide reading but strongly influenced by her own childhood experience at school where:

> *Yes, (I was) well behaved and got on with my work. I just feel that there was a lot of potential that I had that was totally wasted because assumptions were made about me. Too young at the time to know but I do feel it came back to my background and my family and where I lived and that influenced how they treated me and that's why college was never even mentioned.*

Although Paula did well at school it was always expected that she would go out to work. It was only later when she had been working in a bank for some years and had become a mother that Paula asserted her agency in response to the prevailing occupational structure and culture of the bank. She began to compare herself with her (predominantly) male colleagues. *"They didn't see things in the same way and I did more work than them"*. She began *"...questioning the moral issue of the job I was doing and I thought I can't do this for the rest of my life ...I just thought there had to be more to life than this"*. This feeling helped Paula to overcome some longstanding, negative feelings about further study: *"Before I felt I hadn't proved my potential, I knew I was capable of more but was always quite scared of getting above my station"*.

It prompted Paula to start getting books on sociology and politics out of the library and then to apply for an Access course. (An Access course prepares adults for study in higher education):

> *And (the Access course) fired me and oh its just... yes I felt I fitted and I thought I made this happen – this is what I want to know about and this is some of things that I have never been quite been able to explain. Yes I can see why I am being ... I am what I am.*

Paula had a more conventional adult learning identity than Peter:

> *I think that's just me as a person. I think whether it be learning or whatever I do need to be and I need to know what I am doing and set myself targets to do it and deadlines and I couldn't bear to go to bed at night knowing that something that needs to be done hasn't been done.*

This methodical approach allied to her acknowledged 'thirst for learning' served her well on the Access course and later at University. Paula's belief, however, that people and institutions have made assumptions about her, continued as an adult student at university. While at one level she thrived in HE through her love of the subject, well-developed reading, reflective approach and highly developed organisational skills, she still lacked confidence, like several of our project participants, in a university environment:

> *You never lose that. I don't think you ever lose that – you learn to live with it but you don't ever lose that. You always think I am not worthy of this. That's something I feel and you still think that you shouldn't be here and you are a con – you know how did I get here and I slipped through the net and I shouldn't be here.*

An important part of this was the use of language. Like Peter, Paula recognised that:

> *Language is used to exclude particular people and this was a real barrier in the learning environment. ...This is something that colleges and universities often forget; they assume that their audience have all been educated in a similar way to them. This increases the workload of students from non-traditional backgrounds.*

In response to this, however, she made a different distinction about language. She identified two different codes of language which she used (one in university, one at home) - she saw this as an advantage in her work as a teacher:

> *I can communicate with some parents far more effectively than other teachers because I can put things in a way they understand. They do not feel patronised or intimidated when I speak to them, and consequently a good relationship can develop.*

Despite her periodic feelings of being unworthy, Paula was successful at University. Thus, she was able to compensate for these negative feelings by specifically choosing courses and tutors which helped her make full use of her life and work experience in her studies, by making use of the peer support of fellow mature students and by using her highly organised learning approach to good advantage. One of the key factors in stimulating her HE learning and shaping her learning identity was the use and acknowledgement of her life experience, a common feeling amongst adult students in the overall Grundtvig study:

> *I think the key factor was taking into account life experience... using the experiences that mature students have got. The more I go on the more I realise that learning whether it's at a school, a college or a university, they are so narrow in the way that they teach or assess.*

Thus Paula was able to make active and meaningful connections between her own experience and sociological theory that was productive for her studies, for example in an impressive final dissertation which focused on children, class and health. Paula's learning identity is very much tied into her working class habitus which appears to be narrower and less expansive than Peter's:

> *I see myself not as moving between class. I see myself as having achieved something within and saying 'yes' I am working class and this is what I have achieved. But I wouldn't want to think that my roots have changed. I looked at some of the other people I worked with and think, no I am not like you and don't want to be like you.*

So Paula's structural position was more fixed than Peter's, although she was still able to exercise her agency to good effect in HE. This difference is certainly partly gendered, with Peter, coming from a strong working class background but having more opportunities to develop his wide ranging agency and cultural interests and cultural capital as a single man. In contrast Paula's agency was very much restricted initially by class and family assumptions, only emerging later in her life in direct reaction to the structural unfairness of a gendered work-place. Another key difference was in social capital. While Peter studied alongside his fellow trade unionists and could draw on that particular social capital, Paula, as a working class mature student, felt very much in the minority alongside mainstream younger students.

In both instances their learning identities changed as a result of their engagement with higher education. Both became successful in HE through linking their own subjective aims and their different learning identities to what they understood as the objective requirements of HE success. Peter was able to temper his love of radical ideas, difference and debate with an academic discipline and conformity that he knew was necessary to succeed in HE, as part of moving on to further educational work both personally and within the trade union movement. Paula was able to build on and translate her experience into appropriate academic language and concepts while making full use of her strategic and organisational skills in pursuing her studies and her ultimate goal of teaching and supporting kids from backgrounds like herself.

Conclusion

Our research project suggests that learning identities are complex and do not develop in any predicable or linear way, that they can be affected by a number of key personal, interactional and institutional factors. What is particularly important for non traditional adult students is how they inter-connect with prior established learning and other identities. In following the Bologna process in attempting to open up higher education to a range of new and different students, universities may need to reflect on and adapt their approaches to teaching and support in order to make universities more socially inclusive, to understand better the circumstances and attitudes of these new students and to support them in developing positive learning identities for their learning at university and beyond.

These two case studies above illustrate how learner identity is shaped and transformed through the dialectics of structure and agency. The self is an ongoing biographical project, for as Shilling stresses: "The building of a cohesive self is a never ending process precisely because of the individual body's unfinishedness and openness to cultural influences" (1999: p.558). Studying in higher education develops and transforms an individual's learning identity and habitus through the interaction of structure and agency. Adult students leave changed persons, yet for many, they continue to identify themselves as being working class. They do not lose their working class cultural capital but build up their intellectual and social capitals which are then superimposed on their classed self and identity.

References

Abbott, A (2001). *Chaos of Disciplines,* Chicago: University of Chicago Press

Alheit, P and Dausien, B (2002). The 'double face' of lifelong learning: Two analytical perspectives on a 'silent revolution'. In *Studies in the Education of Adults,* Vol. 34, No. 1, Spring, pp 3-22

Alheit, P and Dausien, B (2000). 'Biographicity' as a basic resource of lifelong learning. In P. Alheit, J. Beck, E. Kammler, H. Salling-Olesen, and R. Taylor, *Lifelong Learning Inside and Outside Schools,* Vol.2, Roskilde: ESREA

Anthias, F (2005). Social Stratification and Social Inequality: Models of Intersectionality and Identity. In F. Devine, et al, *Rethinking Class: cultures, identities and lifestyle,* New York: Palgrave Macmillan

Antikainen, A., Houtsonen, J., Kauppila, J., Huotelin, H. (1996). *Living in a Learning Society: Life Histories, Identities and Education,* London: Falmer Press

Archer, M S (2003). *Structure, Agency and the Internal Conversation,* Cambridge: University of Cambridge Press

Barnett, R (2003). *Beyond All Reason: Living with ideology in the university,* Buckingham: SRHE/OUP

Bauman, Z (1997). *Postmodernity and its Discontents,* Cambridge: Polity Press

Becker, H S, Geer, B and Strauss, A (1961) *Boys in White: Student Culture in Medical School,* Chicago: Chicago University Press

Bloomer, M & Hodkinson, P (2000). Learning careers: continuity and changing young people's dispositions to learning. In *British Educational Research Journal,* 26, pp 528 - 597

Bourdieu, P. (1977). *Outline of a Theory of Practice,* Cambridge: Cambridge University Press

Bourdieu, P (1990). *In Other Words: Essays Towards a Reflexive Sociology,* Cambridge: Polity

Bourdieu, P. (2000). The biographical illusion. In P. Gay, J. Evans, and P. Redman, (Eds) *Identity: a reader,* London: Sage

Bourdieu, P & Wacquant, L J (1992). *An Invitation to Reflexive Sociology,* Cambridge: Polity

Brookfield, S (1994). Tales from the Dark Side: a Phenomenology of Adult Critical Reflection. In *International Journal of Lifelong Education (Japan),* Vol. 13, No. 3 pp203-216

Castells, M. (1997). *The Power of Identity, The Information Age: Economy, Society and Culture,* Vol II, Oxford: Blackwell

Côté, J E & Levine, C G (2002). *Identity, Formation, Agency & Culture: A Social Psychological Synthesis,* Mahwah: Lawrence Erlbaum

Crossan, B., Field, J., Gallacher, J., & Merrill, B. (2003). Understanding Participatiion in Learning for Non-traditional Adult Learners: learning careers and the construction of identities. In *British Journal of Sociology of Education,* 24.1, pp 55-67

Dawe, A. (1970). The two sociologies In *British Journal of Sociology,* Vol.21, pp207-218

Delanty, G. (2001). *Challenging Knowledge: The University in the Knowledge Society,* Buckingham: SRHE/Open University Press

Denzin, N. K. (1989). *Interpretative Interactionism,* Newbury Park C.A.: Sage

Devine, F. Savage, M. Scott, J. and Crompton, R. (2005). *Rethinking Class: cultures, identities and lifestyle,* New York: Palgrave Macmillan

Emirbayer, M. and Mische, A. (1998). What is agency? In *American Journal of Sociology*, 103, pp962-1023

Giddens, A. (1991). *Modernity and Self Identity: Self and Society in the Late Modern Age*, Cambridge: Polity Press

Jenkins, R. (1996). *Social Identity*, London: Routledge

Johnston R. and Merrill B. (2004). 'From old to new learning identities: charting the change for non-traditional adult students in higher education'. In ESREA Proceedings: *Between 'old' and 'new' Worlds of Adult Learning*, Wroclaw: University of Wroclaw, pp 153-166

Johnston R. and Merrill B. (2004a). 'Non-traditional students - tracking changing learning identities in the inter-face with Higher Education'. In C. Hunt (Ed.) *(Re)generating Research in Adult Learning and Teaching*, Sheffield: SCUTREA/University of Sheffield, pp 141-149

Marx, K. (1885). *The Eighteenth Brumaire of Louis Bonaparte*, Hamburg: Germany

Merrill, B. (1999). *Gender, Change and Identity: Mature Women Students in Universities*, Aldershot: Ashgate

Merrill, B. (2001). *Learning Careers: Conceptualising Adult Learning Experiences Through Biographies*, ESREA Biography and Life History Network Conference, Roskilde: Denmark

Merrill, B. (2007). Recovering Class and the Collective in the Stories of Adult Learners, pp 71-89. In L. West, B. Merrill, P. Alheit, and A.S. Andersen, (Eds.) *Using Life History and Biographical Approaches in the Study of Adult and Lifelong Learning: European Perspective*, Hamburg: Peter Lang

Pahl, R. E. (1989). 'Is the emperor naked?'. In *International Journal of Urban and Regional Research*, 13, pp711-720

Savage, M. (2000). *Class Analysis and Social Transformation*, Buckingham: Open University Press

Scott, P. (1998). Mass Higher Education: A New Civilisation? In D. Jary, and M. Parker, *The New Higher Education: Issues and Directions for the Post-Dearing University*, Stoke-on-Trent: Staffordshire University Press

Shilling, C.(1999). Towards an embodied understanding of the structure/agency relationship. In *British Journal of Sociology*, Vol. 50 No. 4, pp543-562

Skeggs, B. (1997). *Formations of Class and Gender*, London: Sage

Thompson, E. P. (1963). *The Making of the English Working Class*, London: Gollancz

West, L. (1996). *Beyond Fragments: adults, motivation and higher education* London: Taylor Francis

10 The Impact of Drama on Young Offenders' Learning Identities and Careers

Nalita James and Bethia McNeil

Introduction

In late modernity, in which young adults have become exposed to a range of choices and risks that were previously unavailable to them (Beck, 1992, Giddens, 1991), transitions to adulthood have become increasingly non-linear, and individual experiences and outcomes complicated and unpredictable. As part of their transition between compulsory education and employment, young adults will be faced with competing dilemmas and forced to make choices that have the potential to shape the rest of their lives (Lawy, 2000). For many young adults, such experiences are compounded by the erosion of social and geographical structures such as the traditional youth labour market, and family and housing transitions (see Sandford et al, 2006, p. 252-53). Those without the necessary 'social capital' (Raffo and Reeves, 2000), particularly young men, can find themselves subject to the greatest insecurities, as they try to effect previously predictable school-to-work transitions without qualifications or skills (McGivney, 1999). Reduced opportunities for successful transitions can lead to young adults adopting what Stephen and Squires (2003, p.145) describe as 'alternative careers'. This is particularly so for young offenders, whose learning identities (dispositions) are compounded by their subordinate positions in the prison setting, and thus overlooked rather than being perceived as an integrated understanding of their transitional experiences. Clearly, movement of young adults through different social contexts and statuses can affect the nature of their engagement with learning (Lawy, 2002).

This chapter will address this issue in more detail by examining how, for young male offenders, engagement in learning and the development of a learning career can impact upon their learning identity, and subsequent transitions. We will draw on the findings from a nine month pilot study, joint funded by the Arts Council England and the then Department for Education and Skills (DfES). The study sought to explore the use of theatre as a site for learning, and the methods and process of drama as 'tools' in supporting personal and social development among young men in custody within a closed Young Offenders Institute (YOI) in the East Midlands, UK (see James and McNeil, 2006 for a detailed discussion of the study).

In researching young offenders' lives, France (2007) has argued that issues of social context are important in understanding social action and criminal behaviour. Central then to our discussion is the interplay between individual agency and identity, circumstance and social structure (Wyn and White, 1998). We firstly examine the young offenders' understandings of their formative experiences of learning prior to prison life, and the complex interactions between their experiences and pathways into crime. We will also explore the young men's structural positions in the prison setting and the impact this has upon their learning identities and perception of agency. We then move on to explore the impact of drama on the young men's learning careers and identities during a time of uncertainty and risk in their lives as they embark on a transitional journey, from prison life to life 'on the outside'. We conclude by arguing that drama has a fundamental role to play in the wider shaping of young offenders' transitions and learning careers, as it offers the time and space to explore images and projections of the self and identity. In turn, empowering moments can emerge in which young offenders act as agents in seeking routes out of offending, and develop new projects and orientations for learning.

Learning identities and participation in learning

Our research draws on Bloomer and Hodkinson's (2000) notion of learning identity (dispositions) and learning career (positions) to understand how young offenders' formative experiences (such as education) can inform their identities and the dispositions they hold towards learning. These concepts have been developed as a way of theorising the movement of the individual through different social contexts and statuses, and in turn the transitions that can occur in terms of engagement with education and/or employment opportunities. Bloomer and Hodkinson's empirical research shows the complex combination of positions and learning identities. It also describes the complex relationships that young adults can have with learning, particularly in terms of how social and cultural influences inform different orientations to education, "transforming dispositions to learning that make up the young people's learning careers" (Hodkinson and Bloomer, 2000, p. 200). They also recognise that young adults' dispositions towards learning can be conditioned by their formative experiences of gender and class. As in Cieslik and Simpson's (2006) research, these concepts have explored how past events can condition patterns of engagement in young offenders' learning, yet more crucially how such dispositions and participation in learning can be transformed. Lawy (2000) argues that not only can dispositions provide a framework through which individuals can make sense of the world, but can provide opportunities for young adults to make sense of their previous experiences, in the present, and inform the development of future action, identity and learning.

Whilst Bloomer and Hodkinson's (2000) concepts provide a useful approach to understanding young offenders' dispositions to learning, and how their subjectivities shape their agentic action, it is also important to place greater emphasis on agency and structural contexts in the transformation of their learning identities. As noted by Cieslik:

> There is a neglect of how social contexts can offer enablements and constraints for social actors and that these structuring qualities of social contexts are in part conditioned by the sorts of resources and dispositions that actors bring to these situations (2006, p. 239).

One way to understand young offenders' perceptions of and dispositions towards learning is through the use of drama. The techniques of Forum Theatre (Boal, 1998)[1] particularly, can expose young offenders to "more diverse forms of social interaction and to new events and changing circumstances...' (Bloomer and Hodkinson" 2000, p. 594). The methods and processes of drama also illuminate how such experiences have been shaped by wider social and economic structures. The approach encourages them to "express themselves by taking an active role in determining the content and form of the drama and to experiment with new forms that are relevant to them" (Conrad, 2005, p.38). Drama then is able to provide a form of learning such as that achieved in daily life, and can play a part in developing knowledge and skills acquisition (Henry, 2000). It is these imaginary worlds that are the basis for learning through drama. Through the freedom of creativity then, young offenders can engage in a journey of self-discovery and risk as they draw on their experiences. This in turn can help them to begin to make sense of the structural contexts they inhabit using images, ideas, characters and stories that make up a piece of drama about their social world. This process places emphasis on the agency of the young people by focusing on the social and constructed nature of reality within their lives and unpacking the inequalities, relationships and social structures that make this up (see also Carroll, 1996). The potential learning benefits of this process are vast as the young people can find a level of involvement that goes beyond that found in more formal 'sitting and listening learning' prison scenarios. This is because no one is excluded, as the experience of exploring perspectives requires initially only that any participant has experienced something, at some point, in the most basic way (James, 2006).

---

1   The work of Forum Theatre takes its inspiration from the work of Augusto Boal. Forum Theatre is a theatrical device in which a problem is shown in an unsolved form, to which the audiences, who are active participants, are invited to suggest and enact solutions. The problem is always a symptom of oppression. The spectators try and bring the scenario to a different conclusion, in which a cycle of oppression is interrupted. Many different solutions are enacted in the course of a single forum workshop. The result is a pooling of knowledge, tactics and experience whilst at the same time enacting out scenarios for real change in our everyday lives.

Research context and methodology

Current Government initiatives around penal policy signal a stronger emphasis on the effective resettlement of offenders. Within this, offender learning and skills policy focuses on the acquisition of skills for employment, including literacy and numeracy and vocational learning. Movement into sustained employment is seen as central to reduction in and desistance from (re)offending. However, there is also recognition of the importance of personal and social development in supporting young offenders to make the transition from custody back into the community. This is also seen as fundamental in enabling young offenders to explore the circumstances that lead to their offending behaviour, and to manage the risks and challenges they will face on release. The Youth Justice Board (2002) recommends that education provision for young offenders is not only about providing skills for the workplace but has an important role in personal development, improving self-esteem, increasing understanding of responsibilities, extending choices, increasing aspirations, and improving life chances. Research (see, for example, The Howard League for Penal Reform, 2006, Lyon et al, 2000) has consistently highlighted young offenders' negative experiences of formal education, and the impact on their learning careers and identities. Such research has contributed to the ongoing development of informal and non-formal approaches to learning with young offenders and young adults at risk. Within this, the arts are recognised as making a particular contribution to engaging and motivating young offenders, offering learning relevant to the context of their lives, and "have proved to be effective in raising participation in other learning and skills activities" (DfES, 2005, p. 27). Arts Council England note that the arts have a 'significant and unique role to play' in offering young offenders effective learning and career pathways (Arts Council England, 2005, p.14). Drama and theatre, particularly, are seen as offering exciting, inspirational and challenging activity, with the "power to transform lives" (Arts Council England, 2005, p.2).

In light of this context, we wanted to understand the young offenders' attitudes to, and experiences of learning, and the transformative impact of drama in challenging and reshaping their attitudes and learning identities. To do this, we needed to give voice to the young offenders' experiences - something which is not possible in quantitative research (Shah, 2006, p. 210) in order that we could uncover their understandings of their social worlds. Rather than identify the young men with their past or current offending behaviour, we sought to remove their 'criminal agency' (see also Stephen and Squires, 2003), and regard them as participants (actors) in a creative process through which their potential as learners could be developed and explored - to address the whole person "without prejudice" (Arts Council England, 2005, p.17). To achieve this, our research design used an ethnographic approach to the study that allowed us to research "from the inside" (Emond, 2004, p.105) and to adapt to the existing culture of the young men, and their social world (Skeggs, 2001).[2] As Hammersley and Atkinson (1983) note, initial perspectives are important in giving insight into the experiences and lives of young adults. As part of this process, we visited the prison prior to the drama programme commencing to gain an understanding of the social context we would be researching.

As prison settings are difficult places to work (Liebling, 1999, p.151) we felt it important to adopt a range of research methods that were justifiable and ethical. We recognised the importance of adding to our understanding of the young men's experiences by exploring the broader social and cultural processes that impacted on their lives (France, 2004). Firstly we undertook a group interview with the young men to begin to contextualise their formative experiences of education and learning, including within the custodial context. This interview also provided an impression of the nature of interactions between the young men (as peers and as 'inmates'), the staff (both security and education) and within the prison as a community in which the production of meanings, identity and status were important to these young men. A further purpose of the interview was to begin to develop the research relationship as well as give them the opportunity to 'suss us out'.

Secondly, through the drama programme, we engaged in participant and non-participant observation of two groups of young male offenders in terms of the learning taking place and skills development. Each group was set up to have a maximum of ten participants, to enhance opportunities for creativity, interaction and learning. Establishing relationships with the young men, and the resultant degree of access to their everyday lives, was vital if observation was to be accepted by them. The researchers also had to ensure that consideration was given to what participation in this project might mean for them. As Mason (2002) notes, relationships in the research setting can develop and change over time, either becoming close, or difficult and challenging. We had to find the "right distance" between ourselves and the young men (Bazanger and Dodier, 2004, p.14), and live through and manage the relationships we developed as we immersed ourselves in the research setting.

Finally, we conducted one-to-one semi-structured interviews to explore the young men's learning identities and careers to further understand their relationships with learning. To a degree, these interviews were 'biographically focused' (see also Macdonald and Marsh, 2005) as we explored their personal histories and formative experiences of learning, particularly in relation to how these experiences had contributed to the formation of their identities. Further, we explored the young men's experiences of transition - their perspectives on

---

2   We formed part of a wider project team that also included two drama practitioners from a national theatre company, and two *Skills for Life* tutors from a Further Education College.

the drama activities they had been involved in, and the changing patterns in their learning identities and career. The interviews also allowed for an exploration of the young men's views of their future roles and values.

The drama programme
A critical element of the research study was the ten-week drama programme which was offered twice a week on a voluntary basis to the young men as part of their educational provision in the prison. Those who took part in the programme had little or no experience of drama. It was held in the prison chapel - a large open space with big windows and tables along the walls, which allowed a degree of physical expression and openness that the young men arguably were unable to achieve in other education provision, or possibly anywhere else within the prison. The young men identified the chapel as a very different space to their classrooms as it had no broken windows or furniture. It was also perceived as a quiet space that was 'more chilled.'

The drama programme offered a creative process requiring a level of involvement that drew directly on the experiences, the character, the very persona of the young men. This involved a high level of ownership organically built into the learning process that was bounded and framed within the young men's experiences, where nothing is right or wrong, where there can be no failure, and where the individuals agree that they are just playing at making things up, whilst remembering, albeit subconsciously, that learning is taking place (James and McNeil, 2006). Through this process, the drama practitioners created a negotiated and shared understanding of the young men's roles and responsibilities as 'actors' that was based on trust and respect. This approach also helped to develop confidence and communication skills so that the young men and drama practitioners could work effectively together and share life experiences. It further created a safe environment in which the young men could bring different qualities and learn from each other (Shah, 2006). From there, it was possible to develop characters and stories through a creative process. Personal and social skills became critical as ideas began to be expressed, explored and negotiated.

The Impact of Drama on Young Offenders' Learning Transitions

The research participants were aged between 18-21 and were from a wide area across England including the East Midlands, parts of the West Midlands and the London region. The majority of the young men held ethnic minority group status. Many of the young offenders were a long way from home, having been previously held in other custodial establishments. Some were remand prisoners; others had convicted but were waiting to be sentenced. Many had young families or girlfriends; others were due to become a father; some had no contact with their immediate families at all. All of the young men taking part in the drama programme had left compulsory education before the age of 16, with some saying they had never attended school. Many of them had re-engaged in learning by participating in education activities in the prison, including numeracy and literacy, as well as practical-based courses such as carpentry and engineering.

Learning identities: formative experiences of learning and the prison context
The young men's dispositions to learning were influenced by their formative experiences of education, including school and prison education. All claimed to have hated school, and expressed strong negative opinions towards teachers, lessons and the formal education system itself. At the heart of this negativity was often a sense of feeling belittled or powerless, and a frustration at being compelled to participate in learning which was not seen as relevant to their lives. The young men did not see themselves as learners, and indeed, their dislike of school, and education more generally, actively contributed to the development of their powerful and protective prison identities. Education in prison was viewed as being instrumental in gaining employment, the sole aim of most of the group, and was consequently something to be endured. Prison education provision was framed as a route to gaining valuable qualifications, rather than an experience of learning new skills and qualities, yet it seemed to involve a constant negotiation that strongly impacted upon their learning identities and perception of agency. For example, the young men resented the discipline in the prison setting that 'leaked' into their education classes. They spoke of receiving warnings from teachers for not working hard enough or being actively engaged in classes, even where they were repeating sessions or work programmes due to administrative errors. These warnings had a very real effect on their lives in the prison, and their motivation to fully participate in learning. In these cases, the young men's learner identities incorporated elements of hostility towards formally structured education. Some, however, were focussed on where they wanted to be in the future, and what they needed to achieve from education to get there, but saw themselves as being held back by the regime and bureaucracy within the prison:

> *I have been doing the same thing for 5 or 6 months. I started the damn course again, so today I thought I am going to ask again about level 2 literacy. Why do they get angry and refer me from the unit, and then I get a warning...because they do not tell you where you are going...* (Jason)

'Prison identity' was something that all the young men took very seriously. For example, Kyle referred to the need to *"wear a mask"* in prison, to create and maintain an institutionalised identity that would *"get you through"* your time inside. Part of this mask involved a lack of opportunities for expression and voicing opinions, and stood in direct opposition to exploring learning identities. One young man reflected that they were not allowed to ask questions in prison. As Damon said: "W*e don't think. That's why we're in here. You have to think for us"*. Kyle felt that his mask would be dropped when he was released, and he would *"return to normal"*. Others understood that their style of communication was an integral part of their identity, beyond the prison context. It was often closely linked to where they grew up and the background with which they aligned themselves. Consequently, changing the way they communicated, whether in specific situations or as part of larger changes in their outlook on life, was seen as *"not being true to yourself"*:

> *I don't think you can change the way you speak... that's how we speak [in London], that's how it is with the whole image... I don't think people can change that, that's how I am... to change my accent or try to speak like something I'm not, that ain't going to happen...*
> (Elvis)

Participating in drama: The transformation of learning identities
In engaging the young men in learning about the theatre process, the drama practitioners required high standards of performance and behaviour. This meant that even for the most challenging participants, or those who lacked confidence in their ability 'to do it,' they knew that their achievements were genuine. Particularly pertinent to this was the way in which the young men felt they were spoken to and treated by the drama practitioners. Neil saw this as a positive experience; it influenced his desire to participate, and impacted upon how he was perceived in this space - as an actor and not a criminal, and how he perceived himself:

> *[The drama practitioners] talk to you, like, I don't know, like you ain't a criminal. I hate being classed as a criminal... I hate it... It's just not like being in jail, it's like being at a course somewhere else, if you know what I mean..., you're doing this and, like, having a laugh, you ain't worried about nothing, you're just, like, you learned it, but you don't look at it like that.*

This approach played a central role in supporting the young men to develop greater awareness of their identities and actions within a shared context, and also to creatively express their own experiences. It allowed the young men to safely explore their thoughts and feelings and issues relevant to their lives, in creating characters and the challenges they might face. Consequently, they were developing a context within which to explore their agency. This was one of the main assets in the development of the creative process that drew on their experiences, and developed skills and qualities. During the final session, they reflected that taking part in the drama programme had *"given us confidence"* (Damon), *"supported them to learn some interesting things...[like] team working, acting...and learned how to listen"* (Lance), and had *"made [them] think..."* (Neil).

Their new self-confidence and their developing communication skills led to shifts in the attitudes and behaviours that had led them into offending. This was particularly evident in the interviews with the young men who had completed the drama programme, all of whom were soon to be released from prison. Their narratives suggested that over the programme's duration, they had reflected on their learning histories and developed new projects and orientations for learning. This was particularly evident in Neil's interview about the critical incidents in his life. His imminent release from prison, and the fact that his girlfriend was due to have a baby prior to his release, together with reflection on these experiences, had pushed him into taking part in the drama programme. He reflected upon how the drama programme had given him space to think, not only about himself, but also about his new family, and life on the outside:

> *I mean, like, to get work.... Cos before, like, I didn't want to get up for work in the morning. But, like, [drama] made me think that, it's made me think that, you know, it's better when you, like, you've got something else... keep you motivated and that...* (Neil)

He also reflected upon how his involvement had developed his motivation and confidence. This occurred most strongly as he got more involved in the acting and creativity, presenting ideas about how particular characters could be developed, drawing on his own experiences in defining their identities.

The development of the young men's personal and social skills also went beyond the prison context. It showed that engagement with the drama, and the learning that was taking place, was a subjective experience bound up with other life events. For the young men, taking part in the drama programme had, at some level, given them time to explore issues and experiences relevant to their own lives. This had introduced new perspectives and knowledge about themselves, specifically in terms of what was achievable for them in employment and/or education, and also, in attitudes and behaviour towards other people. Their accounts of formal learning had indicated negative experiences of schools, in which they didn't attend, learned nothing, or didn't really care. However, the shift in attitudes, where they seemed to have a vision of life 'on the outside,' now included participation in further education and learning. Hassan, Jason and Kyle had started the process of thinking about what educational opportunities might be available to them on release. For Elvis, who had a girlfriend and children, he too wanted to 'achieve', to make something of his life not just for himself but his family. He wanted to apply the skills he had developed through the drama programme. This included understanding the importance of respect, tolerance and patience for other people.

The creative processes involved in drama provided opportunity to shape the young men's identity and skills by reinventing or drawing upon existing personal identities. For both groups, this was linked to the importance of developing characters where the young men could project their own personalities and experiences on to it. From this, characteristics were identified, and then interrogated or explored within challenging scenarios. The notion of keeping scenes real and representing what would happen on the street gave the young men a freedom of expression which drew on their very personas, their 'knowledge' and experiences that made them who they were. It is here that drama can be distinguished from other creative processes. The young men were invited to take their stories, their life experiences, and act them out: "...*to live out an aspiration or an ambition inherent within creating fiction"* (drama practitioner) whilst also provoking or challenging situations or contexts which are within their frame of reference.

The opportunity to develop characters and stories then became important in developing self-awareness and identity. For example, the development of the character 'Spiker' was an intrinsic part of Elvis' identity, as he commented: *"That's my name, so that's what I'm sticking to".* Through this process of creativity and reflection he had space and time to explore his perceptions and attitudes towards a number of issues, and to begin to consider how not only how he saw himself, but how others saw and reacted in response to him. This was particularly evident in the way he identified with, and spoke to, his children. Elvis admitted that his general style of communication involved 'slang' or what he termed *"street speak".* The only occasion that he would deliberately avoid this style of communication was in front of his children. It was evident that his attitudes towards learning had altered as a consequence of his caring role and responsibilities, and associated changes in his identity and relationships:

> *When I'm speaking to my kids obviously... you've got to change your tone of voice... I wouldn't talk in a slang way to my kids. I don't want them to be like on the street, like just how I was, yeah, at the age of 15, running away from school, innit, like up to nothing and ending up in jail, you know...*

Discussion

This chapter contributes to our understanding of how drama has a fundamental role to play in the wider shaping of young offenders' transitions and learning careers. It demonstrates how drama can create a social space in which approaches to behaviour can be explored collectively (Turner, 2007), as well as a transitional space in which individuals can reflect upon themselves and take on new roles (Hughes and Wilson, 2004), voice their opinions and create their own meanings (Conrad, 2006). Loi and Dillon (2006, p.364) contend that educational environments that claim to foster creativity must incorporate potential for analysis and the transference and synthesis between and across disciplines. In the study, the creative processes of drama involved role-play and characterisation from personal experiences and drawing on the young men's own personalities and experiences as they reflected on their social world and perceptions of their own lives. They did not always feel comfortable with this process, however it seemed to provide a level of learning and achievement with a strong sense of ownership and personal commitment built in without any sense of judgement. To do this also required the young men to explore their own situations and the place of such learning in their wider life course experiences.

In the prison context, drama can do much to constructively (re)engage young offenders in learning since it offers a non-threatening and non-judgemental context to explore life situations and reframe identities through make believe. Within the prison, the chapel became a 'creative space': an environment adapted to accommodate the fluidity of collaborative, integrated work, where ideas are analysed, synthesised and applied (Loi and Dillon, 2006, p.365). For the young men, the context of the prison chapel was particularly important in ideologically distancing them and their negative experiences of prison life. It provided the space to create imaginary worlds that became metaphors to link their personal experiences with the unknown, or outer, social world. The exploratory creation of 'metaphoric worlds' provides different perspectives that result in learning which can be integrated into other life experiences over time (Henry, 2000, p.56). This process of creative engagement with characters, perspectives and opinions can challenge fixed assumptions and attitudes, providing positive reinforcement and challenging negative behaviour. Consequently, the process has a more sustained effect because the context in which the learning transition occurs, and the degree of both cognitive and creative engagement that learners require, is more memorable (Silvis 2002).

France and Homel (2006) argue that the choice available to individuals and the structural circumstances in which they find themselves are influential in shaping their lives. For the young men in the study, their predispositions (values and beliefs) had been shaped by their experiences and orientated them towards a particular view of the future, which included their involvement in crime.

Alongside their negative experiences of education and schooling, their criminal activities had played a positive role in shaping their identities and lives, and offered a form of social inclusion (Armstrong et al, 2006). This in turn had led to fragmented lives resulting in learning careers that were not always linear, and creating what Cieslik (2006, p.247) describes as 'reticent learners.' Cieslik and Simpson (2006, p.225) have observed, "individuals over time come to reflect on their learning histories and develop new projects and orientations for learning". The young men's learning careers were intrinsically bound to concepts of the self, and of identity. Drama methods had provided the young men with a means to reflect on their learning careers and "act their way into better thinking" (Turner, 2007, p.182). In the study, there were often long-term experiences (such as a pending birth of a child) which influenced the young men's transformation. So where in the past, they had been reticent about education or employment, they were now more receptive to such opportunities. In this sense, the young offenders had begun the process of reframing their learning identities, as also observed by Conrad (2005, p.38): "like drama, our social reality is constructed and can be reconstructed". The drama had provided ways for them to start the process of projecting themselves into the "adult activities of their culture and rehearse their future roles and values" (Wagner, 1998, p. 33). They now expressed the self-belief that they could achieve and have a future and were keen to find employment or continue their education by going to college.

It can be argued that this process is not only an enriching experience for young offenders, but allows them to instigate their own actions, thereby achieving a sense of agency. As Turner (2007) notes, young offenders can try out different behaviours and responses that are other than their own, gain insight and greater awareness of their lives, and shows them that they can take on different, and more positive roles in society. In our study, the young offenders wanted to apply the skills and qualities they had developed, to other areas in their lives, in particular employment. They also articulated the need to apply these skills to their family and friends, to be responsible for themselves and others in their lives and to adopt different attitudes and behaviours. Identities too can be created and sustained as individuals give meaning to the social contexts in which they find themselves (France and Homel, 2006). The young men's structural circumstances provided a learning context for the 'playing out' of their social lives. The prison context was critical in this process, as they struggled with changing perceptions of their social identity as criminals. This in turn made them question their identity and reassert themselves in order to survive the experience intact. They could do this through drama, creatively exploring aspects of their prison lives and beyond. It can be argued that improvising different scenarios can provide opportunities for the young men to negotiate their identities, as well as allows them to resist negative identities and possible criminal futures (Armstrong et al, 2006).

Conclusion

The methods and processes of drama are particularly important for young offenders, especially where their previous life experiences have often given them little confidence or impetus to engage in the process of learning. They offer the possibilities to develop new learning opportunities that are not only more adaptive to the lives of young offenders but also embrace the diversity of their experiences and actions. We would also argue that drama has a fundamental role to play in the wider shaping of young offenders' learning careers as it can provide a forum within which they are free to make mistakes. By offering the time and space to explore images and projections of the self through improvisation and performance, learning can take on distinctive meanings and significance at a particular stage in the young offenders' life course. They can begin to recognise something of fundamental importance about their dispositions and assert their agency in exploring what they desire for their lives - in this case, to seek pathways out of offending and develop new projects and orientations for learning.

References

Armstrong, D., France, A. and Hine, J. (2006). *Pathways into and out of crime.* Final Report, London: Economic Social Research Council.

Arts Council England (2005). *The arts and young people at risk of offending,* London: Arts Council England

Baszanger, I. & Dodier, N. (2004). Ethnography: Relating the part to the Whole, in D. Silverman (Ed.) *Qualitative Research. Theory, Method and Practice,* London: Sage.

Beck, U. (1992). *Risk Society: Towards a New Modernity,* London: Sage

Bloomer, M. & Hodkinson, P. (2000). Learning careers: Continuity and change in young people's dispositions to learning. In *British Educational Research Journal,* 26 (5): 583-597.

Boal, A. (1998). *Legislative Theatre: Using Performance to Make Politics,* London: Routledge.

Carroll, J. (1996). Escaping the information abattoir: Critical and transformative research in drama classrooms. In P. Taylor (Ed.) *Researching Drama and Arts Education,* London: Sage.

Cieslik, M. (2006). Reflexivity, learning identities and adult basic skills in the United Kingdom. In *British Journal of Sociology of Education,* 27 (2): 237-250.

Cieslik, M. & Simpson, D. (2006). Skills for life? Basic skills and marginal transitions from school-to-work, *Journal of Youth Studies,* 9 (2):213-230.

Conrad, D. (2006). Entangled (in the) sticks: Ethical conundrums of popular theatre as pedagogy and research. In *Qualitative Inquiry,* 12 (3): 437-458.

Department for Education and Skills (2005). *The Offender's Learning Journey: Learning and skills provision for adult offenders in England.* Available at: *http://www.dfes.gov.uk/offenderlearning/uploads/documents/adult_OLJ_V0.5a.doc* Accessed 1 February 2006

Emond, R. (2003). Ethnography in practice: A case study illustration. In: A. Bennet, M. Cieslik, and S. Miles (Eds.) *Researching Youth,* Hampshire: Palgrave Macmillan.

France, A. (2004). Young people. In: S. Fraser, V. Lewis, S. Ding, M. Kellett and C. Robinson (Eds.) *Doing Research with Children and Young People,* London: Sage.

France, A. (2007). *Understanding Youth in Late Modernity,* Maidenhead: McGraw-Hill/Open University Press.

France, A. & Homel, R. (2006). Societal access routes and developmental pathways: putting social structure and young people's voice into the analysis of pathways into and out of crime. In *Australian and New Zealand Journal of Criminology,* 39 (3): 295-309.

Giddens, A. (1991). *Modernity and self-Identity: Self and society in the late modern age.* Cambridge: Polity Press.

Hammersley, M. and Atkinson, P. (1983). *Ethnography: Principles and Practice,* London: Routledge.

Henry, M. (2000). Drama's ways of learning. In *Research in Drama Education,* 5 (1): 45-62.

Hodkinson, P. & Bloomer, M. (2000). Stokingham sixth form college: institutional culture and dispositions to learning. In *British Journal of Sociology of Education,* 21 (2): 187-202.

Hughes, J. & Wilson, K. (2004). Playing a part: the impact of youth theatre on young people's personal and social development. In *Research in Drama Education* 9 (1), 57-72.

The Howard League for Penal Reform (2006). *Out for Good: Meeting the resettlement needs of young men,* London: Howard League for Penal Reform

James, N. (2006). 'Actup!' Theatre as education and its impact on young people's learning'. In J. Somer and M. Balfour (Eds.) *Drama as Social Intervention,* Canada: Captus Press.

James, N. & McNeil, B. (2006). *Theatre as a Site for Learning: The Impact of Drama on the Development of Oracy among Young Adult Offenders,* Available at: www.niace.org.uk/research/yalp

Lawy, R. (2000). Is Jimmy really so different? Learning and making-meaning in work and non-work contexts'. In *British Journal of Sociology of Education,* 2 (4): 591-604.

Lawy, R. (2002). Transition and transformation: the experiences of two young people. In *Journal of Education and Work,* 15 (2): 201-218.

Liebling, A. (1999). Doing prison research, breaking the silence. In *Theoretical Criminology* 3 (2): 147-173.

Lyon, J et al (2000). *'Tell them so they listen': Messages from young people in custody,* London: Home Office

Loi, D & Dillon, P (2006). Adaptive educational environments as creative spaces. In *Cambridge Journal of Education* 36(3): 363-381.

McGivney, V. (1999*). Excluded Men: Men who are Missing from Education and Training.* Leicester: National Institute of Adult and Continuing Education

Macdonald, R. and Marsh, J. (2005). *Disconnected Youth? Growing up in Britain's Poor Neighbourhoods,* Hampshire: Palgrave Macmillan

Mason, J. (2002). *Qualitative Researching,* second edition, London: Sage.

Raffo, C. and Reeves, M. (2000). Youth transitions and social exclusion: developments in social capital theory. In *Journal of Youth Studies* 3 (4) :147-166.

Sandford, R.A., Armour, K.M. and Warrington, P.C. (2006). Re-engaging disaffected youth through physical activity programmes. In *British Educational Research Journal,* 32 (2), 251-271.

Silvis, E.L. (2002). *Creative Curriculum: Including the Visual Arts in Public Schools,* Available at www.ac.wwu.edu, accessed 3 December 2005.

Stephen, D. E. and Squires, P.A. (2002). Adults don't realise how sheltered they are. A contribution to the debate on youth transitions from some voices on the margins. In *Journal of Youth Studies,* 6 (2): 145-164.

Skeggs, B. (2001). Feminist ethnography. In: P. Atkinson., A. Coffey,. S. Delamomt, J. Lofland and L. Lofland (Eds.) *Handbook of Ethnography,* London: Sage.

Shah, S. (2002). Sharing the world: The researcher and the researched'. In *Qualitative Research,* 6 (2): 202-220.

Turner, J. (2007). Making amends; an interventionist theatre programme with young offenders. In *Research in Drama Education,* 12 (2):179-194.

Wagner, B.J. (1998). *Educational drama and language arts: What research shows.* Portsmouth, NH: Heinemann.

Wyn, J. & White, R. (1998). Young people, social problems and Australian youth studies. In *Journal of Youth Studies* 1(1): 23-39.

The Youth Justice Board (2002) *National Specification for Learning and Skills. Available at: http://www.yjb.gov.uk/Publications/Scripts/prodView.asp?idproduct=50&eP=PP Accessed 1 February 2006*

11 The Symbolic Power of Knowledge: Exclusion Mechanisms of the 'University Habitus' in the German HE System

Peter Alheit

1. Introduction

It is of course polemical to talk of the *'university habitus'*. There is no such thing as *'the'* habitus. We know that different faculties develop their own habitual little quirks: the medics, the jurists, the economists, certainly the theologians and probably the educationists as well (see Alheit, 1995). I am very interested in these differences and I will be looking at them in the course of my chapter. But first of all I want to focus on the broad experience of a group of students, with whom I have – in the frame of an international basic research project and three follow-up studies with a practical orientation – been working intensively over the past ten years.[1] The group was one we in our international research team called 'non-traditional adult students'[2] (see definition below) – people who have come to the university after pursuing a career or women who have been child rearing and who spontaneously experience this institution as 'strange', 'removed from reality' and 'arrogant'.

German universities – as our international comparative studies research identified[3] – are surrounded by an aura of exclusiveness, regardless of what one studies. People coming to the university from non-academic professional milieus are beset by feelings of inferiority when they attend degree courses. They feel stupid, too old, inflexible and somehow just not belonging. There does, therefore, seem to be a 'university habitus', a symbolic power of knowledge surrounding the weird fuss about the excellence of German universities. And that distinguishes them from Danish, Swedish or Finnish universities, and even more so from the universities in Great Britain.

But this does not mean that 'non-traditionals' will fail. Some develop – in Foucault's sense – such successful 'technologies of self' (Foucault, 2004) so that

---

1   LLP project, Access and Retention: Experiences of Non-Traditional Learners in HE (RANLHE- 135230-LLP-1-2007-1-UK-KA1-KAISCR)
     Grundtvig projects: Promoting Reflective Independent Learning in Higher Education (PRILHE - 113869-CP-1-2004-1-UK-GRUNDTVIG-G1); Learning in Higher Education (LIHE -100703-CP-1-2002-1-UK-GRUNDTVIG-G1)
     TSER project, University Adult Access Policies and Practices Across the European Union and their Consequences for the Participation of Non-Traditional Students (SOE2-CT97-2021)
2   A new mature student entrant (by age in respective countries) with no previous HE qualifications whose participation in HE is constrained by structural factors.
3   See footnote 1.

they manage the hurdles of exclusion without any problems. It means however that studying in Germany – and by no means only for the 'non-traditionals' – has become a subtle challenge and that this condition is becoming more acute.

True, this hidden hypothesis must be empirically proved. I am going to put forward four interesting 'anchor cases' of so-called 'gate-keepers'[4] of university faculty cultures. These are actors who provide a 'frame' for students in counselling, and moderating and therefore have a forceful effect on their status passage to study. They make transparent in different ways what could be termed the symbolic power of knowledge.

After discussing the case studies I examine the notion of a 'university habitus' which can be universalised – quite aside from the faculty cultures – in the German university system.

2. 'Gate-keeping' in faculty cultures

When I speak of faculty cultures I take up a plausible concept of Becher (1987), who combined the categories *'pure'* verses *'applied'* and *'hard'* verses *'soft'* as heuristic aids to a four-field table (see Fig. 1):

Figure 1: Four-field scheme of the faculty cultures (according to Becher, 1987)

categories	'hard'	'soft'
'pure'	e.g. physics, chemistry, biology, mathematics	e.g. history, philosophy, literature
'applied'	e.g. mechanical engineering, electrical engineering	e.g. social sciences, education, social work etc.

The *natural sciences* recognise the combination *'hard'/'pure'*. Their method of understanding is described as cumulative, fragmented, universalist, quantitative, simplifying and abstracting. The goal of knowledge is the discovery and causal explanation. Its social forms are seen as convergent, closely linked, politically well organised, competitive and goal-orientated. The scientific output is a high rate of publication. Physics, chemistry, biology and mathematics are seen as typical representatives of this.

In the combinations *'soft'/'pure'* the *classical sciences* and parts of the social sciences are to be found – with the distinguishing mark of being holistic, idiographic, particularising and case-oriented, qualitative and complicating. The goal of knowledge is understanding and interpretation. The social forms are divergent, individualistic, loosely structured and person-orientated. The rate of

4 Cf Behrens & Rabe-Kleberg, 2000; Struck, 2001 (already White, 1950).

publication is by comparison relatively low. History, theology, English literature, philosophy, but also partial areas as in sociology are seen as typical representatives of this.

For the combination *'hard'/'applied'* we have the *technical sciences*, which are goal-centred and pragmatic, functional and effective, also heuristic and concerned with quantity and which intervene in the physical environment. The goal of their knowledge is the development and application of techniques and products. They are described as entrepreneur-like and cosmopolitan, role-orientated with professional norms. Patents count here in lieu of the rate of publication. Mechanical and electrical engineering are seen as typical representatives.

The combination *'soft'/'applied'* stands finally for the *applied social sciences*. They have an orientation in terms of both function and practice. It is a matter of professional practice in interactions. The goal is the drawing up of reports and procedural plans. They are aimed externally, locally linked and for the most part directed at government. Instead of publications counselling is often at the forefront. Typical representatives here are social work and social education, the education sciences in their teaching aspects and to some extent jurisprudence as well.

This arrangement is of course rather rough and stereotyped. It does not cover all subject cultures evenly. It is difficult to place in these fields the complex phenomenon of the medical faculty culture. The increasing significance of the economic sciences cannot be covered properly in this scheme either. Nevertheless, the arrangement does give us the opportunity of an initial approach which facilitates our dealing with the case studies referred to above. The case studies involved interviews with experts, in each case four representatives of the faculty cultures described.

2.1 'Hard' and 'pure': The 'exclusive habitus'

Professor Schmidt is a highly renowned representative of natural scientific psychology at a traditional university with a historical reputation. He describes his scientific career as follows:

> *Well, H-town is really the end of a long way. I have already had chairs at many other universities. I studied in Hamburg, did my doctor's degree and got my post-doctoral qualification in Kiel and then became professor for psychology. Then I had various offers – at the TH Aachen, then at the University of Düsseldorf. That is where I had my first chair. Then I was offered a professorship back in Aachen. Then I had here, erm, here again a chair, but the people at Aachen called me back again. And from there in, erm, 1982 I was called to H-town. In between I was called to Würzburg, well, before*

that I did work at a number of other universities and finally I just found myself here in H-town. But then, that was because I really wanted to come here. Well, that's it really, that's the way things went.[5]

Successful scientific careers in a 'pure' and 'hard' faculty seem to require a 'long way'. But it is not the experiences which are made on this way which are significant, but clearly the quantity of the stations. Our hero accumulates eight calls for a professorship. Insiders know that this, particularly since his third call, means not only 'intellectual' but also 'economic capital'. But that is not the point for 'Herr Schmidt'. He gives the impression – notwithstanding the reputation he has acquired – of being fairly reserved. True, it appears to him to be important to emphasise his third call as his 'first chair'. All the other ones are of course further 'chairs'. His coquetry with the *just found myself here* at the end of the passage is a deliberate understatement. H-town is the crowning of an extremely successful career. Here he builds up a research institute with an international reputation and he trebles the number of people working in his subject. Schmidt finds his self-esteem by no means just by his own achievements. It is the subject itself which marks him out:

Our faculty is very popular, er, we can only take every fourth student. And they are all well above average. You've got to be firm in the saddle in the natural sciences, erm, statistics for example, plays a central part here. Basic knowledge in mathematics is also an important prerequisite. The English language too is essential for us because most of the literature is written in English today. The Germans too write mostly in English. In other words, our demands on the students are high. We have a reputation to lose.[6]

Mr Schmidt has fantasies of exclusiveness. His ideal students belong to the scientific elite as he uses criteria such as: *'firm in the saddle in the natural sciences'*, *'basic knowledge in mathematics'*, *'the English language'*. His experience with 'non-traditionals' makes him sceptical as to whether the older students can fulfil the high demands of the faculty. As proof of this he gives two examples:

I remember two ladies. One, I think, had not quite finished, who after a period of study which had lasted much too long, with dreadful, really a dreadful amount of effort, has done her best to finish. I think

---

5   Transcript Schmidt (2002, unpublished), p. 1.
6   Ibid, p. 5.

she'll probably manage it, but it's real torture and what comes out in the end will probably be pretty under-average. Another has just given up. We tried to make her change her mind. She had got quite a long way. She had written, er, a diploma thesis, which she really couldn't manage. We gave her a hand, er, just as far as we could. But then she said she really didn't want to carry on with this stress.[7]

The picture of the *dreadful amount of effort* points clearly to the desirable alternative: the highly intelligent student who tackles the considerable demands of the faculty with interest and without any problems. The dimension of the 'hard' and the 'pure' has without doubt a male connotation. Women are under-represented in such faculties. So it is not surprising that Herr Schmidt can think of *two ladies* who failed to meet these demands. But even the social gesture of *giving a hand* has a patriarchal basis and carries a pejorative note.

Professor Schmidt is a vigorous exponent of the excellence initiative at his university. His wish is for his subject to be able, in the near future, to choose its students itself. 'Non-traditionals' would then certainly be welcome – provided that they fulfil all the criteria facing the elite of the normal students. Mr Schmidt is interested in 'exclusiveness'.

2.2 'Soft' and 'pure': The 'ambivalent habitus'
Professor Mueller is a theoretically oriented sociologist at a place with a high reputation in his subject at a classical university. His career is certainly not as brilliant as that of Mr Schmidt. But he has also applied for various *'chairs'*, although not always with success. He attributes the failure of his ambitions to the fact that, as he puts it himself, he comes *'from a left-wing corner'*. He makes it his business to bring his faculty, which also on account of his 'left-wing' profile only has a marginal position, more into the centre of attention. And that he seems to have achieved:

And now the position is that our subject and our faculty is in the first place no longer an outsider, is no longer out in the wings and secondly has given up the left-wing profile. It has become more normal and therefore more recognised.[8]

One could see this process as a subtle move towards conformity, since the change of profile of the subject also has effects on teaching. Professor Mueller states that students in previous years were more politically involved, but in a scientific sense not really enlightened. It is now in his opinion a matter of raising

---

7   Ibid, p. 8.
8   Transcript Mueller (2003, unpublished), p. 4.

the scientific demands and presenting a clear *'curricular structure'*. This is particularly relevant in the case of mature students, who do bring in important experiences, but who often cannot let go of these experiences. They must therefore have a firm methodical scientific grounding and also intensive training in sociological theory. *'Sociology is not social work and not spontaneous action either'*, says Mueller, *'but a demanding science calling for intelligent and responsible students'*.

An unconventionally pretentious attitude can be detected in these statements. It is not the straightforward distinctive exclusiveness of Professor Schmidt. Mueller firmly emphasises that sociology must remain open for unconventional student careers. But between the lines one notices a sort of socially implied 'excellence bias' – which is however fatal for the 'non-traditionals'. They experience a climate in the faculty full of double-bind messages: *'You are welcome, but not, if you please, the way you are.'* The faculty habitus is ambivalent. The socio-political openness of the faculty is countered by the studied concern for institutional recognition.

2.3 *'Hard' and 'applied': The 'pragmatic habitus'*

Professor Markert is a 'hands-on' person. What concerns him is the subject, not his own person. In his self-presentation he does not talk about his career, but he constructs, as it were, his 'world':

> *Okay, my special subject is here Technical Mechanics. I myself, er, studied Mechanical Engineering with all theoretical branches of mechanics.*
> *Mechanical engineering is divided up into a large number of special subjects. I'd say the most important branches of engineering are on the one side construction, on the other calculation and perhaps on a third side the science of materials. And for me, well, I'd fall into calculation with my special subject – and of course inside calculation into the theoretical groundwork.*
> *Mechanics is a subject coming from physics, and physics belongs to the natural sciences. The natural sciences describe nature. But the engineering sciences, they do not only describe nature, but change nature somehow. Engineers build machines for example and buildings, and mechanical engineers build machines for some purpose. And for this they need the principles of physics, especially the principles of mechanics. Mechanics is, er, the science of movement. Movement covers also the special case of non-movement. This is a partial area of mechanics, which one calls statics. Statics is, well, a very broad area, which is handled by construction engineers – because buildings are supposed to move about as little as possible.*

In mechanical engineering on the other hand there is a lot more movement, that's why there is a lot of interest in so-called dynamics, another area we have to cope with. This means that the subject which I represent is so to speak in the middle, connecting natural sciences and the practice of engineering.[9]

In this fascinating account of the world one cannot help but be reminded of an association from the kindergarten, that convincing statement of Gyro Gearloose: *'To the engineer it's always clear'* (rough translation of a famous self-ironic joke-rhyme in German: *'Dem Ingenieur ist nichts zu schwör.'*). And yet one does not get the impression from Mr Markert that he wants to claim with it any exclusiveness for his subject. It is a matter of 'feasibility' and – interestingly – also of 'maintenance'. This metaphor (which, by the way, also touches an educational utopia) expresses empathy for the subject, a certain love for the subject, which possibly takes away some of its 'hardness'.

Perhaps it is no accident that Markert's remarks on teaching, and particularly with regard to students with unconventional educational backgrounds, display a similar outlook. He emphasises at the outset how important to him the students are who bring practical experience with them. *'That is a fantastic prerequisite for our work climate'*, he says. But he does not neglect to say that this group as a rule shows considerable gaps in knowledge, especially in mathematics. His way of handling this problem is however neither distinctive nor pretentious, but pragmatic. He sets up so-called *'bridging courses... which'*, as he says, *'bridge the gap between school and the requirements of the university'*.[10]

The picture of the bridge is certainly not chosen at random. It is a central symbol of the engineer's art, but the metaphor takes over the function of *'communication'*: communication between science and practice. There is behind this 'bridge-building' by no means just a project related to the subject, but a social one too. Professor Markert proves that he is therefore also a successful 'engineer in matters of university didactics'.

2.4 'Soft' and 'applied': The 'inclusive habitus'
The fourth 'gatekeeper', Mr Graf, is typically not a professor. He does not even have a doctor's degree and works as a teaching social worker at a reform university:

I am a social worker by background: first of all Abitur, then I studied social work, was a social worker for some years, had here contact

---

9   Transcript Markert (2002, unpublished), p. 1f.
10   Ibid, p. 7.

with the university through projects with students, as supervisor and then found myself here in the reform process of the university.[11]

The formulation *'a social worker by background'* shows more than a professional placing. The statement could almost be read as social positioning. Graf was, as he emphasises, *'for 20 years a consultant for professional practice studies'*[12]. And he identifies himself in his present position as the *'Dean's consultant'* still with the social work 'milieu of origin'. In his description of the professional field he displays a similar empathy like Professor Markert in Engineering. However, it is not 'feasibility' which is with him in the forefront, but 'responsibility'. *'For this profession you must have a certain amount of experience in life and above all a sense of responsibility'*[13], he says. And this is precisely what in his opinion qualifies unconventional students for study. But Graf does not deny the problems of this special group:

> *Well, one of the greatest problems we have is the key qualification, which means handling texts. Students with professional experience cannot do this at all. And we face difficulties here right up to the exam... And the other thing is this vagueness. We do not have here any leading subject, there is no science of social work, though there is a crown of auxiliary sciences which one can draw upon from all sciences. Anyone studying here will be first of all completely confused... and there is no foundation there for understanding that.*[14]

Graf describes the problems, however he does not place the responsibility with the students, but with structural dilemmas of the subject, and he develops an idea about the way in which these difficulties can be resolved:

> *Well, my theory is, and I come from the field of practice myself, that in social work and everywhere where it's a matter of developments, of educational processes, that there relationships play an important part. .. My strategy is, I manage to establish a relationship with the students, which makes it possible for them to accept me as a model on the one hand and on the other for them to want to show: 'I can do that too.' Perhaps this would in former times been called educational tact, I call it building up relationships and it works.*[15]

---

11   Transcript Graf (2003, unpublished), p. 1.
12   Ibid., p. 2.
13   Ibid., p. 5.
14   Ibid., p. 10.
15   Ibid., p. 14.

'Educational tact' is a wonderful characterisation for a habitus, which can only be described as 'inclusive'.

3. The draw of the university's social space

It might seem reasonable to compare systematically the four habitus configurations laid out above and to qualify them from an educational standpoint. But that would not get us very far from a sociological point of view. We did not have to wait for Bourdieu's amusing polemical study on the *Homo Academicus* (1988) to discover that there are different places of rank in a relationship matrix. Physics and increasingly the neuro-sciences are at the forefront, while social education and social work come right at the bottom (cf Alheit, Rheinländer & Watermann, 2008).

In other words, the 'inclusive habitus' of a gatekeeper in social welfare, which is probably most attractive to ourselves, must be qualified against the backcloth of the low prestige of the subject which exercises little influence. The *'exclusive habitus'* of the natural science psychologist links up with the prestige of the 'powerful subjects' and shines out therefore over the whole university field. We can observe this influence very clearly in the *'ambivalent habitus'* of the sociologist, who achieves the growing recognition of his subject only through conforming or, as he puts it himself, through *'normalisation'*.

If we imagine the social space of the university once more and, following Bourdieu, identify the symbolic capital which relates to the subject cultures, then the four-field diagram presented at the outset turns into a convincing educational and power-political figure of relationships (Figure 2, page 170).

The 'soft' subject cultures, which certainly have cultural capital, fall clearly back behind the 'hard' subject cultures, which have much more social capital and not only inside the university field. Parameters outside the university – such as the support policies of the German Research Foundation or the new government initiatives of excellence – support the process of segregation, which itself produces a *'prestige suction'* in the direction of the 'exclusive habitus', which is just turning into the *'university habitus'*.

I would like in conclusion to make this clear with an empirical observation, which has to do with this group of 'non-traditional students' (cf Alheit, 2005) which we have been researching and thinking about (see Figure 3, page 170):

Peter Alheit

Figure 2: The social space of the subject cultures

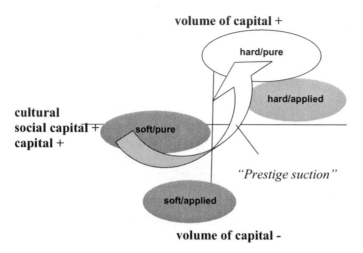

Figure 3: Entrance channels of 'non-traditionals'

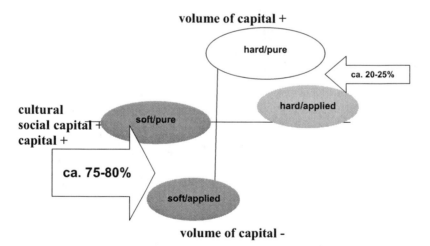

It is by no means surprising that the great majority of the 'non-traditionals' opt for the subjects with low prestige. Provocative, however, is the fact that in this group's success in study is lower than with those who choose the hard subjects (cf Alheit & Merrill, 2004; Alheit, 2005; Alheit, Rheinlaender & Watermann, 2008). The reason given by those concerned is to be found in the irritating double-bind messages which we met in the analysis of the *'ambivalent habitus'*, those hidden claims of exclusiveness which are covered up by superficial offers of opening. In other words, the 'prestige suction' towards exclusiveness damages the climate of study also in the soft subjects. The *'university habitus'* is clearly a ubiquitous phenomenon at German universities.

References

Alheit, P. (1995). Patchworkers: Biographical constructions and professional attitudes - Study motivations of adult education students In: P., Alheit, et al. (Eds.) *The Biographical Approach in European Adult Education*. Vienna: Edition Volkshochschule, pp. 212-231.

Alheit, P. (2005). Passungsprobleme: Zur Diskrepanz von Institution und Biographie – Am Beispiel des Übergangs so genannter nicht-traditioneller Studenten ins Universitätssystem' In: H., Arnold, L., Böhnisch,.and W., Schröer, (Eds.) *Sozialpädagogische Beschäftigungsförderung. Lebensbewältigung und Kompetenz-entwicklung im Jugend- und jungen Erwachsenenalter*. Weinheim, Munich: Juventa, pp. 159-172.

Alheit, P. and Merrill, B. (2004) Biography and narratives. Adult returners to learning. In: M., Osborne, J., Gallacher, and B., Crossan (Eds.) *Researching Widening Access to Lifelong Learning. Issues and approaches in international research*. London, New York: Routledge Falmer, pp. 150-162.

Alheit, P., Rheinlaender, K. and Watermann, R. (2008). Zwischen Bildungsaufstieg und Karriere. Studienperspektiven nicht-traditioneller Studierender In: *Zeitschrift für Erziehungswissenschaft*

Becher,T. (1987). Disciplinary Discourse In: *Studies in Higher Education*, Vol. 12, pp. 261-274.

Behrens, J. And Rabe-Kleberg, U. (2000). Gatekeeping im Lebenslauf – Wer wacht an Statuspassagen? Ein forschungspragmatischer Vorschlag, vier Typen von Gatekeeping aufeinander zu beziehen In: E. M. Hoerning (Ed.) *Biographische Sozialisation*. Stuttgart: Lucius and Lucius, pp. 101-136.

Bourdieu, P. (1988). Homo academicus. Frankfurt/M.: Suhrkamp.

Foucault, M. (2004). *Sicherheit, Territorium, Bevoelkerung. Geschichte der Gouvernementalität I*. Frankfurt/M.: Suhrkamp.

Struck, O. (2001). 'Gatekeeping zwischen Individuum, Organisation und Institution. Zur Bedeutung und Analyse von Gatekeeping am Beispiel von Übergaengen im Lebenslauf' In: L. Leisering, R. Mueller, and K. Schumann, (Eds.) *Institutionen und Lebensläufe im Wandel. Institutionelle Regulierungen von Lebensläufen*. Weinheim: DSV, pp. 29-54.

White, D.M. (1950). 'The 'Gate-Keeper': A Case Study in the Selection of News'. In: *Journalism Quarterly*, Vol. 27, pp. 383-390.

12 Practicing Critical, Reflexive and Autonomous Learning Among Students of Higher Education. A Polish Case Study

Ewa Kurantowicz and Adrianna Nizińska

Higher education is now one of the most dynamically changing social institutions in Polish society. The changes touch legal, economic and cultural aspects. The first concerns ownership transformations (e.g. setting up public universities). The second, ways of financing education and scientific research (e.g. tasks connected with self-financing of schools, payment for studies and economic calculation based on the profits and losses of an educational institution). The third change is connected with the sphere of values and ideas of a 'university' as practiced within institutions of higher education (e.g. professionalisation and the vocational shaping of academic education).

What is rarely discussed in Poland is what changes institutions of higher education should undergo in relation to pedagogy and in what ways working with students should be transformed. The discourse on the process of learning in higher education institutions is somehow absent, and as a result changes in teaching approaches take place very slowly. They are only introduced through the commitment of young academics or through new technological approaches. In practice they are usually implemented without reflection or in non-compliance with any system of teaching activity (e.g. the project or portfolio methods). What are the reasons for the lack of a serious debate on learning in higher education institutions in Poland? Why is this problem ignored? The most frequently heard answer is that 'students are adults' and this is used as a justification for not changing teaching approaches in higher education. We think that the debate on these issues in Poland is still not seen as a crucial one, but as second-rate. The difficulties of making such a debate public are rooted deeply in the mentality of both academic teachers as well as higher education students.

The lack of discussion can be caused by a tacit knowledge/ reception and cultural *a priori* consolidation of a 'proper' definition of the concept of learning as an instrumental process, based on acquiring, remembering and recreation of information given by an expert/teacher. Referring to critical theory one can say that the domination of such a vision of learning is a derivative of the domination of instrumental and technological rationality over communicative rationality: Polish social sciences are still dominated by a positivistic discourse, despite the presence of alternative paradigms.

The research on Promoting Reflective Independent Learning in Higher Education (PRILHE)[1] project made it possible to gain information about critical,

---

1   The project involves seven countries: The UK, Germany, Poland, Sweden, Spain, Finland

autonomous and reflective learning in relation to Polish non-traditional students who studied in higher education at a time when the latter were rather unstable, even revolutionary or, being more precise - 'refolutionary' (from reforms). Partners in the PRILHE project produced quantitative and qualitative reports based on empirical research which emphasised how different contexts and experiences of academic practice in various European countries may determine the very course of reflective, critical and autonomous learning and its promotion.

In this paper we want to present a Polish context of Critical Autonomous Reflective Learning (CARL[2]) learning and its role in higher education institutions. Using the literature review produced by the project and the interviews and learning diaries of the Polish participants in the PRILHE project we will use a qualitative approach to interpret our data.

Between cultural and economic order: the Polish context of higher education

Three spheres of transition in the Polish higher education system can be identified: the most general is connected with social and economic transitions; the second one is connected with higher education institutions themselves, while the last one is connected with the learning of individuals in these institutions. These transitions occur at three levels: macro, meso and micro. This approach was taken by Bourgeois, Duke, Guyot, Merrill (1999) and also Johnston and Merrill (2005) in a handbook written for a Socrates Grundtvig EU project *'Learning in Higher Education: Improving Practice for Non-traditional Students'*.

In the Polish context the biggest transitional spaces are the events between 1980 and 1989 which brought about changes in Poland. In the analyses of different phenomena we cannot (we do not want?) to become 'detached' from these events. We think that these significant social events had, and still have a crucial impact on higher education institutions as they are an element of the wider social system as well as the mentality of adult learners. However, the

---

and Portugal. The key objectives are to identify the learning processes which enable non-traditional adult students in higher education to become reflective independent learners through examining study skills, self management, learning to learn as well as analysing learning and teaching styles. The project is focused on non-traditional undergraduate adult students, which is why one of the most important aims is identifying and examining the relation between learning from everyday life experience and learning in higher education.

2   The project team reviewed the terminology of the project title (Promoting Reflective Independent Learning in Higher Education) during the period of the project to reflect more closely what the voices and experiences of adult students and lecturers were telling and used instead Critical Autonomous Reflective Learning (CARL).

changes and their effects which took place in 1980 and later after 1989 differ in principle from one another despite the fact that they were shaped by the same social forces.

Summarising briefly, there were two crucial features of the transition in 1980: the strategy which consisted of transforming society (but not taking over the power) and also the introduction of the ethical dimension in public and political activity (Koczanowicz 2005, p. 123 - 124). In contrast, the transition year of 1989 was concerned mainly with the transformation of the political and economic systems. It can be stated that the effects of these decisive years were embedded in two different social spheres: the cultural and the economic. The effects of the transformations of 1980 are visible in the system of values (individual and socially shared) and cultural models based on co-operation and trust in others, and on the category and hierarchy of social actors. In 1989, however, the changes and their effects are more visible in the sphere of everyday life practice, both in the social and individual dimensions. Economic transformations connected with categories such as ownership, work, financial resources, etc. created new divisions in society which resulted from the economic value of an individual or a group rather than from their cultural background. Many researchers of modern Polish reality state that the achievements and effects of the first turn (1980) are shaded (often replaced) by the effects of the second one (1989). In our chapter we will restrict ourselves exclusively to the nearest and local perspective.

Significant enlightenment and emancipation traditions of European universities constitute a cultural context of their functioning. However, in the 20th century this context was clearly changed and the changes altered the role of science, knowledge and scientists in the modern world. The crisis of the enlightenment notion of truth as the target of education was replaced instead by pragmatism, commercialisation, marketing rules for the functioning of universities, individualisation and reshaping university career of scholars and scientists as well as the idea of universality of higher education. All these factors are bringing on drastic transformations in the world of academia. In Western Europe these transformations of higher education have been gradually growing since the 1960s and in Poland within the last 15 years, which undoubtedly has represented a cultural shock for our society (Malewski, 2000). The result of these transformations is the dramatic increase in the number of higher education institutions. Until 1990 in Poland there were 126 higher schools - exclusively public institutions. By 2004 there were already 427 higher schools, including 301 non-public (owned by associations, foundations, enterprises, private owners).

Higher education in the perspective of the cultural and economic consequences of the transformations in years between 1980 and 1989

The transformation in 1980 maintained the high position of traditional university professors in the ranking of social status and trust. It was believed that academic knowledge as a target of business activity of an institution of higher education is an autotelic value fostering freedom and the discovery of truth as well as undertaking tasks of an emancipatory character (Malewski, 1999). This type of myth was sustained also by the organisation and policy of higher education institutions. It is worth emphasising that higher education up to 1989 was of a selective character. The limited number of higher education institutions, the limited number of students and admission regulations created numerous barriers to accessing higher education. This was despite the fact that the former communist authorities used the idea of promoting widening access to people from the working and peasant classes (so-called preferential points were given for people from the working and peasant classes)[3]. However, this remained mainly at the level of propaganda, because in reality the number of students from these backgrounds did not change. On the other hand, this exclusivity was one of the factors which ensured high social status (prestige and respect) to institutions of higher education, and to academic teachers as well as to graduates.

After 1990 higher education in Poland started its 'adventure' with the free educational market. The effects are very diverse. The growing non-public institutions of higher education have to compete with public ones and either had to adhere to the existing academic myth or create a new image for higher education institutions within the new conditions of political and economic transformation. There was an educational boom which took place in the second half of the 1990s which increased student numbers - from 500,000 in 1990 to about 2,000,000 in 2005. Paradoxically, the problems on the job market (the necessity for training and improvement) and the possibility of enriching educational opportunities through these institutions increased the importance of higher education, but students chose higher education mostly for instrumental reasons rather than for autotelic motives. Employment prospects (future, present, lost) became very often the main factor and criterion by which an individual chose their subject of study in higher education. However, at the same time it did make higher education more accessible.

We wish to concentrate on the micro dimension: on the learning of students in higher education institutions. The students experience a period of instability, searching for self-identification in the overlapping cultural and economic orders, in which they have to function. Institutions of higher education - formerly solid,

---

3   Act of higher education as of 31 March 1965

stable and sustaining historical and cultural continuity - become a transitional space.

Being an adult student in HE - Polish students' stories: Developing as an independent/autonomous reflective learner

Researching adult students in higher education revealed how they developed significantly as independent/ autonomous reflective learners. First of all, adult students stress a different attitude towards their self. In the interviews they told stories about how they became aware of their self and role outside of higher education in the family or work environment and how they started to see themselves as a mentor, guardian or a critic. This new path they followed was influenced by the educational challenges they were experiencing and even if this 'awakening of a new consciousness' was not a part of the official curriculum, it was definitely a side affect of becoming an adult student. Very often this particular way of 're-inventing' oneself also helps the student to realise how valuable their life experience may be and what kind of benefits they can get from it:

> *What I mean is that already now, that is, I am the oldest when it comes to age and with life experience and these young people who have various problems come to me for, as I think of it, some amateur advice, but not only because I am older than them, but also because they know that I study such a subject. And, privately, I have such a young neighbour who has some problems with his parents, I mean his mother has problems with abusing alcohol. The boy is 20 years old and is slowly getting entangled in this environment. Also he comes to me and he has nowhere to go and no-one to talk to, I help him.* (SW nr 1)

Another way of understanding the concept of independence is a new look at the idea of learning. Students who were interviewed very often talked about how they realised that there is more than one way of learning. They have not only learnt how to collect materials on their own or select teaching materials but also to listen to other students and refer to their experiences. Some of the students stop at this level of creating their understanding of being an independent/ autonomous learner, but for others it is just a step to another level - one can have not just different attitudes to learning in itself, but also towards knowledge. Some interviewed students pointed out that they have discovered that knowledge can be created jointly through discussion and not solely by written text:

That is, while doing a Bachelor's degree I became convinced that education opens the door to the world and despite everything, it is possible to change oneself, to learn and get to know. Because, before doing the degree I thought that I already knew everything, and if so, only some courses, training workshops about working with children. This gives me knowledge and improves my qualifications. But, when I was doing the bachelor degree, then suddenly my orientation to this changed. The outcome was completely different and therefore it was easier to start these studies because I knew that it would somehow be translated into my outlook about the world. (SW nr 3)

What I like most here is that there are mostly lectures. What I like is that you can be very creative during classes, that you can say something wise yourself on the basis of your own experiences or on the basis of literature, you can show here your creativity, you can create a theory/concept which will be adopted by the others or which can be discussed. We do not base only on a concrete bibliography - from literature we have to read this and we only base on it - the truth still takes place on the basis of a free discussion and this is the nicest thing as we learn most from this. (SK nr 3)

Thoughts about how they are developing their skills to learn independently on their own are also in the student's diary:

The history lecturer is amazing! He really knows what he means and here it is very rare... I can't wait to get infected by his knowledge. I admire him and would like to know all this. At home I take 'The History of Silesia' and I read and read, nothing will stop me - the book is fascinating! Tomorrow I will start writing the paper he told us to do, but maybe I could start already today? I'm off to the library, museum and I search, but with such a determination, that my feet start burning...! Oh no, I'd better slow down... I have to stop, otherwise I'll exhaust myself.

What a group I have.... Only 'stars and starlets'. Everyone fights to get a chance to talk, they kill each other with their eyes, generally the atmosphere is dull. My wallet has become very thin due to the constant buying of presents and flowers for the lecturers - all these are ideas of our prefect and her assistant. Bribery is the first step to hell according to me...they don't want to learn, they only think of collecting money and of meetings...they say that it has got a purpose - less stress. The lecturers are then 'relaxed' and appreciated and our plans turn out well. Total rubbish! I'm getting fed up with this. Next time I don't give any cash, I will be condemned. But I don't care about that, as a matter of fact I study here in order to learn something and be a little wiser than them [other students]

Learning and teaching approaches

Many of the students in their interviews told stories about how they have moved from the point when they were scared and full of doubt about whether they can manage learning at an academic level to the moment when they realised that they are completely capable of accomplishing it. They were getting rid of some old habits, brought from primary and secondary schools, and opening up towards new ways of learning, and this time - not like their early educational experience - they have had a chance to develop their own, very individual strategies. Their creativity was stimulated and their personal interests in particular subjects engaged them. Once they realised that learning does not have to be just about memorising theories they have more flexibility in perceiving potential sources of improving their learning and making it easier, for example, by using their prior life experiences from different fields to enrich the process of learning.

Another important issue for adult students was the learning atmosphere, as many students stressed how different it is to be part of a learning community where freedom of speech and ideas are appreciated, wanted and respected and how it contrasts to their experiences and memory of initial education:

At the beginning maybe not all the lecturers; but they spoke quickly and my hand was not used to it, as I spend all the time at the computer, so I couldn't keep up with writing. I was accumulating something in my head and I thought that I would never take any notes. This was terrible at the beginning. Then I tried to write only key words, but this depends on lecturers, because when he lectured in a nice way I remembered a lot of things… And sometimes if something was not OK and I lost the plot then I lost most of the lecture and this was one thing. But, I say, it was at the beginning, in fact the first year was like that. (SK nr 4)

Nobody disturbs me, nobody discriminates against me in any way and generally speaking I'm glad, about lecturers, because I have noticed here a little that such trends are more dominant here - there is freedom in this school, isn't there? I have noticed here that here critical theory is promoted. I mean here Habermas and the Frankfurt school. And, because I'm very interested in it, and, because, you know, I really like it that here are, as a matter of fact, it seems to me that there are such trends to freedom. And, you know, that for example, during classes you can say what you really think. (SW nr 4)

Some subjects are easier, more understandable, but in others there are some new words, concepts, for example, when we are starting this logic now, then your brain stops working correctly. And the course History of Pedagogical Thought is a cool thing and interesting, as it somehow relates to history, to some things that you know. You listen to it as if to some fairytales. While learning, what helps is that first of all I have to understand what it is about. I don't like such things when somebody talks to me with some words which I don't understand and do not know at all what he is aiming at. (SW nr 6)

Learning with others

Besides the learning process, the social dimension of becoming an adult student seems to be very important to the interviewees. Because of the age diversity some of the students were anxious at first about fitting into a mixed group, finding a position within it and finding some level of understanding with others. Day by day they experienced a lot of help from each other in terms of organisational matters (travelling, learning/teaching materials, communication in transferring information). But what was rather less usual and less frequent was joint studying of the teaching/learning contents, probably due to the distances between their home towns and cities. On the other hand, this distance makes logistic cooperation between the students from the same groups even more important, because they were dependent on each other in case of longer absence. For example, being given notes, teaching materials, or information they missed while absent.

Another benefit of the mixed group seems to be the synergy produced by a diversified group - different points of view, different levels of experience, peer evaluation. It was not only about getting help from other people, it was also about learning by being with others:

I got on well with the young people and it seems to me that they also accepted me, as they come or sometimes they call me at work: "Listen, have you got maybe the topics or this or that, can I come and make a copy". So I see that we get on well and they are not afraid, as they could go to other young people instead, couldn't they, but they come to me. So I understand this as being that they have accepted me, too. (SK nr 4)

This means that I feel good, I have nice female schoolmates, I'm the only man in the group and generally speaking I feel very good. (W nr 4)

You know, in our group there are younger and older students than me, but the communication is very good. We all get on well, we all help each other, all of us lend notes to each other, make copies, call each other, exchange materials, so there are no problems. (SK nr 3)

Also I was a little afraid what it will look like, as, you know, my age is...how to say it, there is a big age difference and I was afraid of such a clash with these young people. How we will cooperate? Yet, we cooperate very well, we understand each other and we are so relaxed that..., it means I generally like such young people ... How I perceive it is that in such a mixed group I have a possibility of a viewpoint...let's assume how I approach at this age generally the teaching and studying at all. For example, being present during lectures. (SW nr2)

Relationship with lecturers

Most of the interviewees evaluate their contact with lecturers in a very positive way. This impression of being surrounded by nice, friendly, helpful people was even more astonishing for the students because of certain expectations they had, based on their previous educational experience. Students not only valued lecturers according to their professional knowledge, but also very often because of their attitude, openness, availability, readiness for a partnership and interest in students' personal lives and problems they were facing. That was probably the reason that students complimented such 'human – oriented' lecturers for possessing all the required skills and having more influence on the students than those of their lecturers with a 'profession-oriented' attitude:

I am completely amazed because I have such not nice memories, particularly from the secondary school and that is why when I see here what attitude the lecturers have, and even when a lecturer once said very nicely that it is Us who are for You, and not You for Us, this is something totally different from what I had experienced at school. (SK nr 4)

Positively, very positively, I had always been scared that I would not have anything in common with lecturers, with professors, I thought that they are very inaccessible people and what turns out - these people are so warm, so open. What's more, my professor helped me a

lot with my thesis. She knew about my situation. I am really very grateful to her. (SW nr 2)
*As a matter of fact, the contents of the lectures referred to my life's situation and... sometimes I wanted so much to escape from these thoughts, but attending the lectures I come back, I must come back as during lectures I hear things which exactly refer to my situation. But this strengthens me in a different way, I am stronger. (*SW nr 2)

Institutional environment & impact on learning

In this area some students report a lack of information and a problem with contacting school authorities which is important to a student like Deans of different faculties, the Dean of Student Affairs, or the Director. Some of the students would like to engage in a school's scientific life like attending an open lecture with famous professors, seminars and workshops. Their feeling is that university and academic life is more geared towards full-time young students. As a result they feel that part-time adult students do not receive as much institutional support as full-time students.

They also complain about the locality and geography of the campus. Many buildings are separated from each other and from the main building where the administration and Deans' offices are located. This causes some difficulties for adult students. The main building is also where the library is situated. This is an important issue for students from small towns at a distance from the campus. They cannot depend on the library in their own towns because they do not have the academic resources which they need for their studies and many feel bitter about inaccessibility of the library:

I don't know, today I reported such one remark, as I know that the university organises meetings with various professors, but if you are not in Wagonowa street {the main building of the university}*, then you don't know it. And if there had been a notice... because I would have known that there was a meeting with a professor and for sure I would have done my best to have come, but I wasn't. And, actually, if, it would be better, if there was one university building. Yes the buildings are very scattered and I don't like it but apparently there is some necessity for this. But it would be good, if everything were in one place.* (SW nr 3)

Being a part-time student is not an easy task. It takes a lot of skills to combine all aspects of everyday life (finance, partners, family, social life etc.) with the new role, as one can read in the example from one student's diary:

Today I had to be at school by 9.00. As it always happens on Saturdays I have more housework duties. By 9.00 I had done my shopping, prepared breakfast for my children and taken them to my mother-in-law's. My daughter is only 4 and I'm afraid to leave her with my 10-year-old son. And I was late for the lecture. After lectures it is sometimes hard for me to understand why there are so many theories, different definitions and terms that academics use.

When I have classes on Sunday, I always have to find a person who will go with my son to 12 o'clock mass in church. Because my child will take his First Communion this year, the priest checks the attendance of all communion children. Sometimes it is difficult to combine home duties with school and learning. But this day was more pleasant to me than the others as the classes lasted only till 3.15pm and I could come back home to the children more quickly.

Starting my studies cost me so many sacrifices and I have the impression that we are brushed off here. Not even a single teacher was happy that their classes are attended by several students who travel 250 kilometers, instead - every teacher asks us why we come to such a faraway school and whether we are eager to come, because they wouldn't be...

Interaction between public & private life

Polish students seem to be very aware of the connection between their private life and their student activities. Many of them stressed the interaction between learning and family life. Both men and women emphasised the need to sort out family life and fulfill their parental duties and then their studies. An important experience of being an adult student is learning how to cope with everyday life obstacles in order to undertake their studies. The non-traditional Polish students are also aware of the connection between professional life and their studies. They did not only use the knowledge and skills obtained through the university education in their professional life but also some of them expected or experienced professional promotion or at least growth of status in their work as a result of being a student:

I mean my dream has always been to take up studies, I wanted to improve my education, but I had finished a secondary school and took a break. At that time somehow our marriage was very good, I was very satisfied with my work so we had this time for ourselves, in a way. We travelled a lot, we had a lot of friends then, but already then I wanted, it means I had always wanted I said to myself that when I'm over 40 I will start studying. And just then I did it and in

> *this saddest period of time for me, because I was fired after 26 years*
> *of work, but I think that I'm very happy that I am here. In this*
> *difficult period I got a very good support from professors and*
> *lecturers and they helped me with this difficult period, though it*
> *hasn't finished yet for me, has it. But they helped me to overcome it.*
> (SW nr 2)

Learning identity - how it has changed/ is changing

Students, when asked to evaluate their own learning in terms of personal development, present totally different positions. For some of them keeping interest in ideas, theories and concepts they have learnt while studying is a natural consequence of ongoing development processes. Such a way of perceiving their personal development is also an important aspect of becoming a critical and independent learner.

Another example of developing and reconstructing a new learning identity is the ability to use knowledge and theories to achieve a new consciousness, point of view or perspective. This kind of change can also have an impact on the collective identity of the generation, family or community - to see the history in a new light, to re-construct the common identity. For others change was not so deep but was related more to obtaining new skills, such as being well organised and capable of fulfilling many tasks at the same time:

> *I think that I am still changing and developing. I'm more and more*
> *interested in philosophy classes, but also in social psychology. Today*
> *there is going to be the first one, but in philosophy {I am changing*
> *and developing} more and also I'm particularly interested in*
> *philosophy of personalism, and if I want more I have been reading*
> *recently the works of Karol Wojtyła. This is such a small diversion*
> *from work.* (SW nr 1)

> *For sure - this course* {Community Education and Development[4]} *of*
> *studies. This subject of study as, practically, these, you know, these*
> *subjects, which had been really allowed me to understand. This*
> *being in just this, this is living on these territories. I was born here,*
> *but I know that my parents travelled here. And when I go on holiday*

---

4   The student is talking about the course that concerns the history of regions and local communities of Lower Silesia, which, amongst others, refers to resettlements of people organised by the state (often compulsory) after World War II (into western regions, the so-called regained lands) from Eastern and Central Poland.

somewhere in the Zamość or Kielce {East and Central Poland} *regions, I knew that there was something wrong. Because they had never talked about it in the primary school that there are such or such people. There is a town, a community of residents, but we didn't talk about this region* (the history of this region before 1945). (SK nr 1)

Yes, for sure, even if only because I am better organised. It helps me in family life, at work, in professional life. Certainly it works in a way that, despite the fact that Saturday and Sunday are free days, aren't they, then you must get up in the morning and get organised. Be organised all the week, later, taking into account these classes and work and home. Therefore it surely helps, because if a person organises everything, he is so mobile, first of all, and secondly he is so disciplined. (SK nr 3)

It was difficult for me to learn again how to learn, but I care about good marks, mainly because of the children, whom I expect to have good marks at school and university (diary) *Being an adult student is not easy. You must take into account a lot of unfavourable circumstances like a displeased boss, a lonely, neglected spouse, an 'orphan' child and a general lack of free time for yourself.* (diary)
It wasn't easy for me to become a student, so I mustn't allow a failure to happen. Even if I must perform the hated job of a telemarketer, I will always have a satisfaction that it was my choice and my will to study, executing my life plans and developing internally. In my heart of hearts I count on the fact that my studying will be used "for what it is intended" [work as a school counsellor] *I hope that this is not just incurable optimism I dream to work behind the door with an inscription 'School counsellor' ...and then I can be on a diet till the end of my life.*

Conclusion

We want to relate the research results presented in this chapter to the typology of adult students' learning styles. For this we draw on the work of our German partners in the PRILHE project: Peter Alheit and Anissa Henze (Figures 1, 2, pages 188 - 189).
Our data proves that the mentioned types are present also among Polish students. However, we want to focus on a type of learning characteristic that is typical for the Polish context and which emerged in our research but not in the

research findings of other partners in the PRILHE project. Polish non-traditional adult students can be situated between the dependent/reflective dimensions. The dimension of reflectivity refers to the internal transformation of a student, who - taking up tasks connected with learning 'in a new way' discovers their autotelic value and how this is connected with the practice of everyday life.

However, learning also leads a person to reflect on their own life in all its dimensions (personal, professional and family). The stories of those interviewed clearly show this transformation, which can be called an educational shock. The paradox of the Polish type of learning of non traditional adult students consists of the fact that its second dimension is dependence. It can be present in the dependence of a Polish student on 'a traditional vision of university', which inhibits their criticism towards educational institutions. This burden of the inherited 'university idea' is the reason for a rather affirmative relationship towards these institutions. The criticism of higher education institutions is of a 'technological' character and relates to such spheres as: organisation of classes, poor equipment in the teaching rooms, etc. In the sphere of values, knowledge, the process of teaching-learning and the very institution, a significant group of Polish students show significant dependence. This type identified by the research was called by us 'jumping learners' (Figure 3, page 190).

Functioning between reflectivity and dependence are two separate worlds. The first world is one dominated by a critical and reflective attitude while the second world consists of devotion and loyalty towards culturally recognised ideas and values. The first one is a private world, which concerns 'I' and the nearest surroundings. The second one, in contrast, belongs to the public sphere. In the era before 1989, Poles practiced the skill of living in two spaces: private and public, which differed in principle from one another. Perhaps these skills are still used by non traditional adult students in a learning situation. We also think that arguments for supporting this thesis can be found in the findings of a comparative research study on the German, Czech and Polish mentality, undertaken by Alheit (2006) and which has recently been published in Poland. In this research the writers identified the model of Polish mentality in the following way (Figure 4, page 191).

The picture of the Polish mentality indicates two categories that are seemingly contradictory: they are (post)modernism and tradition. The university as an academy, its representatives and creations (knowledge) are perceived by non traditional adult students as being an institution which supports tradition and social continuity. Therefore, the attitude of Polish students towards learning within the space of the university is compatible with the suggested mentality type in Peter Alheit's research:

Mentality... responsible both for the long-term reproduction of structures and for its simultaneous and successive modification, experienced by social actors as internal locus of control. For this reason, mental models of orientation, constitute the principal element of socialisation process. We acquire them through our biographical experiences and compose it into individual structures of biographical knowledge (2006, p. 29).

The link between macro-social mentality and individual biography, shown in the above quotation, is shaped not only by the present, but also by historical experience which is specific to a given country (compare Alheit 2006). In our research which is based on narrative and autobiographic materials this model of mentality is clearly imprinted. Looked at from this perspective it is no wonder that the learner type of 'jumping learners' was found only in the Polish research. Further arguments are provided by the results of Piotr Stańczyk (2007) research. At the present stage of market transformations of higher education the feature of students' **dependence** on the structure and the institution of higher education is rather strengthened than weakened. It is connected with the instrumentalisation of learning and its effects. Stańczyk, who researches meanings given by extramural students to their learning processes at the higher level states that ' of bearing the costs of their own education, in the context of the labour market leads to economisation of meanings given to the studies' (2007, p. 56). On the other hand, the economisation of meanings is supported by the attitude of the academy and its culture, where the market rules make us redefine the social role of university again and again and which, "carrying out the production in the atmosphere of reducing costs and popularisation of education symptomatically approaches the canning factory, moving away from the ideals of freedom, which defined them at the very beginning" (Stańczyk 2007, p.57).

Therefore, does there exist a chance for adult students learning, whose aim will be the change (learning to change), and not the adaptation or instrumentalisation of effects? Is there a hope for 'leaving' by adult students the field of 'dependence' on the institution? The results of our research indicate that students who practice reflection (even if it focuses on their own individual and private life) are able to better resist the culture of higher education institutions.

Figure 1

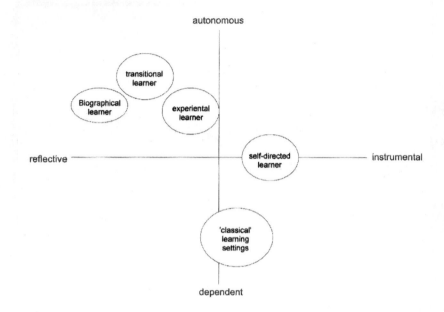

Figure 2

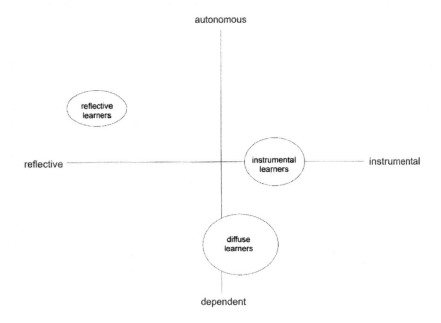

Figure 3

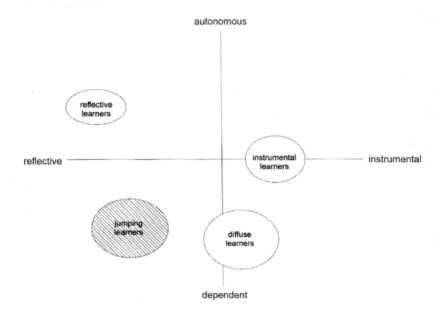

Figure 4

"Jumping learners" and concept of Polish mentality by P. Alheit:

modernisation

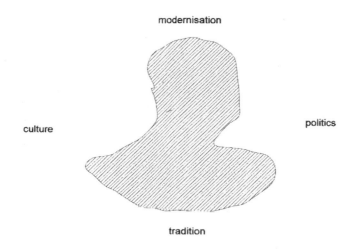

culture   politics

tradition

Scheme of Polish „mentality concentration"

References

Alheit P. (2006). Biografia i mentalność. Narracyjne badania relacji pokoleniowych w Niemczech Wschodnich, Polsce i Czechach: Teraźniejszość Człowiek Edukacja, nr 3 (35) pp 7-33.

Bourgeois E., Duke C., Guyot J.L., and Merrill B. (1999). *The Adult University.* Buckingham: OUP.

Johnston R. and Merrill B. (2005). *Enriching Higher Education: Learning In Higher Education: Improving Practice for Non-traditional Students. A Handbook.* Socrates Grundtvig Adult Education: The University of Warwick.

Koczanowicz L. (2005). *Wspólnota i emancypacje. Spór o społeczeństwo postkonwencjonalne.* Wrocław: Wydawnictwo Naukowe DSWE TWP

Malewski M. (1999). Szkoła i Uniwersytet - odmienność społecznych funkcji, odrębność edukacyjnych światów. *Teraźniejszość Człowiek Edukacja* 2(06), p. 21-34.

Malewski M. (2000). Od misji życiowej do roli zawodowej. O kryzysogennej ewolucji kompetencji w nauce. *Teraźniejszość Człowiek Edukacja* 3(11), p. 77-90.

Stańczyk P. (2007). Wykształcenie, rynek pracy i "lepsze życie" w perspektywie znaczeń nadawanych przez studentów zaocznych. *Teraźniejszość Człowiek Edukacja* 1(37) p.41-58.

13 Building a Knowledge and Learning Society in Portugal: Adult Students in Technological Schools and Higher Education Institutions

Ana Maria Ramalho Correia, Dulce Magalhães de Sá, Ana Cristina Costa, Anabela Sarmento

1. Introduction

Lifelong learning (LLL) has received increasing attention in recent years. It implies that learning should take place at all stages of the "life cycle and it should be life-wide, that is embedded in all life contexts from the school to the work place, the home and the community" (Green, 2002, p.613). The 'learning society', is the vision of a society where there are recognized opportunities for learning for every person, wherever they are and however old they happen to be. Globalisation and the rise of new information technologies are some of the driving forces that cause depreciation of specialised competences. This happens very quickly in terms of economic value; consequently, workers of all skills levels, during their working life, must have the opportunity to update "their technical skills and enhance general skills to keep pace with continuous technological change and new job requirements" (Fahr, 2005, p. 75). It is in this context that LLL tops the policy agenda of international bodies, national governments and non-governmental organisations, in the field of education and training, to justify the need for LLL opportunities for the population as they face contemporary employability challenges. It is in this context that the requirement and interest to analyse the behaviour patterns of adult learners has developed over the last few years.

When the biographies of adult students are studied they reveal uncertainty and sometimes a lack of confidence concerning their potential. However, some students have developed approaches to deal with these difficulties and have become independent (autonomous) learners. This situation may be related to the pathways chosen during their lifetime. As a consequence, we may have different identities emerging from different institutions. Is this choice dependent on how they lived before? And has this choice affected the way they learn and develop their autonomy and independence? Are teachers and tutors prepared to address these changes?

This chapter introduces a case study of adult students in Portugal. It was developed by the Portuguese partner of the PRILHE (Promoting Reflective Independent Learning in HE) project consortium. This was a project funded by the European Commission Socrates Adult Education Programme (113869-CP-1-2004-1-UK-GRUNDTVIG-G1PP). In Portugal, adults may choose Higher

Education Institutions[1] (HEI) or Technological Schools (TS) to pursue their education. The case study shows that there are similarities and differences between students from technological schools and universities, mostly related with the approach students use to learn and the way teachers take this into consideration. It seems that TS have 'best practices' that should be shared with the other institutions.

The chapter is organised as follows: first, we contextualise LLL development as an element within the political objective of creation of the knowledge economy, especially in the context of the European Union Lisbon Agenda, linking education with employment. The different access routes non-traditional adult students can take to access universities in the Portuguese higher education (HE) system are then briefly described. The PRILHE project, its main objectives, the participant institutions in the consortium, and the methodology used to gather and analyse data are briefly explained. Finally, the results of the Portuguese case within this project are presented and discussed.

2. The knowledge economy as a political objective: linking education with employment

The efforts to actively move towards the knowledge economy in Europe started back in 2000 with the Lisbon European Council putting forward the vision for Europe in the 21st century. The defining statement of the EU policy-makers' setting of the goal for the EU economy to:

> ...become the most competitive and dynamic knowledge-based economy in the world, capable of sustainable economic growth with more and better jobs and greater social cohesion . . . (Lisbon European Council, 2000),

highlighted the link between education and employment, between skills and prosperity and identified the successful exploitation of information and communication technology (ICT) as the means to achieving economic growth and full employment (Zantout, 2007:134). A well educated and well-trained population is essential for social and economic success of countries and individuals and for the expansion of scientific and cultural knowledge. It is in this context that the European Union:

> faced with the problem of [...] the rapid changing market demands on skills sets of human-capital and concurrently the problem of

---

1 In Portugal, higher education comprises university and polytechnic education, both public and private, all with different aims, programmes and characteristics (Portugal, 2005). The term universities is used in this chapter to refer to any of these.

maintaining the employability of its ageing populations over their whole lifespan, expresses the political will to utilize lifelong learning in order to overcome these challenges (Tuschling & Engemann, 2006, p. 454).

Lisbon's ambitious goal was that:

. . . the number of 18 to 24 year olds with only lower-secondary level education, who are not in further education and training, should be halved by 2010 (Zantout, 2007, p. 136).

This illustrates how, in the European Union, LLL is occupying a prominent position "within all attempts to change and connect the educational framework of Europe" (Tuschling & Engemann, 2006, p. 453). So the quest for finding novel solutions to resolve the skills shortage problem and achieve the targets is still ongoing. In Portugal for example the initiative *"Novas Oportunidades"* (Portugal, ME, 2006) is offering, since 2007, new routes for adults, recognising their prior learning, acquired via informal and non-formal ways. In parallel, there is a new drive - via promotion of LLL and acquisition of IT skills - to increase the number of adults in the country who have completed secondary education. Hopefully, this will increase student numbers entering higher education.

However, as these are just very recent developments, this chapter concentrates on routes for adults to access higher education existing up until 2006, as explained in the following section.

3. Access routes for adult students

Adult access to HE in Portugal has been recently revised (Decree-Law n° 64/2006, of 21st March, Portugal, 2006a) which regulates access of adults students who have not completed the traditional route of studies. However, up until the year 2006, adult access was through one of three possible routes (Correia & Mesquita, 2006, p. 214-226):

- Via a traditional route - adults followed all the stages of the education system. In the situation where circumstances may have dictated an interruption of their normal education route and they decided to return, they re-entered the system at an age greater than the norm but progressed through all the steps. This was the route which the majority of the adult population took, while attending HE, in Portugal.
- Via a special route previously designated (until the year 2005/2006) by *Exame Extraordinário de Acesso ao Ensino Superior –* in this case, the

assessment of candidates capabilities to access HE was the exclusive responsibility of the HEI; the candidate selection was made according to what each HEI considered more appropriate to each course and to each candidate, through the evaluation of his/her professional curriculum and through theoretical and practical examinations (*provas teóricas e práticas*) to evaluate the competences considered fundamental for the course selected by the candidate.

- Via attendance at *Cursos de Especialização Tecnológica* (CET)[2] – this attendance was undertaken under the auspices of an agreement, or protocol, with at least one HEI. These protocols - agreed between the provider of CET and HEI - stated the programmes of study that candidates, who finish a CET, can undertake, as well as establishing the conditions for recognition of training for advanced entry, within those HE programmes without the need to sit the National HE Access examination.

These were the possible ways an adult could choose to (re)enter HE in Portugal, up until the year 2006. Although there seems to be a number of different possibilities for adults to pursue a higher level of education, what the statistics say is that the number of adults (re)entering HE is very low (Correia & Mesquita, 2006:216).

While Europe is trying to prepare its human resources to be competitive and to develop the necessary skills and competences, the results vary across the Continent. It is in this context that the PRILHE project, described in the next sections, appears[3].

4. The PRILHE (Promoting Reflective Independent Learning in HE) project – a brief introduction

As a consequence of the policy push for lifelong learning – at national government, European Commission (EC, 2006) and Bologna Process (Bologna, 2007; Eurydice, 2007; EC, 2007) levels – more adults will, hopefully, take part in HE. Adults bring with them a wide range of life experiences to the learning process. The use of these experiences, in the HE curriculum, can assist academic learning and enable adult students to become independent (autonomous) and reflective learners. It is also recognised that to study throughout life requires the development of some additional skills and competences. Taking this into consideration, the project PRILHE (Promoting Reflective Independent Learning

---

2 *Cursos de Especialização Tecnológica* (Technological Specialization Courses) are post secondary courses, non university education, Level 4 of the EU (Decree-Law nº 88/2006, of 23rd May, art nº 3, Portugal, 2006b).

3 PRILHE project Webpage, http://www.pcb.ub.es/crea/proyectos/prilhe/project.htm

in HE) funded by the European Commission Socrates Adult Education Programme had as its main objective, 'to identify the learning processes which enable adult students in HE to become independent and reflective learners'. The overall aim was to identify models of good practice in HEI to share across Europe, in order to improve policy and teaching practices in this field. The project was developed by a consortium of European HE organisations, in seven countries – namely, the Centre for Lifelong Learning, University of Warwick, United Kingdom (coordinator); ISEGI, Universidade Nova de Lisboa, Portugal; Centre for Extension Studies, University of Turku, Finland; Department of Education, Georg August Universität Göttingen, Germany; The University of Lower Silesia, Poland; CREA, University of Barcelona, Spain; Department of Education, University of Stockholm, Sweden.

Within this research, both quantitative and qualitative methods were used to determine how students organise their studies and to discover their learning experiences.

4.1 Portuguese case study
In this chapter we present the Portuguese results, in particular the learning experiences in the Technological Schools (TS) and in the HEI (Polytechnic Institutes and Universities).

4.1.1 Methodology
In this section we explain the methodology used to select the target as well as the consideration given to the choice of the sample. Afterwards we present the procedures used to select and analyse data. By acknowledging the need for assessing the learning processes of adult students, the study aimed to identify possible differences between their learning experiences in the TS and in the HEI. Therefore, the main objective was to verify if students organise their studies similarly, when they enrol in a TS or when they enrol in a HEI. Within this scope, the study focused on eight important topics, which the literature considers key factors in the learning process, helping or preventing the student to become more autonomous and independent:

a) Role of work/life experience in the learning process
b) Individual organisation of learning
c) Reflection of contents
d) Framing of the learning process
e) Dialogue in the learning process
f) Learning motivation
g) Learning approach
h) Instructions and space for individual organisation

4.1.2 Target population and sample

The adult student is considered to be a person over 25[4] years old who left school with few or no qualifications, who has been out of the educational system for a long time, has no previous higher education experience, and comes from a disadvantaged group (one or more of these conditions may apply; Bourgeois *et al.*, 1999).

In Portugal, the number of students, fitting this description, have been much reduced (in 2005 only 3776 adults applied to enter HE and only 901 have been admitted). Knowing that the number of traditional students who enrolled for the first time in HE in the year of 2005 was 86,000, one can see that the number of adult students represents around 1% of the total number of students in HE (Correia & Mesquita, 2006, p. 216).

As outlined above, to access HE in Portugal students can choose to enrol in a TS, to obtain a CET which is a certificate of level 4 (more practical courses) then progress to a HEI in the terms described above or to enrol in a HEI which offers courses at level 5. Taking this into consideration, the target population for this exploratory study comprised students enrolled in TS and in HEIs. The sample is not representative of the adult population in TS and /or HE in Portugal. The objective at this stage of the research methodology was only to determine if the factors found in the literature and described above were valid for that population. Through in-depth interviews of adult students from TS and HE, carried out in the subsequent phase of the research, these factors were studied in detail.

4.1.3 Data collection and processing

A Web-based system was developed to collect the data; this facilitated the compilation and analysis of data, and a sample of 149 validated questionnaires was obtained (48% from students enrolled in TS, and 52% in HEI). In order to motivate the students and thus increase the rate of questionnaire return, presentations of the project were made in some institutions (both TS and HEI). The information provided also aimed to get unbiased answers. Following each presentation students were asked to fill the questionnaire online as soon as possible.

4.1.4 Questionnaire and analysis framework

The questionnaire was divided into several sections. A first set of questions aimed to collect students' personal information such as socio-demographic characteristics. The second set of questions focused on the eight categories of factors established in the study design. Although not explicitly organised and

---

4   In Portugal, it became 23 years of age, according to the Decree-Law n° 64/2006 (Portugal, 2006a)

ordered by topics, for each category some statements were prepared; students were asked to classify each one according to a 7 point Likert scale, ranging from 'totally agree' to 'totally disagree'. Failure to answer was also noted. The eight categories that have impact / importance in the learning process are as previously listed and their descriptions are detailed as follows:

1. **Role of work/life experience in the learning process** – Work experience means specialized knowledge (related to the profession) and competences (e.g. talent for organisation, ability to be critical, team spirit...). It was necessary to establish the role of the above-mentioned work experience in the learning process. The statements included for this category are the following:
   - *"My work/life experience doesn't support my learning in higher education"*
   - *"I am learning from the work/life experience of my fellow students"*
   - *"Lecturers value my work/life experience"*
   - *"My previous work/ life experience affects my current learning"*

2. **Individual organisation of learning** – On the one hand one might say that learning is an individual issue; on the other one might have a clear idea of how learning should be undertaken. The point of view of the student was the aspect of relevance. The statements included here are the following:
   - *"I have changed my approach to learning since I came to higher education"*
   - *"The way I learn is taken account of by lecturers"*
   - *"I am unsure how lecturers expect me to learn"*
   - *"I have a clear idea how I learn"*

3. **Reflection of contents** – The statements reflect the importance of sharing of opinions and comments from lecturers regarding their performance and participation in critical debates. The statements included here are the following:
   - *"The exchange of different views is important to me"*
   - *"In general, lecturers expect me to reproduce what I am taught"*
   - *"Lecturers encourage critical thinking"*
   - *"I like to engage in critical discussions in informal situations"*
   - *"I like to engage in critical discussions in seminars, etc."*

4. **Framing of the learning process** – The statements deal with contexts of learning. To what extent is learning influenced by prior life experience or by specific learning situations? This category comprises the following statements:
   - *"My background (personal, social, work, etc.) plays an important role in my learning"*
   - *"I can't separate my feelings from my learning"*

- "*My life experience prevents me from opening up towards new knowledge*"
- "*My learning is affected by the situation in which I learn*"

5. **Dialogue in the learning process** – The statements deal with the relevance of communication with other people during learning; they included the following:
   - "*I prefer to work in groups*"
   - "*I learn best on my own*"
   - "*My peers are useful to my learning*"
   - "*I learn best through interaction with others*"

6. **Learning motivation** – Here, it was asked which motives and expectations caused the student to take up his/her studies and how they influence their learning process. This category comprises the following statements:
   - "*Sometimes I don't know why I am taking this study*"
   - "*The expectations of others towards me to be a successful learner have a great influence on me*"
   - "*I am an organized learner*"
   - "*I am studying because I want to progress in my career*"

7. **Learning approach** – Everybody develops individual approaches to learning in the course of his/her learning life. Here, the personal way of learning, as well as the aims pursued with it, are the aspects under investigation. This category comprises the following statements:
   - "*Learning is for me quite easy*"
   - "*Learning must have a practical outcome*"
   - "*I am an experimental learner*"
   - "*I am rather cautious when I begin something new*"
   - "*I also learn for the sake of the learning itself*"

8. **Instructions and space for individual organisation** – For some people it is helpful to get clear instructions on how to organise their learning process; while others need space to proceed individually. In the following, the learning conditions the student prefers are the aspects being researched, using the following statements:
   - "*In my learning I definitely need support*"
   - "*All strict and rigid instructions disturb my learning*"
   - "*Without clear instructions learning is quite difficult for me*"
   - "*I learn best when I organise my learning process on my own*".

In the analysis stage, for each category, students' opinions from the two sub-samples (students enrolled in TS and in HEI) were compared. The average response rate to each question was above 97%.

5. Results and Discussion

Although the sample is not representative of the adult student population in TS and HE in Portugal, the main goal is to obtain insights for the factors that have impacted on the learning process of those students. The results are given for the students of the two sub-samples; comparisons of their learning experiences are made through a detailed analysis of the eight *knowledge and learning categories* previously described.

Determining the students' learning processes, provided an indication of how their life experiences might be used to assist academic learning and enable adult students to become more independent (autonomous) and reflective learners. Moreover, this approach was also expected to contribute to the development of guidelines / recommendations to increase the success of adult students in HE.

Characterisation of the students
Technological Schools' students

The majority of the TS' students in the sub-sample are male (77%) and the most frequent age group is from 25 to 34 years of age (73%).

Figure 1 shows the distribution of male and female students by age group. Adult students represent approximately 75% of the sample of TS students.

Figure 1 – Distribution of female and male students from TS by group age

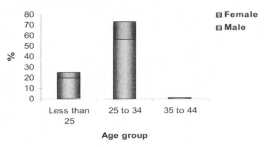

Approximately 76% of the students have been out of the educational system for less than 5 years, 19% of them discontinued their studies for 5 to 10 years, and almost 5% did not engage in the educational system for more than 10 years. Considering just the adult students (Figure 2), approximately 31% of them have been out of the educational system for more than 5 years. However, approximately 43% of them have participated in some kind of short course since their studies have been discontinued, whereas this is equal to 28% among the students with less than 25 years of age (Figure 3).

Figure 2 – Number of years that the adult students from TS have been out of the educational system (%)

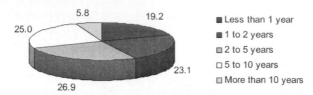

- Less than 1 year
- 1 to 2 years
- 2 to 5 years
- 5 to 10 years
- More than 10 years

Figure 3 – Distribution of students from TS that participated, or not, in some kind of short course since their studies have been discontinued (%)

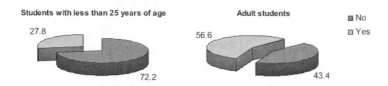

Students with less than 25 years of age

Adult students

- No
- Yes

Approximately 85% of the adult students are employed or have an occupation, whereas this percentage is equal to 79% for students with less than 25 years of age.

Higher Education Institutions' students

The majority of the HE students in the sub-sample are male (65%) and the most frequent age group is from 25 to 34 years of age (82%). Figure 4 shows the distribution of male and female students by age group. Adult students represent approximately 92% of the sample of HE students.

Figure 4 – Distribution of female and male students from HE by group age

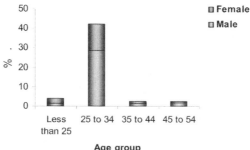

Only 18% of the HE students have been out of the educational system for less than 2 years, 24% of them discontinued their studies for 2 to 5 years, and 58% did not engage in the educational system for more than 5 years. Considering just the adult students (Figure 5), approximately 84% of them have been out of the educational system for more than 2 years.

Figure 5 – Number of years that the adult students from HE have been out of the educational system (%)

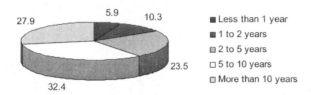

Approximately 68% of the HE students have participated in some kind of short course since their studies have been discontinued, whereas this percentage is equal to 71 among the students with less than 25 years of age (Figure 6).

Figure 6 – Distribution of students from HE that participated, or not, in some kind of short course since their studies have been discontinued (%)

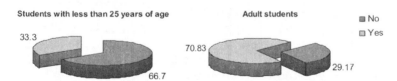

Most of the adult students (67%) have a full time job. Approximately 14% of the adult students enrolled in HE are unemployed, whereas this percentage decreases to zero for students with less than 25 years of age.

5.1 Role of work/life experience in the learning process
Both students enrolled in TS and in HE agree that their work/life experience supports and affects their learning. Another common opinion of the two groups of students is that the work/life experience of their fellow students is important in their own learning process. However, their opinions differ on the value that lecturers give to their life/professional experience. Most TS students agree that their work/life experience supports (72%) and affects (79%) their learning. Likewise, many HE students agree that their work/life experience is important (82%) and influences (85%) the way they learn. Approximately 79% of both the

TS and the HEI students consider that they can learn from the professional experience of their colleagues. Regarding the students' opinions on the statement '*Lecturers value my work/life experience*', there is some dissimilarity between TS and HE answers (Figure 7). While in HE only 31% of the students agree with the statement, in TS this percentage increases to 66%.

Figure 7 – Opinions on the statement '*Lecturers value my work/life experience*'

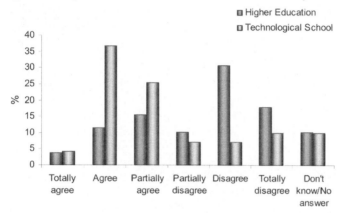

5.2 Individual organisation of learning

Most of the students enrolled in TS and in HE agree that they have a clear idea on how they learn (86% of TS students, and 62% of HE students), but changed their approach to learning since they came to higher education (96% of TS students, and 88% of HE students). For the other components of this category, related with the students' perception on how lecturers recognise the way they learn, there is a strong difference (Figure 8 and Figure 9).

After entering the higher education level (HE or TS), more students from TS (75% against only 27% from HE), consider that lecturers take into consideration the way they learn. In a way, it might support the results of the statement '*I am unsure how lecturers expect me to learn*': the number of students who feel insecure about the way lecturers expect them to learn is higher in HE (47% against 27% for TS). This means that lecturers in TS know and understand their students better, supporting them in the way they learn, helping them to feel more confident.

Figure 8 – Opinions on the statement '*The way I learn is taken account of by lecturers*'

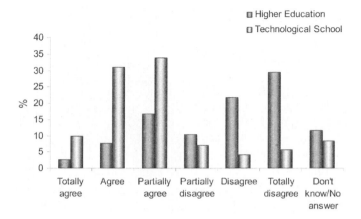

Figure 9 – Opinions on the statement '*I am unsure how lecturers expect me to learn*'

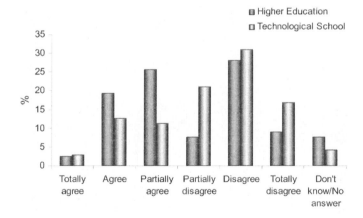

5.3 Reflection of contents

Both students enrolled in TS and in HE agree that an important contribution to their learning is the sharing of opinions and different views (approx. 96%) and comments from lecturers regarding their performance and participation in critical debates. In fact, students like to engage in critical discussions, not only in informal situations (76% of TS students, and 86% of HE students) but also in seminars and other situations where the debate is promoted (79% of TS students, and 64% of HE students). Moreover, the great majority of students consider that lecturers encourage the development of critical thinking (96% of TS students, and 85% of HE students). Nevertheless, most of the students enrolled in TS (83%) and in HE (80%) still have the perception that lecturers expect them to reproduce what they are taught.

5.4 Framing of the learning process

There is almost total agreement in both HE and TS students (approx. 96% in both groups) concerning the importance of background (personal, social and professional) in learning, as well as in the influence of the contextualisation of learning, in the way they learn (97% of TS students, and 87% of HE students). On the other hand, both HE and TS students (97% in both groups) show almost a total disagreement concerning the role that life experiences play when preventing the acceptance of new knowledge. However, there is not a consensus in the students' opinions on what degree their feelings are connected with their learning (Figure 10). Only 38% of TS students and 46% of HE consider that they do not have the ability to separate their feelings from learning.

Figure 10 – Opinions on the statement '*I can't separate my feelings from my learning*'

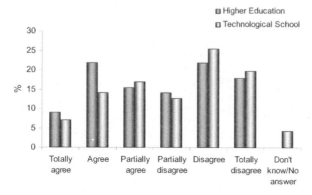

5.5 Dialogue in the learning process

For this category, the similarity between HE and TS students' opinions is mostly present for statements indicating the degree of belief that colleagues are useful in the learning process (approx. 93% in both groups), and that interaction with others is beneficial (approx. 89% in both groups).

The students from TS prefer group work (approx. 90% against 76% from HE). On the other hand, 47% students from HE feel that they learn better alone, against 30% from students of TS.

5.6 Learning motivation

There is an almost total agreement of students' opinions from HE and TS (96% in both groups) concerning the fact that the purpose of studying is to progress in their professional career. Similarities are also present in the conviction that students are organised learners (approx. 80% of the students from both HE and TS). On the other hand, the major difference in this category concerns the doubt *"why am I attending this programme of study?"*, doubt which affects 42% of the students from HE, against 31% of the students from TS.

Most of the students, from both groups, agree that others' expectations of them to become successful learners have a definite influence (72% of TS students, and 67% of HE students) but, the degree of this influence varies between groups (Figure 11).

Figure 11 – Opinions on the statement *'The expectations of others towards me to be a successful learner have a great influence on me'*

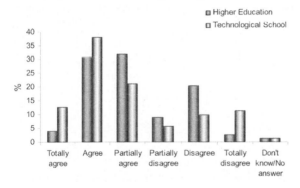

However, both groups recognise that their own expectations and willingness, for instance, to change career or have a better life, is also an influence. Some students answer that they agree with the statement shown in Figure 11, but others disagree or partially agree with the statement. We think that these results might be explained, at least in part, by the Portuguese culture and the last 35 years, after the Revolution. It became important for citizens to have access to HE, Since previous generations, for the most part, could not realise this dream, they try to make sure that their children have the opportunity.

5.7 Learning approach

For this category, the similarity between HE and TS students' opinions is mostly present for statements concerning not only the need for experimentation and for understanding the practical applications of what they learn, but also the pleasure of learning as one of the reasons why the student learns. Approximately 72% of the students, from both HE and TS, are experimental learners (Johnston and Merrill, 2004), and 59% state that learning must have a practical outcome. Almost all students (93% of TS students, and 97% of HE students) learn for the sake of the learning itself. In TS, 63% of the students feel that learning is easy for them, and only 56% of the HE students find it easy. Furthermore, 83% of the students from TS consider themselves very cautious when they start something new, while in HE 71% consider themselves to be so.

5.8 Instructions and space for individual organization

The similarity between HE and TS students' opinions occurs in all statements from this category. The students from HE show themselves as a little more convinced of their need for learning support (77% against 72% from TS), although they also prefer to organise their own learning processes (92% against 91% from TS). On the other hand, the students from TS are slightly more sensitive to situations of rigid or restrictive instructions, in the sense that they disturb their learning (61% against 55% from HE), and to the absence of clear instructions (77% feel it is difficult to learn without clear instructions, against 69% from HE).

6. Conclusion

This study attempts to establish if there were any significant differences between the characteristics of adult students from HEI and TS and the way they learn in Portugal. According to the results, there are both similarities and differences between them. The level of uncertainty regarding the reasons that lead the student to enter a particular study programme is higher for those in HEI. There were more students saying that they didn't know why they were attending that programme of study. It may be because, for mature students in Portugal, there are study programmes which are easier to apply for (social sciences, humanities, management) than others (engineering, medicine). Furthermore, in terms of culture one can feel a social pressure coercing students to attend a course in HE. This probably means that the candidates try to find, not the programme of study that they really want, but the one which seems to be easier and can be completed in few years.

Students from TS said that they are more cautious when they start something new. Students of HE seem to be more carefree; the reasons for this need further investigation but it could be that HE students are more likely to be seeking a new career path which, in Portuguese society, is very much dependent on having a HE Degree.

As for the reflection on content, more students from TS agree that classes contribute to the development of critical thinking. This may be due to the fact that HE classes have a higher number of students and so the opportunities to have discussions are less. Students from HE also say that they prefer discussions and critical debates in informal situations, while students from TS prefer those discussions in a seminar. It is thought that the reason given for the development of critical thinking also applies here – the size of the classes prevent discussions and so HE students prefer informal situations for debates, instead of using the environment of the class.

As for dialogue in the learning process, students from TS prefer group work while those from HE feel that they learn better when they study alone. A reason for this difference may also lie in the number of students in the classes – usually it is more difficult to work in groups with big classes and so the lecturer may avoid those situations, preferring students to work alone.

Regarding life and work experience, students from TS believe that lecturers give some value to their previous experience. Again, it is felt that this may happen because of the smaller classes in TS. Concerning the individual organisation, students from TS said that they have changed their approach to the way they learn. In HE the approach remained the same, probably the same one that the student used in secondary school, not having had the opportunity to develop a new one. Students in TS also say that lecturers take into consideration the way they learn; students from HE feel that they do not know the way lecturers expect them to learn. This may be due to clear objectives not being adequately established at the beginning of the session / study programme in HE.

To sum up, one can see that there are some similarities between HE and TS but that there are also some important differences. These have been identified and some possible explanations for them were provided. Of course, these explanations are speculative but are well grounded in our experience as researchers and lecturers in HE for some years. The next step in this research could be to assess the situation in HE and TS, after application of the PRILHE proposals. The results could further help to develop guidelines/ recommendations to increase the chances of success for mature students.

Studies like the one described in this chapter are extremely relevant to the creation of opportunities for adult students to obtain higher qualifications, in Portugal, in order to overcome the country's shortage of skilled workers and enhance its competitiveness in globalised markets (OECD, 2007; Euridyce, 2007; European Commission, 2007).

References

Bologna Benelux 2009 Secretariat. 2007-, *Bologna Process Official Website*, viewed September 2008: <http://www.ond.vlaanderen.be/hogeronderwijs/bologna/>

Bourgeois, E., Duke, C., Guyot, J. L., and Merrill, B. (1999). *The adult university.* Buckingham: Society for Research into Higher Education and Open University Press, England.

Correia, A. & Mesquita, A. (2006). *Novos Públicos no Ensino Superior – desafios da sociedade do conhecimento*. Gradiva: Lisboa (Portuguese language).

Correia, A. M. R., Sá, D. M. and Sarmento, A. (2006). Web Survey System to Discover the Actual Role of Experience in Learning in Higher Education: a case study. In C. R. Brito and M. M. Ciampi, (Eds.), *New Engineering to a New World*. IEEE & Council of Researches in Education and Sciences, pp. 351-355.

European Commission (2006), *From Bergen to London – The EU Contribution*. Commission Progress Report, CEC- Directorate General of Education and Culture; School Education and Higher Education, Brussels, 24 Jan. (rev3), viewed September 2008: <http://europa.eu.int/comm/education/policies/educ/bologna/report06.pdf>.

European Commission (2007), *Key data on higher education in Europe - 2007 edition* Brussels: Eurydice and Eurostat, viewed September 2008: <http://epp.eurostat.ec.europa.eu/portal/page?_pageid=1073,46587259&_dad=portal&_schema=PORTAL&p_product_code=978-92-79-05691-8>

Eurydice (2007), *Focus on the structure of higher education in Europe. National trends in the Bologna Process - 2006/07 Edition*, Eurydice, Brussels, viewed September 2008: <http://www.eurydice.org/portal/page/portal/Eurydice/PubPage?pubid=086EN&fragment=5&page=1>.

Fahr, R.(2005). Loafing or Learning? – the demand for informal education. *European Economic Review*, vol. 49, pp. 75-98.

Green, A. (2002). The many faces of lifelong learning: recent education policy trends in Europe, *Journal of Education Policy*, vol. 17, no. 6, pp 611-626.

Johnston, R. and Merrill, B. (Eds.) (2004). Enriching Higher Education: Learning and Teaching with Non-Traditional Adult Students. A Handbook. LIHE

Lisbon European Council (23 and 24 March 2000) *Presidency Conclusions*. Council of the European Union, viewed September 2008: <http://ue.eu.int/ueDocs/cms_Data/docs/pressData/en/ec/00100-r1.en0.htm>

OECD. (2007). *Education at a Glance*, OECD, Paris, viewed September 2008: <http://www.oecd.org/document/30/0,3343,en_2649_39263294_39251550_1_1_1_1,00.html>

Portugal. AR. (2005), Lei nº 49/2005, de 30 de Agosto. (Segunda alteração à Lei de Bases do Sistema Educativo e primeira alteração à Lei de Bases do Financiamento do Ensino Superior). *Diário da República, I Série-A*, vol. 166, pp. 5122-5138.

Portugal. MCTES. (2006ª), Decreto-Lei nº 64/2006, de 21 de Março. [Regulamenta as provas especialmente adequadas destinadas a Avaliar a Capacidade para a Frequência do Ensino Superior dos Maiores de 23 Anos, prevista no nº 5 do artigo 12º da Lei nº 46/86, de 14 de Outubro (Lei de Bases do Sistema Educativo)]. *Diário da República, I Série*, vol. 57, pp. 2054–2056.

Portugal. MCTES. (2006b), Decreto-Lei nº 88/2006, de 23 de Março. (Regulamenta os cursos de especialização tecnológica). *Diário da República, I Série*, vol. 99, pp. 3474–3483.

Portugal. ME. (2006), *Novas Oportunidades: Aprender Compensa* – Guia de Acesso ao Secundário, Adultos, viewed September 2008: <http://www.novasoportunidades.gov.pt/ >

PRILHE project, viewed September 2008: <http://www.pcb.ub.es/crea/proyectos/prilhe/project.htm>

Tuschling, A. and Engemann, C. (2006). From Education to Lifelong Learning: the emerging regime of learning in the European Union. *Educational Philosophy and Theory*, vol. 38, no. 4, pp. 451-469.

Zantout, Hind and Dabir-Alai, Parviz (2007). 'The knowledge economy in the context of European Union policy on higher education', *Education, Knowledge and Economy*, vol. 1, no. 2, pp. 125 – 143.

14   Grading and Knowledge: a Matrix of Student Identities

Jan Thorhauge Frederiksen

Introduction

This article discusses the relationship between grading as a structuring element in educational settings, and the identities of students located in these settings. Looking at two forms of professional training in Denmark - Social Educator[1] and to a lesser extent a computer scientist - a comparison between the values embedded in the professional cultures and grading reveal how the cultural settings communicate specific values to their students, and how this communication in turn contributes to a matrix of student identities.

Grading and social practice

The Danish grading system[2] is currently being replaced, as a result of a number of concerns related to globalisation and the interlinking of the European educational systems in the European Area of Higher Education by 2010 through the Europe an Credit Transfer System (ECTS). A great deal of deliberation and committee work has gone into preparing the Danish shift of grading scales, and

---

1   The profession Social Educator is a Scandinavian phenomenon. Danish social educators study for a degree (Bachelor of Professions) at National Institutes of Social Education (NISE). The degree authorises the holder to be employed in Danish public and private social institutions, such as: pre-schools, kindergarten, day care, after-schools, and special therapeutic institutions and social community work. Social educators work with children or adults, including individuals with physical, psychological or social disabilities, or substance abuse. The training lasts for 3½ years including three periods of work-practice. See www.socialeducator.dk/.

2   The current Danish grading scale consists of 10 numerical grades, with varying intervals. The scale is supposed to be used for *relative* grading, that is to say, the individual students are not compared, but are graded in relation to an absolute scale of achievements. In fact, the Department of Education's order about grades specifically says that: '(teachers) may not aim at a particular distribution of the grades (relative grading)' Undervisning-sministeriet (1995). Bekendtgørelse om karakterskala og anden bedømmelse, Under-visningsministeriet. BEK nr 513 af 22/06/1995.. Grades 00, 03 and 5 all means that the student has failed, and must retake the exam. The grade 6 is acceptable, but barely, and 7, 8 and 9 are middle of the scale, 8 being defined as the midpoint. 10 and 11 are grades given to remarkably good achievement, whereas 13 is a so-called exceptional-grade, given only in case the utmost impressive achievements, beyond what can be expected. This concept of an exceptional grade is the only exception in existence to the rule mentioned above, that teachers are not allowed to aim for a certain distribution of grades.

into devising a new scale of grading, yet this process has, at least in Denmark, been characterised by mostly revising the intentions and the presumed inner mathematical workings of the existing scale.[3] Only slight attention has been given to the practical *use* of the current scale, and this attention has mainly focused on grade-averages - are grades subject to inflation, or devaluation? (Undervisningsministeriet (2004), suppl. 3, 4 and 7). Thus there is a lack of research on how grading is practiced. One recent study (Miller, 2004) has studied this to some extent in high schools, but focuses mainly on grades as a form of communication, and especially focusing on the thrice-yearly progression grading in all subjects. Miller's conclusions are that grading, seen from the pupils in high school's point of view, is very much a matter of relations and being visible as an attentive and interested pupil (Miller, 2006). No thorough studies of grading in higher education in Denmark exists[4].

Thus grading is both a formal tool for sanctioning and gate-keeping within the educational system itself, as well as a behaviour-modifying pedagogical device. This constitutes a functional dilemma of grading. On the one hand grades make subjective characteristics *comparable*; on the other hand they do so *subjectively*. It is this double-edged device of control, I wish to examine further here. Being a student at a particular type of educational institution, means being exposed to a certain institutional *culture*, and this article examines examining grading as a *characterising feature* of these cultures[5].

---

3 The Danish Department of Education has collected this preparatory material on their website: http://www.uvm.dk/nyskala/index.htm?menuid=15

4 However, there *are* several different traditions of examining grading, that have been extensively studied: one, where grades are seen as a measure, that may have motivating and/or disciplining effects on students; another, where grades are examined for their ability to predict scholarly aptitude (Choppin, 1990); and finally, one where grades are examined as dependent on gender, age, ethnicity, and class. Only the latter tradition will be relevant for my approach to grading here.

5 It should be emphasised that grading and grade distributions will not in this article be understood as quantitative data. Each grade represents a qualitative deliberation by a teacher, an attempt to objectify the assessment of the student. Any grade is thus a social practice, which just happens to be instantiated as a number. Grade distributions are thus a graphic representation of this objectifying social practice, as it is practiced by the teachers at the institutes examined. In other words, I am neither measuring nor calculating, I am examining *structures* in the way teachers (and students, in collusion) socially are constructing grades, by engaging in the social practice of grading, and examining these structures as an aspect of the particular culture of that educational institution. As a consequence of this approach, I will not consider grading as accurate measures of any real-world phenomena, abilities or skills. I aim to understand the accumulated affect of practices *of grading*, not the effects or precision of grading per se.

Forms of pedagogy and pedagogical devices

When examining educational assessments, it becomes necessary to distinguish between the various ways the relation between the assessor, assessed and the topic of the assessment are construed. For this purpose, the work of English educational sociologist Basil Bernstein is useful. Bernstein describes two pedagogical devices[6]: visible and invisible pedagogy. Pedagogic devices are characterised by first a certain form of control and second, a certain form of power. Bernstein analyses control as forms of framing, that is, the forms of interaction within this pedagogical practice: the form of communication, its order, initiatives and turn-taking, pacing, and evaluation. Framing thus describes what forms of communication are acceptable and relevant within the classroom. Power may then be analysed as forms of classification - that is, distinctions between positions and legitimate categories of meaning (Bernstein, 2000). This could be disciplines - e.g. physics and social studies- and subdivisions of curriculum, e.g. grammar and vocabulary. Framing and classification can be either strong or weak. This is because both classification and framing refer to boundaries drawn in classroom interaction, boundaries between what is accepted or is relevant, and what is not. These boundaries may be quite visible lines of demarcation, as they are between subjects on a timetable, or they may be completely vague, as they are in project- or theme-based work. These two forms of organisation represent respectively strong and weak classifications. In the same manner the framing may be strong - for example, which topics are considered relevant for discussion in a physics class, and the framing may be weak - as in which topics might be relevant in a social studies class.

The distinction between invisible and visible pedagogy thus concerns whether the criteria that are actively organising the classroom interaction (the pedagogic device) are made explicit to students/pupils or must be decoded. We may also consider this as a question of whether student performance is measured: did the pupil learn what was taught? Or whether student competence is evaluated - did the pupil creatively interpret the subject of tuition? When put like this, we may also note that the positioning of the pupil as a target for pedagogy is substantially different. The pupil exposed to visible pedagogy is targeted as an individual. S/he must perform correctly, in comparison with a given template - s/he is one individual of many, who is being measured against a standard. The pupil exposed to invisible pedagogy must interpret and re-tell

---

6   Bernstein describes these as two practical modalities of pedagogical codes but for now, these distinctions are unimportant. The discussion and construction of these concepts can be found in Bernstein, B. (2003). *The structuring of pedagogic discourse*. London, Routledge.

creatively. S/he is targeted as a person, whose inner (inaccessible) competence must be outwardly illustrated, in order to be interpretively evaluated.

Invisible pedagogy and social educators

Søren Gytz Olesen has utilised Bernstein's work describing social educator training in Denmark (Olesen, 2005:337). He describes the educational principles, in which the students must find their way, as "…a mixture of friendly intimacy and admonitory raised fingers…" (op.cit). Students are confronted by these educational principles especially through the manner of control they are subjected to within an invisible pedagogy:

- Control is implicit
- Students are not required to learn specific skills
- Criteria of evaluation are ambiguous
- Progression within the content of the training is merely implied
- Criteria of relevance and legitimacy are ambiguous (Bernstein 1974)

One may note in passing, that this list inversely describes the visible pedagogy, which is characterised by strong framing and classification, and thus presents itself to students in the guise of explicit control, and specifically required skills etc. The invisible pedagogy ideologically replaces the individual with the person, which means that the foci of education moves from universal and unequivocal requirements and standards of discipline, progression etc. to the individual interpretation and embodiment of ambiguous and vague requirements and standards. In a word, the students must now interpret and perform, and no longer simply reproduce. As for the teacher, her/his task within the invisible pedagogy is to 'assess the maturity' of the students by interpreting their performance (and not achievements) in the classroom. The teacher must then adjust the challenges presented to the students in accordance with her/his assessment of the student. What in other words is *not* explicit or visible is the criteria of maturity - when is the student 'ripe' for further challenges? Because the student ripens as a *person,* it is not skill-levels that are evaluated but the embodiment and performances of themes taught, which in their turn are interpreted as documenting inner qualities. Olesen describes the resulting implicit requirements of the students thus:

- The student is authentic, that is, s/he will recount the private story of her/his life, perhaps never told before?
- S/he feels safe, that is, he will do as he is told, and follow instructions from the teacher

- S/he is frank, that is, s/he will expose himself, and put her/his person at risk
- S/he dares to ask questions, that is, s/he subjects himself to the doctrines of the institutions
- S/he learns, that is, s/he is successfully disciplined
- S/he participates with others, that is, s/he both exposes her/himself, and holds something back(Olesen, 2005).

These points describe a pedagogy directed towards the inner life of the student - her/his mind, emotions, the stories of her/his life, motives, etc. This pedagogy attempts to both examine publicly the inner life of the students, and to inculcate a certain attitude towards this examination, namely that publicly examining ones inner life is a prime requisite for social educators. Thus it is necessary for the students to examine their own inner workings, and do so in collaboration with their fellow students, under the scrutiny of their teachers. This the student can do safely, because of the interchangeability of the professional and the personal, and the tacitly presumed integrity of all involved. Thus, the requirements given by Olesen above indirectly provide a description of the cultural and professional ideal the social educator students should aspire to. But how does the student incorporate this in her/his behaviour? How, in effect, is this form of control incorporated by the students?

Self governance

Bernstein arrived at his notion of control through the work of Michel Foucault. The public examination of one's inner life and producing discourses of it is a central part of Foucault's analysis of sexuality (Foucault, 1994:60ff.). It is a central tenet of modern western thinking that the fundamental truth about one's self cannot be enunciated by one's self, but must be interpreted by others in the interplay of what is said and what is not. Truth is only said in what I do not say, in what another might find reason to say of me in the light of what I choose to say of me. According to Foucault this constitutes a new economy of power, which relates to the necessity of government, rather than enforcing. This accompanies a new, fundamental object of governance: population. Whereas the object of the sovereign was the territory (e.g.. When Tycho Brahe was given the island Ven by the Danish king, this gift tacitly included the right of two days of labour a week from all peasants residing on the territory of Ven), the object of the government is the population (e.g. How can the government of Denmark make their population healthier?) The problem of population is not one of requirements, but instead one of promoting certain forms of behaviour. It is, simply put, possible to force labourers to work, but it is not possible to force them to abide by a healthy diet. Thus, a new form of government is necessary:

218   *Jan Thorhauge Frederiksen*

one that subtly instills good reasons for behaving in certain ways, and one that assists us in making choices, as opposed to forcing us, or controlling us behind our backs. In making the truth of one's self an object of interpretation, the person becomes externally related to her/his own behavior. S/he must then employ various technologies of the self, on her/his self, to change her/his self; s/he is being governed from within. This self governance is how students incorporate the requirements of the social educator training. Examining this self governance amounts to examining the relationships between the institutional culture, and the identities of students within this institution: What positions and attitudes are available?

Cultural values of social educator training

The positions that the training make available are to be found in how the training formulate expectations and goals for the students. In the following I will look at formal descriptions of how the students are to be evaluated, followed by some descriptions of what the teachers and students see as the core of the training. These attempt to make explicit the knowledge and skills required of the students, and metaphorically they form the surface of the culture, in which the students are immersed.

The discipline Educational Studies [pædagogik] in social educator training is described in the current order from the Department of Education as follows in Excerpt A. Here, it is required that the student must acquire knowledge/insight and skills related to a set of phenomena, but no requirements are given as to the exact nature of these skills etc. It seems unlikely that any kind of knowledge is acceptable - surely there are, at some level, distinctions as to what kind of knowledge is considered of value to the profession or institution, and what is not. Excerpt B is from the Studieordning[7] of a smaller NISE[8]:

> **A** The student is required to acquire 1) knowledge about social educational work, and the tasks, methods and areas it contains, 2) insight in the relations between social educational work, society in

---

7   Studieordning: formal description of the structure of the training at one particular institution: its form, content, partitioning and the purpose and goals of these.

8   The institutes examined here are: two small (150 students a year) institutes, one in Copenhagen, (Fröbelseminariet) and one in Jutland (Ranumseminariet), two medium (300-400 students), one near Copenhagen (Skovtofteseminariet) and one in Southern Jutland (Esbjerg), And finally two large (500+ students) from two large provincial cities (Odense Socialpædagogisk Seminarium og Jydsk Pædagogseminarium in Århus, Grenå and Randers). All formal documents and grades given at National Institutes for Social Educators are required to be publicly available on the websites of the institutes. It is from these I have collected the materials used here.

general, and the development and well-being of the individual child, adolescent or adult, 3) prerequisites and skills to evaluate and discuss practical, theoretical and ethical questions in relation to preparing, carrying out, and evaluating social educational work. (Undervisningsministeriet, 1997)

Excerpt B complements the previous excerpt, in that it specifies the requirements to be met when students evaluated a period of work practice. While certain legal terms are required knowledge: use of force, duty to lay information, confidentiality. These are regulated by departmental orders, to which the social educators must adhere. The other points required are, however, very ambiguous. What is an acceptable level of knowledge about care or ethics? When is one ethically prepared for three months of work practice? Or, more to the point, what is sufficient preparation within a species of knowledge, as ethics, but no particular tenets or schools? Like the previous layer, any sort of knowledge would do, it seems. Thus, the actual, underlying cultural value demanded here is that of being involved and concerned about the topics of care, ethics, etc:

B The student acquires knowledge about pedagogical work, including use of force, confidentiality, duty to lay information, care, ethics, reflection and learning [...] - The student is prepared theoretically, ethically and practically for his period of practice. (Seminariet & Esbjerg, 2004).

Excerpt C is from the corresponding formal document used at one of the largest Danish institutes for social educators. It describes required achievements from a culture-related project in the middle of the training. Again the requirements are areas of species of knowledge, but not any particular propositions. The students are to communicate competently in crosscultural contexts - but by what standards? The intents with which one enters relations spanning cultural differences is an important parameter in establishing what sort of competence the students should strive to possess. Yet neither is explicated here. There also seems to be some underlying assumptions about how personal experience of foreign or international cultures affects students. Again this may be understood as a demand of personally relating to a topic or theme, not as acquiring a specific skill:

C The student must acquire:
- (experience with) other cultures through working with multicultural or international problems...
- ability to compare, communicate, reflect and analyse cross-cultural aspects in pedagogical work, and tasks
- experience with communicating across international cultures and forms of societies
- personal experiences with and knowledge about conditions of life in foreign cultures (Jydsk Pædagog Seminarium, 2005.)

A final excerpt, D, from an altogether different source, is from the Diploma for the Bachelor degree of Social Educator of a large NISE in the capital - it describes the objective of the degree within the subject Educational Studies.

This reveals implicit connections between being in the field, and knowing; that which constitutes Educational Studies is so closely related to the actual work as social educator, that the students' knowledge and skills are created in the field, and enters the educational context as reflections in a diary, almost a grounded theory of the student's experiences in the pedagogical field. The implication is that in this manner the very exposure to the field will in itself affect the students in particular ways, and forms some manner of learning:

D The objective of the discipline entitled Education Studies is to enable students to analyse and assess educational practice with a view to determining potential actions. Knowledge, theories and notions concerning human relations in the fields of upbringing and education must be acquired by students so as to develop their communicative skills and ability to cooperate in educational contexts. Students must keep individual written 20-page diaries in connection with their preliminary work practice. (Hovedstadens Pædagog-Seminarium, 2002).

These four excerpts from the state legislation, the internal regulations of social educator training and descriptions of the objectives of the training can be characterised thus:

- The objectives of the training is not specific knowledge, but commitment to specific themes
- The actual content of the training is inaccessible from the formal descriptions
- The commitment and exposure to certain themes and phenomena is assumed to influence the students in a particular way,
- The curriculum thus consists of a set of formative experiences, rather than a set of subjects and theories

No formal document directly states what knowledge the training is supposed to contain. Rather than specific skills or knowledge, what the training aims to produce is a certain personal investment in and commitment towards certain valued topics.

Social educator's assessments

In the following, I will look at the distribution of grades. The grades are taken from exams[9] of last two years, at six institutes[10] of social educators of different sizes and geographical location. The four graphs on pages 220 - 221 show the distribution of grades for exams in Bachelor-thesis, Theory disciplines (oral and written), Culture and Activity, and finally all grades together. The numeric distribution is included in the tables below the graphs. These four distributional curves be characterised together as follows:

- Very few students fail
- Hardly anyone fails below 5 (the highest failed-mark)
- Few students in extreme high end of the scale
- Most students in the middle of the scale
- Distribution resembles *normal curve*

The absence of failing students in general may hint at another system of selection in the training. But it also shows that the actual passing is not the most important aspect of these exams. The lack of lower failing marks can be interpreted as the teachers' reluctance to distinguish between failures. This reveals a concern with how the failure is experienced subjectively: being just below the passing grade is a good deal different from receiving the lowest grade on the scale. When taken together with the fact that relatively few students fail at all, this illustrates underlying values embedded in the grading of social educators: the individual experience of the assessment may overrule the need for objectively comparable and precise assessments. The teachers doing the grading

---

9   The social educator training is organised in two types of disciplines: Theoretical disciplines, and Culture & Activity-disciplines The former are Education Studies, Psychology, Social Studies, Health Studies and COM (Communication, Organisation, and Management), whilst the latter, Culture & Activity-disciplines, consist of Physical exercise disciplines, Outdoor Activities, Drama, Music, Art & Craft and Danish & Media. There are both written and oral examinations in the theoretical disciplines, but only an oral in the Culture & Activity-disciplines. In addition, the students must write a final dissertation, the *Bachelor-thesis*. All of these exams are graded individually, by a teacher and a censor cooperatively, and, by decree of the Minister of Education, this grading is not supposed to be comparative, but absolute - as mentioned previously.

10 The same institutes as examined earlier in this paper, see note 8.

Jan Thorhauge Frederiksen

are practicing a species of care - likely the very one, that the students are in effect assumed to commit themselves to, even if (as previously discussed) it is not a professed value of the training. The low numbers of students in the high and low ends of the grading scale and the concentration of them in the middle grades becomes very apparent, when the distributions are shown back to back, as in Graph 5 on page 222.

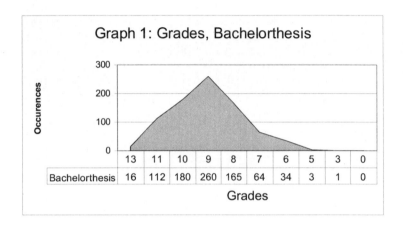

Graph 1: Grades, Bachelorthesis

	13	11	10	9	8	7	6	5	3	0
Bachelorthesis	16	112	180	260	165	64	34	3	1	0

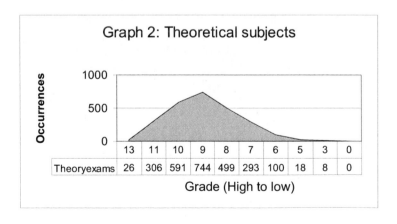

Graph 2: Theoretical subjects

	13	11	10	9	8	7	6	5	3	0
Theoryexams	26	306	591	744	499	293	100	18	8	0

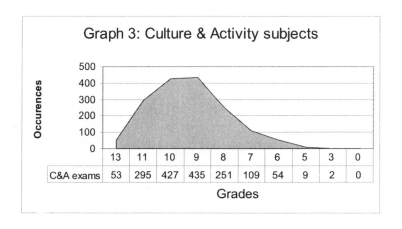

Graph 3: Culture & Activity subjects

	13	11	10	9	8	7	6	5	3	0
C&A exams	53	295	427	435	251	109	54	9	2	0

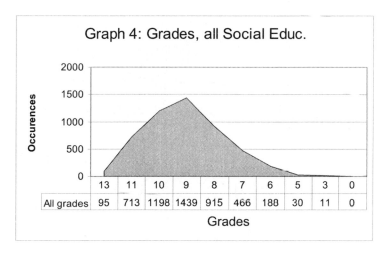

Graph 4: Grades, all Social Educ.

	13	11	10	9	8	7	6	5	3	0
All grades	95	713	1198	1439	915	466	188	30	11	0

Instead of interpreting this characteristic in terms of variance or standard deviations, as the quantitative paradigm would have it, we should stick to seeing this as illustrating the grades that most students find themselves receiving - the mode(s). When shown this way, the middle grades are also shown to be the most ordinary ones, and thus inversely defines when students may experience themselves as extraordinary, by being graded.

Finally, though the graphs plot six different institutions, 11 disciplines, around 100 different teachers and as many censors, and about 1000 different students, the overall distribution of the grading is quite similar. And not only are they similar, but they also resemble a particular distribution, namely the

Gaussian distribution, also known as the normal curve. Graph 6 illustrates the similarity between the 4 distributions, and the normal curve: The four curves have been normalised, and in addition a broken curve plotting a standard normal distribution (μ=9.2, σ=1.1) is superimposed on the plot.

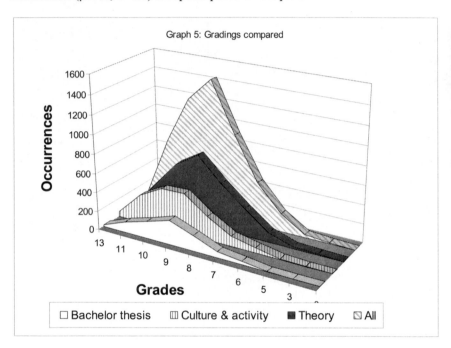

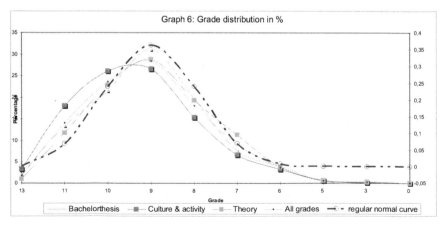

Now, the normal curve is traditionally the only statistical observation that (normality being the expected observation) need not be explained. Quantitative methodology tries instead to reveal deviations from normality, and explain them. But in this case, both origin, and effects of the normality of grading should in fact be examined and explained.[11] Since grading is not a natural phenomenon, nor a reliable (in the classical sense) measurement, the assumption of what is normal must not be taken for granted. If one can in fact locate a standard of normality, this must be a product of the social and cultural setting in which grading occurs.

Put simply, both individual grades and the tools used in performing grading (tasks, exams etc.) are constructed socially, and therefore it is unlikely that they should behave - in the aggregate - as if they were measuring natural phenomena. This amounts to saying that the procedure of grading itself strives to reproduce this distribution and that the distribution does not depict an accurately measured spread of skills or competencies possessed by students. Rather, the curve depicts the structure of the assessing teacher's assumptions and conceptions of the students as a group, and the spread of their abilities.

If one considers the curve and the distribution as part of the culture of the social educator training as a symptom or indicator of the underlying social educator culture[12] the next analytic step is to consider how grades and grade distributions are produced by and reproduce this institutional culture. This regular distribution found above is then produced by assumptions about the distribution of abilities, held by teachers and students in the field of social educator training.

---

11 The normal curve is not to be expected here, strictly mathematically speaking. It describes *the average, aggregated behaviour* of natural phenomena: rolling and adding two dice will follow a normal distribution, but rolling one will not. A single die-roll will be completely random, and exhibit a flat distributional curve. In other words, the metaphorical die the teacher rolls when grading appear to be loaded. It is important to note here, that these similarities are just that: similarities. The similarity does not provide any explanatory power or validity whatsoever.

12 This claim is certainly only true in the aggregation - on an individual level, be it student, teacher, discipline or institution, this distribution is much less apparent, as is noticeable in graph 6. In the individual teacher's grading, there is but a small tendency to grade along the normal curve. There is simply a slight consideration, that one should be neither generous nor stingy with the grades. And even though teachers probably consider this a breakable rule, it does show up when we consider sufficient numbers of grades, as a social structure of the *subjective* judgements performed by teachers. What at the teacher level seems as a small adjustment or moderation in the case of the individual students, appears here, in the aggregate, as a clear systematic adherence to a distribution, by which grading is performed.

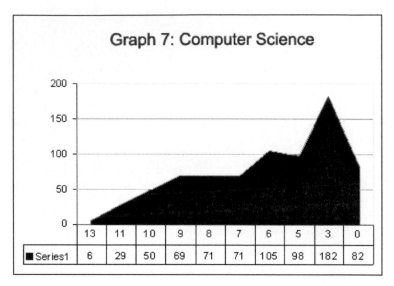

Computer Science Assessments

Above graph 7 shows the distribution of grades given at first year exams in Computer Science, University of Copenhagen[13]. These exams involve a set of questions with few or only one correct answer, seemingly making grading a simpler matter[14]. This curve may be characterised as follows:

- Almost half fail
- Many fail with grades below 5
- Most students below middle
- Extremely few high grades
- Distribution slopes steeply down from low to high

The distribution shows half the students failing and most of these are below grade 5, which is the highest failing grade. Comparing with the social educator

---

13 All data are from The Institute of Computer Science, University of Copenhagen - www.diku.dk. 763 student grades are used here.

14 Of course, the difficulty of the grading is simply shifted to the task of composing the questions, but the very act of grading (and of student comparing each others achievements) appear much more objective, which is likely an important part of the culture of grading in this institution. In passing one may note here that the picture is likely to be more complex that what one may immediately assume - the Masters thesis grading of DIKU is a good deal higher (10.5 average) than the social educators (9.14), indicating that the distribution curves shift shape within the institution.

graphs, the computer science teachers exhibit no reluctance in employing the lower failure-grades. Obviously the similarity to the normal curve is not present in the graph from Computer Science.

In effect, these distributions reveal two very different practices of assessment. One practice exhibits that gentleness and leniency is important and another does not. This relates to the different cultures of the two training settings. First, objectivity would likely be a more important ideal for natural scientists than for social educators. Second, the nature of the foundations of knowledge in the two professions is quite different: Computer science, when applied, may solve certain problems or not - such irrevocable measures of success or failure, or of good practice is rarely present in the social educator's workplace. Third, the nature of relationships is a central part of a social educator's practice and professionalism, whereas it has little bearing on most aspects of computer science. These three aspects of knowledge accuracy and species of knowledge matter reveal the interconnection between grading practices and the two professions. They address the issue of how the culture of an educational institution comes to be, and hint that we might find answers in both the knowledge foundation, and in the nature and dynamics of the training's relations to the field and practitioners [15].

Thus, the different grading practices seen in social educator training and computer science indicate that there are different assumptions underlying the culture of the institutions - both about the profession, the practice and the students.

Grades doing educational culture

The concepts of governmentality from Foucault may explain this. In a famous quote, Foucault says that "People know what they do; they frequently know why they do what they do; but what they don't know is what they do does" (Dreyfus and Rabinow, 1986:187). Thereby he describes the difference between what the subject sees, and what his position, and all comparable positions does as a whole. The structure of the grade distributions seen here is a cumulative effect of what all of the grading teachers do - this is how the culture of the institution presents itself to the students. Put bluntly, the *position* 'grading teacher' wants to grade by the normal curve.

The teachers evaluate their own grading practices, and adjust them, if they are immoderate. Not because they are so ordered, but because grading does not (literally) make sense without, and because they are exposed to subtle suggestions that they should: they are required to make all grading averages

---

15 A much more detailed discussion of these issues may be found in Olesen (2004)

publicly available, there is a general concern in the organisation of censors[16] that grades have become subject to inflation[17]. The Department of Education has recently introduced a new system of grading, and in the manual[18] for this system, an assumed distribution 'nation wide, seen over time' is described, not that the teachers are required to follow it, they should just keep it in mind. And the union of social educators students are worried by students passing too easily and grading being too generous[19].

These conditions are the Foucauldian concept of government targeting teachers as a population. The teachers are being governed from within themselves. It becomes rational to relate practice and distribution of grades to the ideal intruding upon it, and to take measures that remedy any faults in one's own grading. The arguments about whether grading is inflated illustrates that grading is not spoken of as a performance but as a measurement. The grade is assumed to reflect the students' absolute positions on an absolute scale reliably - that is in an implicit stable relation to grading in all comparable situations. How students themselves speak of grading reflect this. Grades become something they deserve or not. Grading is a situation, where students may or may not avoid exposure by skirting dangerous subjects or questions, and the hidden truth of one's self. The students cannot themselves define their relative position in the classroom - they must disclose it in exams, and perhaps attempt to control the interpretation of this confession, by skirting some topics and delving in to the other etc. Grading as a practice establishes an axis and a scale of abilities or aptitude, which the students use to understand and position themselves within. Their degree of embracing or distancing themselves from the culture of the institutions could then be another axis in this matrix.

The expectations of the students are being presented in the grading, and the grading then attempts to reflect the students' behaviour, which is led by these expectations. Grading is a way for teachers and students to speak and look at each other and themselves, which both enables comparison, and self-control within the context of educational assessment: "He didn't deserve that grade" or "I deserved a better grade than what I got" or "I did not deserve this".[20]

---

16 [:censorformandskabet]
17 www.censorformandskabet.dk/sekretariatet/download.php?blobId=2
18 www.uvm.dk/nyheder/7b.htm?menuid=6410
19 www.pls.dk
20 Writing this article, I have come across several teachers who have let students propose their own grading – and who were pleased to see that the students were quite moderate and sensible in this. Thinking of grades as a medium of self governance makes it clear that such grading experiments only reveal the extent to which this cited vision is entrenched in educational practices.

Institutional culture and student identity as a matrix

Comparing the characteristics of the grade distributions reveals a little more of how these two educational cultures differ. An overview of the characteristics found previously is in the following table.

Grade distribution characteristics	
SOCIAL EDUCATOR	**COMPUTER SCIENCE**
Few in extreme high end of the scale	Extremely few high grades
Very few students fail	Almost half fail
Most students in middle of scale	Most students below middle
Hardly anyone fails below 5 (the highest failed-mark)	Many fail with grades below 5
Distribution resembles normal curve	Distribution slopes steeply down from low to high

These two sets of characteristics communicate very different frameworks of self-governance to the student embedded in these educational cultures. When considering her/his own position in the span of student positioning available within either computer science or social educator training, these students must relate themselves to this framework. As the students try to make sense of the educational setting they are embedded in, they subjectively translate the social landscape provided in the grade distributions to a subjective position and context. This could conceivably look like the following sketches:

Social educator grading characteristic	Subjective translation
Few in extreme high end of the scale	'Being really brilliant is not achievable'
Very few students fail	'Everybody can pass these exams, failure is rare'
Most students in the middle of the scale	'It is not exam-related skills, that differentiate social educator students'
Hardly anyone fails below 5 (the highest failed-mark)	'Difference between failures is unimportant'
Distribution resembles normal curve	'Exam grading reflects skills that are normal - it is like most other areas where we might compare each other'

Computer Sc. grading characteristic	Subjective translation
Extremely few high grades	'It is difficult to get the highest grades'
Almost half fail	'This is difficult, and failure is common'
Most students below middle	'Passing an exam is in itself an achievement'
Many fail with grades below 5	'Many fail to understand how difficult this is'
Distribution slopes steeply down from low to high	'Exam grading reflects skills that are extraordinary and it takes a lot to do well'"

We can predict (at least) one further dimension in the subjective interpretation of these characteristics. First of all, the grades obtained by each student will contribute a great deal to how the characteristics are interpreted. A computer science student, who obtains very high grades will not interpret the relative rarity of high grades as an obstacle, but rather as a further demonstration of her/his brilliance. And a social educator student, who obtains very low grades will vice versa interpret the characteristic leniency of social educator grading as further demeaning.

The first example is then likely to reinforce students' feelings of loyalty towards their educational choice, whereas the latter may produce feelings of disloyalty or an experience of the student being disowned by the social educator training. Both of these examples may possibly result in either student dismissing the importance of grades, although with quite different motivations. That, however, will most likely relate back the general educational cultural values related to grading - and while the characteristics of social educator training grading is such that in all but a few examples grading will seem unimportant, the opposite is true of computer science. Such considerations as these, relating the grades and the culture of evaluation of the educational institutions, and various subjective conditions, can be understood as a matrix. Relating an axis of institutional setting to an axis of subjective practice, provides a map of students positioning, with an embedded relation to the culture of the institution, the values, and the other students, and their various positioning. Such a matrix may prove an interesting and valuable conceptual device for explorative interviews and fieldwork in these educational settings.

References

Bernstein, B. (1974). *Klasse og Pædagogik: Synlig og usynlig.* Basil Bernsteins Kodeteori. J. Enggaard and K. Poulsgaard. København: Christian Ejlers Forlag.

Bernstein, B. (2000). *Pedagogy, Symbolic control and Identity.* Lanham: Rowman and Littlefield Publishers.

Bernstein, B. (2003). *The structuring of pedagogic discourse.* London, Routledge.

Bourdieu, P. (1996). *The State Nobility.* Cambridge: Polity.

Bourdieu, P. and J.-C. Passeron (1990). *Reproduction in Education, Society and Culture.* London: Sage.

Choppin, B.H. (1990). Prediction of success in Higher Education. In: H. Walberg, and G. Haertel, The international Encyclopedia of Educational Evaluation. Oxford: Pergamon Press.

Danmarks Evalueringsinstitut (2002). *Undervisning i pædagogik - i pædagoguddannelsen og læreruddannelsen,* København: Danmarks Evalueringsinstitut

Danmarks Evalueringsinstitut (2003). *Pædagoguddannelsen.* København: Danmarks Evalueringsinstitut

Dreyfus, H. L. and P. Rabinow (1986). *Michel Foucault: Beyond Structuralism and Hermeneutics.* Chicago: University Of Chicago Press.

Foucault, M. (1994). *Viljen til viden.* Frederiksberg: Det lille forlag.

Hovedstadens Pædagog-Seminarium (2002). DIPLOMA SUPPLEMENT. Copenhagen: Hovedstadens Pædagog-Seminarium.

Jydsk PædagogSeminarium, N. (2005). *Studieordningen,* Jydsk: Pædagogseminarium.

Kvale, S. (1970). *En eksamination av universitetseksamener.* Oslo: Universitetsforlaget.

Miller, T. (2004). *Karaktergivning i praksis. 13-skala og gymnasiet. Dansk institut for gymnasiepædagogik.* Odense: Syddansk Universitet.

Muel-Dreyfus, F. (1997). *Le Metier D'educateur - Les Instituteurs De 1900, Les Éducateurs Spécialiés De 1968. Minuit,* Collection. Le Sens: Commun

Mørch, S. I. (2002). *Den pædagogiske kultur.* Århus: Systime Academic

Olesen, H. S. (2004). Har professioner en fremtid, og kan de professionelle skabe den? In: K. Hjort, *De Professionelle,* Roskilde: Roskilde Universitetsforlag.

Olesen, S. G. (2005). *Rekruttering og rekonstruktion - om praktikker og italesættelser i pædagoguddannelsen. Afd. for Pædagogik.* København: Københavns Universitet.

Seminariet i Esbjerg, (2004). STUDIEORDNING – pædagoguddannelsen: CVU vest.

Schein, E. H.(1994). *Organisationskultur og Ledelse.* Uden sted: Valmuen

Undervisningsministeriet (1995). *Bekendtgørelse om karakterskala og anden bedømmelse.* Undervisningsministeriet. BEK nr 513 af 22/06/1995.

Undervisningsministeriet (1997). *Bekendtgørelse af lov om uddannelse af pædagoger.* Undervisningsministeriet. BEK nr 930 af 08/12/1997.

Notes on Contributors

Dr Barbara Merrill is a reader in Lifelong Learning in the Centre for Lifelong Learning at the University of Warwick, UK. Her research interests are access and experiences of adult students; gender, class and adult education; learning careers and identities; citizenship and community and radical education and biographical methods. Her books include *Gender, Change and Identity: Mature Women Students in Universities* (1999); with Linden West, Peter Alheit and Anders Siig Andersen, *Using Life History and Biographical Approaches in the Study of Adult and Lifelong Learning: European Perspectives* (2007) and with Linden West, *Using Biographical Methods in Social Research* (2009). She coordinates the ESREA Access, Learning Careers and Identities network and is a member of the ESREA Steering Committee.

Prof Dr Dr Peter Alheit is the Chair in General Education at Georg-August-University Gottingen, Germany and the Director of the Department of Education. His research interests include sociology of education, international comparative educational research, biographical research, studies on culture and mentality, and research in lifelong learning. Recent books: *Die vergessene Autonomie" der Arbeiter. Eine Studie zum frühen Scheitern der DDR am Beispiel der Neptunwerft* (with Hanna Haack), Berlin 2004; *Shaping an Emerging Reality – Researching Lifelong Learning* (with other authors), Roskilde 2004; *En el curso de la vida. Educación, formación, biograficidad y género* (with Bettina Dausien), Valencia 2007; *Using Biographical and Life History Approaches in the Study of Adult and Lifelong Learning: European Perspectives* (edited with Linden West, Anders Siig Andersen and Barbara Merrill), Frankfurt am Main et al. 2007.

Professor Gert Biesta (www.gertbiesta.com) is Professor of Education at the Stirling Institute of Education, University of Stirling, Scotland, UK and Visiting Professor for Education and Democratic Citizenship at Örebro University and Mälardalen University, Sweden. He conducts theoretical and empirical research and is particularly interested in the relationships between education, democracy and democratisation. He has published on the philosophy and methodology of educational research, relationships between research, policy and practice, theories of education, democratic learning in everyday settings, vocational education and lifelong learning, teachers' professional learning, and the civic role of Higher Education. Recent books include: *Pragmatism and Educational Research* (with Nicholas C. Burbules; Rowman & Littlefield 2003); *Beyond Learning: Democratic Education for a Human Future* (Paradigm Publishers 2006); *Improving Learning Cultures in Further Education* (with David James; Routledge 2007); *Democracy, Education and the Moral Life* (co-edited with Michael Katz and Susan Verducci; Springer 2008); *Contexts, communities and networks* (co-edited with Richard Edwards and Mary Thorpe; Routledge 2008).

Professor Ana Maria R. Correia is Professora Catedrática Convidada at ISEGI-UNL, Portugal. She is also Investigadora Coordenadora (Senior Researcher) at *INETI* (*Instituto Nacional de Engenharia e Tecnologia Industrial*), an R&D organisation under the Ministry of Economy and Innovation. and researcher at *CEGI - Centro de Estatística e Gestão de Informação*, of UNL. Her research interests include knowledge and innovation management, strategic information management/competitive intelligence, lifelong learning in higher education and e-learning, information resources, information literacy. She has been involved in several European and national research projects. Since 1998, she has served as the Portuguese representative on the *Information Management Committee* (*IMC*) of the *NATO/RTA* (*Research and Technology Agency*).She is an Honorary Fellow of the *Institute of Information Scientists*, London, UK. Recent publications include with Mesquita, A. (2008). *The role of Lifelong Learning in the creation of a knowledge-based society for Europe* and with Sarmento, A. (2008) *The development of a knowledge-based society – Challenges for e-learning and adult students in Higher Education.*

Ana Cristina Costa is a lecturer and research assistant at Instituto Superior de Estatística e Gestão de Informação (ISEGI), Universidade Nova de Lisboa (UNL), since 1998. She is a member of the University Council, the University Senate, and the Pedagogical Council of ISEGI-UNL. She is a Ph.D. student of Engineering Sciences at Instituto Superior Técnico, since 2005. Her main scientific research area is geostatistics for environmental applications. She has several refereed publications not only on this subject, but also in other statistical fields. She has collaborated in several research projects, both national and international in which she contributes to the development of applications with the SAS System software.

Dr Rob Evans lectures at the University of Magdeburg, Germany. Born in London, the author studied Slavonic languages and history at the Universities of Leeds, Brno, Leningrad, and Tübingen. After working in adult, further and higher education, he gained a Masters and Doctorate in Education with the Open University (UK). Since 1977 he has worked in Germany, Italy and Egypt. His main research interest is learning biographies, employing a mixture of methods, including conversation and discourse analysis and electronic corpora. Recent publications include: *Learning discourse* (2004) Frankfurt, Peter Lang and "L'entretien auto/biographique et les paroles" (2008), *Pratiques de formation (Analyses)*, 55, December 2008, Université Paris VIII.

Professor John Field is a professor in the University of Stirling, Institute of Education, where he directs the Centre for Research in Lifelong Learning. His research interests include the historical, social and economic dimensions of adult learning, He has published widely, including recent books on social capital and on theories of and policies for lifelong learning. He was involved in a large national ESRC project on Learning Lives.

Jan Frederiksen is an External Lecturer and Ph.D. fellow at the department of Psychology and Educational Studies, Roskilde University, Denmark. He works mainly within the field of the sociology of professions, in particular professional training and educational reforms. He has several recent Danish-language publications on these topics. Other areas of research include mixed methods, combining correspondence analysis with qualitative analysis.

Dr Patricia Gouthro is an Associate Professor in the Graduate Studies in Lifelong Learning programme in the Faculty of Education at Mount Saint Vincent University in Halifax, Nova Scotia (Canada). Her research interests include critical and feminist theory, women's learning experiences, and citizenship. A couple of her most recent publications are 'Active and inclusive citizenship for women: Democratic considerations for fostering lifelong learning' in the *International Journal of Lifelong Education* (2007) and 'Reason, Communicative Learning, and Civil Society: The Use of Habermasian Theory in Adult Education' in the *Journal of Educational Thought* (2006).

Paula Guimarães is a Ph. D. candidate in Education (Educational Policies). She is a researcher at the Unit for Adult Education of the University of Minho where she coordinates the research activities of the Unit. She is interested in various issues in the field of adult education, namely in adult education policies in Portugal and in the European Union and non-formal and informal adult education. Her recent publications include *Políticas públicas de educação de adultos em Portugal: diversos sentidos para o direito à educação?* [Public policies of adult education in Portugal: different meanings for the right to education?]. *Rizoma freireano 3. Educación, ciudadanía y democracia*, N.º 3 (http://www.rizoma-freireano.org) (2009) and "Reflections on the professionalisation of adult educators in the framework of public policies in Portugal". *European Journal of Education*, Vol. 44, No. 2, Part I, pp. 205-219 (2009).

Tamsin Hinton-Smith is a Research Fellow at the University of Sussex, UK. Her specialist research areas are gender, education and qualitative research methods, all of which she teaches courses on to undergraduate students. She has carried out several pieces of research exploring the learning experiences of lone and teenage parents, including access, barriers and solutions, funded by the Economic and Social Research Council and the European Social Fund. She has also raised two children as a lone parent while completing her own studies.

Dr Nalita James is Lecturer in Employment Studies in the Centre for Labour Market Studies at the University of Leicester, UK. Her research interests include: identity, work and learning, with particular focus on the impact of creativity on young adults learning transitions and skills development. Methodological interests include the ethics of researching young adults. With Bethia McNeil, she recently co-directed an Arts Council/DFES study entitled: 'Theatre as a site for learning: the impact of drama on the development of oracy among young adult offenders.' Recent publications include 'Actup! Theatre as education and its impact on young people's learning,' in J.Somer and M. Balfour (eds.) *Drama as Social Intervention,* Canada, Captus Press, (2006) and 'Ethics and access in research in education,' in A. Briggs and M. Coleman (eds) *Research in Educational Management,* London, Paul Chapman (with Hugh Busher, 2007). She is currently developing the next phase of the drama/young offenders study with Bethia McNeil as well as researching and writing about the impact of Creative Partnerships on creative professionals' learning careers and identities.

Dr Rennie Johnston is a freelance researcher and practitioner in lifelong learning, community development and community-based research. He previously worked at the University of Southampton, New College where he was Co-ordinator for Research and Development, worked with a range of community groups and social movements and organized and taught courses in lifelong learning and community studies. He has participated in a number of European-wide projects, most recently with the University of Warwick in the area of auto/biographical research. He has written widely on adult learning for citizenship, community education, experiential learning and auto/biographical research and is co-author and editor, with Pam Coare, of Adult Learning, Citizenship and Community Voices, NIACE, 2003.

Dr Dulce Magalhães de Sá graduated from the Universidade Nova de Lisboa (UNL) and as a postgraduate from University of London and Universidad Pontificia de Salamanca. Her professional experience includes the UNL, the Agency for the Information Society Development of the Portuguese Government, and the National Geographic Information Centre of Portugal. She has several refereed publications and is author of two books concerning Information Technology and Programming
Techniques and Languages.

Bethia McNeil is Project Manager: Apprenticeships, Local Wellbeing Project, at The Young Foundation. Bethia is leading the Apprenticeship Pathfinder, part of the Local Wellbeing Project, about Apprenticeships for 16-18 year olds. She has previously worked for NIACE and The National Youth Agency, where her work focused on researching and developing effective approaches to learning and personal development with young adults, aged 16 –25. Her areas of expertise include Apprenticeships, informal and community-based literacy, language and numeracy provision for young adults, work with young offenders, the development of training and frameworks to support practitioners in their work with young adults, a range of qualitative research methods and creative consultation with young adults and practitioners, and experience in working with young adults outside formal education, training and employment. Her recent publications include: (2008) *Working with young adults: Supporting literacy, language and numeracy.* NRDC and with Ainsley, A, O'Callaghan, M, Parrott, A and Thomas, H (forthcoming 2009) *Developing young adults' oracy through employability*, NRDC

Amélia Vitória Sancho, University of Minho, Portugal, where she was a member of the Unit for Adult Education. She was a trainer and a researcher from 1979 until 2007. She was responsible for the training sector of the Unit and was also a researcher in the Research Centre in Education. She has published extensively in the field of adult education, namely on second-chance education and adult education in voluntary associations. Now she is retired and involved in adult and lifelong education in a senior academy.

Anabela Mesquita Teixeira Sarmento is Professora Adjunta at ISCAP (School of Accountancy and Administration of Porto, Portugal). In 2007, she was appointed Vice Dean of ISCAP. She is also a Member of the Agoritmi Centre at Universidade do Minho. Her research interests include knowledge and innovation management, impact of information systems in organization, lifelong learning in higher education and e-learning. She has been involved in several European and national research projects. She has published widely in this field. She serves as a Member of the Editorial Board and referee for IGI Global. She also serves as Associate Editor of the *Information Resources Management Journal* and the *International Journal of Technology and Human Interaction*. She is a referee for the *Journal of Cases of Information Technology*. She has also been evaluator and reviewer for European Commission projects.

Michael Tedder spent most of his professional teaching career in a further education college in Cornwall. Between 2001 and 2004 he was a college-based Research Fellow for a large-scale research project, *Transforming Learning Cultures in Further Education.* From 2004 to 2008 he worked on the project, *Learning Lives: Learning Identity and Agency in the Lifecourse* in the School of Education and Lifelong Learning at Exeter University. His research interests include: life history and biographical research; adult and community learning; the experiences of young people on vocational courses in FE; notions of professionalism in post-compulsory education. Recent publications include with Jones, P. & Mauger, S. (2008) *Listening to Learners,* Adults Learning; (2007) *'Making a choice? Insights from using a life history approach to researching access students'.*(2007) Journal of Widening Participation and Lifelong Learning 9(2).

Dr Simon Warren is Lecturer in Critical Policy Studies at the Institute for Lifelong Learning in the School of Education at the University of Sheffield, UK. His research interests are in the areas of Policy Sociology, race equality and education, and learning in the context of social action. Simon is co-convener of the ESREA Migration, Racism and Xenophobia Research Network and a member of the Editorial Board of *Race Ethnicity and Education*. Selected recent publications include with Sue Webb (2007) Challenging lifelong learning policy discourse: where is structure in agency in narrative-based research, *Studies in the Education of Adults,* Vol. 39, No.1, Spring 2007; Migration, race and education: evidence-based policy or institutional racism? *Race Ethnicity and Education* Vol. 10, No. 4, (2007) and Resilience and refusal: African-Caribbean young men's agency, school exclusions and school based mentoring, *Race, Ethnicity and Education,* Vol. 8, No. 3, (2005).

Professor Sue Webb is Professor of Continuing Education and Director of the Institute for Lifelong Learning in the School of Education at the University of Sheffield, UK. Her research interests are lifelong learning and higher education, particularly increasing understanding in the adult learning community of how and why adults engage in learning and succeed or not. This interest reflects an ongoing concern with research themes such as social differentiation and the continued ways that differences such as class, gender, race, age and disability impact on explanations of success or failure, and on learners' decision-making and identities. Recent publications include with Simon Warren (2007) Challenging lifelong learning policy discourse: where is structure in agency in narrative-based research, *Studies in the Education of Adults,* Vol. 39, No.1, pp 5-21 and with Ibarz, T & Webb, S. (2007) Listening to Learners to Investigate the Viability of Technology –driven ESOL Pedagogy, *Innovation in Language Learning and Teaching* Vol.1;2.

Index

Governance 16, 217–18, 228 n.21, 229
Government 10, 17, 18, 39, 58, 101, 103, 125, 148; *see also* Policy
Governmentality 16, 227–8
Grading and identity 16, 213–31
Grounded theory 84, 101–2, 115, 220
Guilt 117, 119–20

H

Habermas, Jürgen 106–7, 179–80
Habitus 13, 15, 50, 56–8, 129, 132, 134, 136, 140–1, 161–71
HE *see* Higher education
HEIs *see* Higher education institutions
Henze, Anissa 185
Higher education (HE) 50 n.2, 51, 53, 161–71, 213–14; access routes 115, 125–6, 195–6, 198; and exclusion 15, 51, 108, 161–71, 176; institutions 10, 14, 129, 173–7, 186–7, 193–211 (*see also* Universities); and non-traditional learners 14, 15, 113–27, 129–43, 195–6; *see also* individual entries
Hodkinson, Phil 129–30, 146–7
Homeplace 100, 102, 103–4, 106, 108
Humanistic approach 76, 131

I

ICT 67, 194
Identity 9–12, 17, 22, 35, 40, 45, 53, 127, 129–31, 184; adult educators 9, 11, 76, 78; 'caring' 54, 57, 58–9, 60, 61; gendered 11, 54, 123–5, 132, 133–4; lone parents 117–20, 124, 127; professional/workplace

41–2, 65, 66, 74, 76, 81, 82, 90; social educators 16, 213–31; working class 14, 124, 129–43; young offenders 16, 145–59
Incidental learning 68–9
Inclusion 51, 59 n.10, 61, 97, 100, 109, 141, 156, 167–8
Independent learning/learners 15, 173–91, 193, 196–7, 201
Individual organisation of learning 197, 199, 200, 204, 208, 209
Individualisation: learning 97–100, 106, 107, 109, 175; modern life/society 9, 20, 53, 122, 123–4, 125–7, 130; narrative 68
Inequality 14, 22, 98, 99, 124, 147
Informal knowledge 13, 20, 35, 65, 81, 173
Informal learning 10, 11, 20–1, 35, 108, 148, 195; in the workplace 13, 65–79
Information and communication technology *see* ICT
Information technology *see* IT
Initial education 72, 78
Initial vocational training 19, 24
Institutional: cultures 9, 50, 123–4, 187, 213–14, 218, 225–30; habitus 15, 161–71; environment 182–3; identities 131, 134, 141; pressures 11, 14; structures 18, 106, 132; support 35, 97, 101, 103–5, 108, 134, 141, 182; *see also* Further education; Higher education; Universities
Instrumental learning 115, 131, 137, 151, 173, 176, 187–**90**
Interviews 12, 17 n.1, 23–8, 33–47; HE students 174, 177–85; professional/workplace 13, 81–96, 163–9; women 49–63, 97, 100–5;

European Studies in Lifelong Learning and Adult Learning Research

Edited by Barry J. Hake, Henning Salling Olesen and Rudolf Tippelt

European Society for Research on the Education of Adults – ESREA

This series is dedicated to the publication of edited volumes of selected papers that have been presented at conferences and seminars organised by the European research networks of ESREA.

ESREA is a scientific association of researchers throughout Europe who are engaged in the study of adult education and adult learning. ESREA is devoted to the promotion of high quality interdisciplinary research on all aspects of adult education and adult learning. Since 1991 its activities include:

- stimulating a European-wide infrastructure for research activities
- specialist European research networks with annual seminars
- triennial European Research Conferences
- encouraging the graduate training of researchers
- promotion of a range of research publications

The ESREA website can be visited at: http://www.esrea.org

www.peterlang.de